Cosmopolitan Culture

Alfred Stieglitz, "The City of Ambition, New York," 1910.
(THE DOROTHY NORMAN COLLECTION)

Cosmopolitan Culture

The Gilt-Edged Dream of a Tolerant City

Bonnie Menes Kahn

Atheneum ♦ New York ♦ 1987

Simon & Schuster
Rockefeller Center
1230 Avenue of the Americas
New York, NY 10020

Simon & Schuster and colophon are registered trademarks of Simon & Schuster, Inc.
Designed by The Sarabonde Press

Manufactured in the United States of America

10 9 8 7 6 5 4 3 2 1

Library of Congress Cataloging-In-Publication Data
Kahn, Bonnie Menes.
     Cosmopolitan culture.
     Bibliography: p.
     1. Cities and towns—Cross cultural studies.
2. City and town life—Cross cultural studies. I. Title.
HT151.K28   1987   307.7'6   87-17429

ISBN: 0-7432-4403-6

Permissions and picture credits continue on page 311

For information regarding the special discounts for bulk purchases, please contact Simon & Schuster Special Sales at 1-800-456-6798 or business@simonandschuster.com

Acknowledgments

I would like to thank Professors Daniel Bell and Stanley Hoffmann at Harvard University for their encouragement and interest. Professor Bell's interest in Babylon in particular and his support for the work in general made this a better book. I benefited as well from the advice and example of Aida Donald, Karen Rosenberg, and Monique Stark and from suggestions by David J. Harris and James V. Aidala, Jr., also at Harvard University.

I would like to thank Professor Richard A. Muller for facilitating my work at the University of California at Berkeley.

This work also owes a great intellectual debt to scholars with whom I studied at Princeton University, especially the historian Carl Schorske and my advisor there, the late Morroe Berger.

John Brockman and Katinka Matson made the publication of this work possible, and I owe them my deepest thanks.

I would like to thank Thomas Stewart, Susan Leon, Ann Keniston, and all the people at Atheneum for their enormous enthusiasm and dedication.

Thank you, Ron.

San Francisco
March 1987

Contents

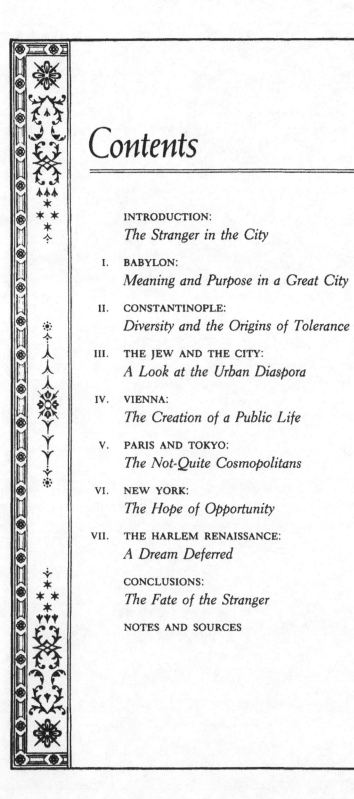

Introduction

The Stranger in
the City

*M*uch of the world is the color of mud. And many of the world's people have scratched out a life where chance left them, toiling endlessly at whatever toil they inherited, hoping for little. Mean-spirited, vulgar, and violent—or hardworking, simple, and decent; it does not matter. Much of the world is that way. Some say it is choice that narrows people's worlds. Some say the choice is taken from them; no one would willingly live in shadow and die leaving only gloom. Not all people are satisfied with the world they have inherited.

The history of all society, then, is a history of struggle—the struggle to control one's life, to enjoy more comfort, experience more beauty, achieve salvation, to make life meaningful. It is struggle to demand that all human beings be treated with dignity. And it also is struggle to enjoy the laughter of grandchildren while knowing the gray truth of the world they enter. The struggle, the gray, is everywhere.

On the horizon there is a spire, or a skyscraper or a minaret, a wall of stone, a ziggurat. The sky breaks open for the skyline of a city and there is, both literally and figuratively, a new horizon. The city is not mud, but brick; not gray, but purple, gold, and silver. It is beauty, wealth, industry, and more people concentrated in one place than is imaginable by most people. Not everyone has admired city life; not everyone has seen beauty in the aimless stares of milling crowds of restless strangers, the monotony of anonymity. The heart of the city, however, is its strangers. The fate of those strangers is the difference between empty walls of glittering dust, and greatness.

The great city, the cosmopolitan city, the subject of this book, is one where diversity has created a temporary tolerance, a thriving exchange among strangers. And the project of the place, by force, by design, by chance or coercion, the project is an attempt to benefit from the presence of newcomers and outsiders. Big cities witness it on a grand scale.

Small towns taste the cosmopolitan fervor whenever a stranger wears a new hat and a local dandy mimics him, when, as in Gogol's *Dead Souls*, a wandering confidence artist becomes a feted curiosity, or when a traveler's tales make captivating listening at an inn. Some listeners are struck and believe, at least a little. Others, mean-spirited or just decent, simple folk, wave away the tales and their teller. Not everyone favors a new horizon.

Sociology was once a new and controversial subject. Now it is not very new and not very beautiful and its substantive controversy has all but disappeared. The city has long interested sociologists, but too often the city itself has been overshadowed by the sociologists' attempts to claim scientific legitimacy, leaving beauty behind. The University of Chicago, home to the "community studies" school of sociology, sent many researchers onto city streets to observe the life of neighborhoods. Robert Park and his Chicago heirs, Gerald Suttles, Elliot Liebow, and still later, Lee Rainwater, have given us detailed accounts of city life seen from the inside: status in the city, income, housing patterns. In recent years the original inspiration of this work has settled into the routine of demography and statistics. Necessary work, it is narrow and impersonal. The smallness of scale which once gave community studies life is now a deadening restriction.

Works by Jane Jacobs and Richard Sennett, broader in scope, still see the city as an established fact; they, too, take the view of insiders. They ask, does the city work well or badly? They see it as a machine driven by the economy or by political power. In order to see the very existence and meaning of the city as a question, the *why* and not the *how,* in order to see the city as an outsider would see it, you have to take a broader view and add wide historical comparisons.

This work attempts several breaks with standard sociological studies of cities. It is historical and treats the whole phenomenon of the city, or one kind of city, a cosmopolitan city, as a question. This is in the spirit of earlier social observers and historians, such as Henri Pirenne or others of the French *Annales* school earlier in this century, but it is not in line with recent studies. The explanation proposed here is distinctly social—

neither wealth nor power nor resources make the great city go. Rather, a social organization, the way people live together, including their ideas and interactions with one another, creates a cosmopolitan culture. Finally, I am interested in history, as many sociologists are today, but I am also interested in beauty, especially the beauty that men and women create, art and artifice. This book is a social essay in the humanistic tradition using historical information.

There are two standard ways of using historical cases. I am doing neither. The first use to which one can put historical data is induction. That is the method as old as the oldest Greeks: learn about the world by adding up all of the observations and knowledge you can gather and use them to draw conclusions. This is the secret dream of all true scholars. Lovers of truth yearn for unlimited time to learn about the world and unlimited wisdom to understand it. There are great works in sociology, such as S. N. Eisenstadt's study of empires or Orlando Patterson's study of slavery, which attempt to gather information from as many historical cases as possible, hoping to approach true inductive wisdom. I have not set about to capture every cosmopolitan city or even most of them. I would admit freely that some cities are more or less cosmopolitan than others; my hope is to convince you to reflect on cosmopolitanism and to think about other cities worthy of discussion. Some may say Berlin or Alexandria or Shanghai, Timbuktu or Marrakech; I have written a Western story in a Western context, due in part to my own preoccupations. And while without inductive reasoning I could never have arrived at many of the thoughts in this book, it is not an exposition of inductive research.

Nor does this book make use of historical cases in the second way. The name some use for this second method, triangulation, sounds gruesome, but it is descriptive. It means making triangles again and again, comparing and comparing to arrive at the common characteristics. I look at two cities, A and B, find their common element, and then move on to city C. Does it have that same characteristic? I compare C and D, find another element, see if it fits city E, then go back and check with my first triangle, and so on. This method draws conclusions by analyzing similarities and differences. The historical sociology of Charles Tilly follows this pattern. Readers who favor this model may find my cities too similar—I have not compared and contrasted them enough; they all seem to contain all the right elements. In short, although I have had to think through these kinds of contrasts, I have not "shown my work." But this book is not an exercise in methodology.

This book is an essay with evidence. It is a theoretical argument, one-half of a debate in which you, reader, are the other side. The cities here, Babylon, Constantinople, Vienna, and New York, not only illustrate the elements I believe necessary to cosmopolitan culture; they do it in a way which might make use of your own understanding. What better way to convince you of the importance of a unifying myth than to speak to you of Babylon, a city of deep importance to all modern cities, part of your dormant cultural repertoire? I hope to use your own knowledge to convince you. I will use beauty to convince you, poetry and music, beauty exotic and familiar. I will use a shared culture in order to argue for a specific understanding of that culture. This book is a social essay in the humanistic tradition.

Finally, although I hope to interest you and amuse and enlighten you, my goal is to persuade you. And if I cannot persuade you directly, showing you that tolerance and coexistence are possible where diversity is favored, telling you that a world of many peoples is a better world, then I will persuade you indirectly. At weary end of your historical travels, you may forget when the Sumerians lived or whether or not Byzantine Armenians wore turbans, and in your newly found confusion the people around you will not look so strange. You will have accepted the stranger.

Not everyone has admired city life. As long as there have been cities, there have been observers and critics. Criticisms of city life are as old as cities themselves and follow very closely the history of cities. The crowding and permanence of cities have made people see them as morbid, unhealthy, or funereal. The first cities may have been no more than cemeteries or shrines, where early settlers left off their nomadic life only long enough to bury their dead. Lewis Mumford, the urban historian, has dubbed these first cities "Necropolis."[1] Even thousands of years later, cities were where people died, not where they were born, and later historians as well as contemporary critics have called the cities of prein-

dustrial Europe graveyards.[2] The stench of plague, and fear, led Boccaccio to write in the introduction to his *Decameron* that Florence
seemed to have breathed its last.[3] If the gallant and handsome and noble
and mighty were laid low, how much worse off the poor and middle
classes who filled fourteenth-century Florence's streets with death and
decay. Boccaccio tells us that the city's true dimensions could be understood only in its tragedy.

> Between March and July more than one hundred thousand persons
> died within the walls of Florence, what between the violence of the
> plague and the abandonment in which the sick were left by the
> healthy. And before the plague it was not thought that the whole
> city held so many people.[4]

Epidemics and overcrowding sound bad enough without the blood
and offal that contemporaries would have taken for granted. In fifteenth-
century London the heads of criminals were raised on pikes and displayed about the city. Even after the eyes fell out or were picked out by
vultures or other scavengers, the wrongdoers were recognizable.[5] Cities
have been seen as immoral and vice as an urban attribute. Long after
the years known as Europe's Dark Ages, the dark hours in Europe were
a dangerous no-man's time. Appearances have changed, but cities are
still criticized as centers of death—if not from disease, then from the
danger of crime and criminals.

While stories of crime make cities sound unsafe, the association of
cities with vice goes deeper than recent crime statistics. For centuries
cities have been criticized as the dwelling place of temptation. In cities
the ancients broke religious law, worshiped foreign gods. In cities the
senses are enticed, exotic desires born. And, above all, social observers
and philosophers were suspicious of the contact with strangers and
strange ways that characterized city life.

The philosopher Jean-Jacques Rousseau criticized the eighteenth-cen-
tury French court as corrupt because each man did not rely on his own
reason but was instead a slave to the opinion of others. The more others
there are, the more the individual is swayed from his own course of
reason. Vice and corruption, Rousseau would argue, come from the

individual's attempt to fit the opinions of others by seeming what he is not.[6] Seeing wealth, one steals to feel wealthy. Seeing alluring women, one buys sexual favors to feel desirable. Seeing beautiful fashions, one adorns oneself to feel important, attractive, knowledgeable. Rousseau's image of city life as court life, as artifice, lies deep within the association of cities and vice. Where there are strangers, there are people to fool.

Influenced by thinkers like Rousseau, American critics of urban life, especially, have seen cities as unnatural, as artifice, illusion, and vice. Even cemeteries, the permanent cities of the dead, are in the United States pastoral or at least suburban. Instead of the stone steps and crypts of Paris' Père-Lachaise, American graves are miniature lawns separated by invisible fences. The land, agriculture, and the simple life of man upon the land have been praised by American philosophers.[7] One American Transcendentalist thinker, Elizabeth Palmer Peabody, praised "true life," which

> although it aims beyond the highest star is redolent of the healthy earth. The perfume of clover lingers about it. The lowing of cattle is the natural bass to the melody of human voices.[8]

But the city? Peabody called it an absurdity, the result of war and not love, and the cause of evil.

If cities were seen as artificial in their origins and unnatural in their animus, they were ugly in their aspect. The critic sought flowers, there were none; the sounds of lowing cattle, the air was empty; the grace of treetops, the expanse of fields . . . Where could the city dweller realize his true nature? Nowhere, the nineteenth-century critic answered. Cities, he said, were unhealthy, immoral, unnatural, and unfree. Thomas Jefferson believed that an urban culture would ruin the American desire for freedom.[9] The great houses were prisons, the great crowds enforcers of social demands and political conformity.

All of these condemnations and more were heaped upon the industrial cities that became western Europe's greatest wonders and abominations. These cities began to grow around the seventeenth century, but they dominated the landscape of the nineteenth. The very word "city" still evokes the smokestacks and squalor of Dickens' England, long after smokestacks have left industry and industry has left the city for the suburbs. The industrial city of the nineteenth century became the symbol of modernity, where technology was housed and architecture transformed, where the marketplace expanded to dominate daily life.

The criticisms of the industrial city have become one of the great legacies of the modern age. Nineteenth-century social reporters not only observed society's ills, but sometimes attacked modernity in its urban form; their criticisms of industry and modern labor shaped much of twentieth-century thought. When Friedrich Engels, the son of a German textile manufacturer, visited Manchester, England, to train for work in the cotton business, he was struck by the exploitation of the workers. His observations, published in *The Condition of the Working Class in England in 1844*, led him, like his colleague, Karl Marx, to condemn capitalist industry and the new slavery of wage labor. While critics like Marx and Engels proposed a future society beyond that which they saw in Europe's cities, conservative critics like Burke or Ruskin pleaded for a return to what went before—agriculture, religion, and feudalism.[10]

The most disturbing consequence of city life as seen by its nineteenth-century critics seemed to be a change in human relationships. The worker, no longer a full human being, existed only to labor and the owner only to buy and sell. Everywhere bourgeois industry left relationships between one man and another cold and calculating.[11] The religious census of 1851 shocked the English public with the remarkably low proportion of English residents who reported practicing religion. The city and industry seemed to stifle spiritual impulses and create a breed of savage, self-interested machines. Even the natural sympathy and joy of family life seemed to evaporate in the steam and smoke of the modern city. A visitor to the industrial city of Mulhouse recounted the life of factory owners there:

> They rise before the sun, spend the day in the fetid gases of the workshops and occupy themselves in the evening by copying columns of figures from big books. When the time pressures [the industrialist], when his vast warehouse is like the Danaides' barrels, always empty only to be refilled, so that there is for him neither

peace nor relaxation, so that it is barely once a week that he remembers he has a wife or watches his children sleep, this fatigue is his joy. . . .[12]

The manufacturer, like the laborer, had become a stranger to his family.

Criticisms of the city grew along with the city itself. But of all the criticisms of city life, past and present, the most powerful is this one: that urban life creates strangers, tearing human beings away from one another, rendering men and women less human. Social scientists of this century have explained that through overstimulation the city dweller becomes callous and blasé, ignoring the feelings and experiences of those around him and hiding his own. The urban world is both impersonal and secretive, the city's twentieth-century critics say, since the individual must try to defend himself against the assaults of a complex setting.[13]

The city as a world of strangers, men and women whose feelings and motivations are hidden, has been a popular subject of film. Alfred Hitchcock's suspenseful dramas often depend on the opacity of strangers—a chance meeting on a train, in *Strangers on a Train,* or on vacation, in *The Lady Vanishes* and *The Man Who Knew Too Much,* begins a long and sometimes violent inquiry into the strangers' real or secret motivations. *Rear Window* at first seems cozy: from his apartment window a bored convalescent follows the activities of his neighbors. Yet what does he really know of their lives? They are all projections of his own inner feelings; apartment-house windows are more reliable as mirrors than lenses.[14] This is contemporary urban criticism: who knows what danger lurks in the hearts of the strangers one passes every day by the hundreds?

Or what affection? Ernst Lubitsch's 1940 comedy *The Shop Around the Corner* ends happily for the shopgirl and the store clerk with whom she works, who find out their love letters have been written for one another. In the shop they detest one another. Yet each feels an inner isolation. So one places an ad, one answers, they correspond, only to find out that they are already acquainted. The inner life of the city dweller, in other words, cannot be guessed by his manner, by his job, by the impersonal or officious way he carries out his work, or by his appearance.

But appearances and all visual cues are essential to the person confronted every day with new things and new faces, as social theorist Georg

Simmel has said.[15] How else can one make judgments? Urban sociologist Richard Sennett says the city holds two kinds of strangers: those who are different but recognizable, such as people of another race, and those who are unrecognizable, strangers whose appearance has little meaning.[16] The city creates strangers by leaving only appearance as a clue to recognition and then imposing sameness, the sameness of business suits or apartment buildings. As fast as a new distinguishing feature is found, crowds of others want it as well. Where appearance reigns, twentieth-century critics of the city claim, anonymity is both a tool and a weapon.

So the city creates strangers, critics claim, by assembling crowds of men and women who hide their inner feelings but search the faces of those around them for clues to guide their behavior. This other-directed anxiety creates what sociologists have called a "lonely crowd."[17] Women wear masks of who they are supposed to be while hoping to attract someone for what they really are underneath. And in men impersonal behavior is lauded; all powerful men must resemble one another. They are reduced to a crowd.

Although the psychology of the crowd has been discussed since the French Revolution, it has been of special significance in our own century as mass media aided propaganda and propaganda aided fascism. The mass society, a volatile world of faceless, nameless, insecure, easily swayed individuals, seemed to some the only explanation for our recent history.

This criticism of city anonymity goes still further. City dwellers, according to city critics, feel no moral responsibility because they have no history—no past to honor, no land to defend, no traditions to follow. Without a past, any man is a stranger. How can you know someone unless you know who he was yesterday and last year? City dwellers are rootless; they have no stake in a particular place, only in city life in general. They have no permanent loyalties. The civilization of giant cities creates homeless, intellectual nomads. So said Oswald Spengler.

According to Spengler, cities were the path of civilization's decline, constructs of pure intellect, pure artifice. His belief that the city warped human relationships was reminiscent of the idea of the city as Necropolis, city of death. Spengler saw the city as fatality and welcomed its demise.[18]

How many suburbanites now believe that their neighborhoods are more stable and responsible, that they have more spirit and dignity than the great decaying cities, not because they fear crime, but because they fear strangers? Spengler's description of rootless cosmopolites, used by Nazi propagandists, was turned against those they accused of being strangers.[19] This is the logical conclusion when critics fear strangers and criticize the city for creating strangers. Are we still subject to the cry "rootless cosmopolites"? Do we still believe that cities create outcasts and undesirables? Once this was used as justification for a war on civilization. Is the fear of rootless cosmopolites alive in today's America's disdain for the cities?

Now, as the numbers of homeless swell, American cities are full of even more displaced persons. Sometimes an urbanite passes a bag lady with fear or disgust. Sometimes it is compassion and generosity. But as long as we unthinkingly accept the criticisms of city life, as long as we believe that it is the city which creates strangers and outcasts, then each individual act of compassion carries with it a wider disdain for city life. As long as we see cities as creating strangers, we fear the city, because we fear for our own spirits. And we move farther away. We move our houses. We move our industries. We siphon off funds. And we hope that we can start again, smaller, cleaner, better. But then we miss the point. This book argues that cities do not create strangers. Cities are the refuge of strangers. Cities are the place for men and women already estranged. And cities are to be judged by their welcome. The city, by definition, is where the inn is, where the boat docks, where the train stops; it is the port of entry to a new life.

Despite all the ills of urban life and the threats of anonymity, men and women have rushed toward city gates, again and again, visiting, moving, tying to gain admission. Cities consist of strangers, first, in the most literal way: most city dwellers were once newcomers. Until relatively recently, the population of cities did not reproduce itself, but depended upon a steady stream of newcomers to counter high mortality rates.

But why did newcomers keep coming? Why did they keep building and rebuilding? Were the newcomers so naïve they believed they could go unscathed by city life? Were they simply so ignorant that they sensed only the outline and reached blindly, groping at fire, trapping the sun? Daedalus may have been Greek, but Icarus is more like a youthful, confident, city-building Roman, insistent on applying to the extreme his father's hard-won wisdom. He was determined to move closer to the excitement.

What is the attraction of cities? Political, economic, and social attractions have drawn strangers into cities, luring them with the promise of something better. Cities consist of political strangers whose aim is conquest—or whose hope is freedom. Cities consist of economic strangers whose drive is ownership—or whose fate is labor. Cities consist of social strangers whose object is the relief of anonymity—or new attachments. All who enter the city are strangers.

The city is a prize worth conquering. Some historians argue that the city was primarily a fortress long ago. Ancient and medieval Western cities, seen in this light, were treasure troves guarded and encased in stone.[20] This need not be the case, though, if we are to understand why outsiders came to the city, hoping to seize control, or even why city walls were built. Cities have been prized for their beauty, their people, and their culture. They have been symbols of material wealth, of spiritual significance, or the very center of order. Peking was built to contain cities within cities. Within the walled Imperial City was the Forbidden or Purple City, the walled residence of the emperor. Within the Purple City, hidden to all but the emperor, were the Sea Palaces, the most natural of pleasure-dome parks, also walled. The walls were both symbolic and religious. But even the most symbolic walls imply outsiders.

As long as there have been cities, there have been outsiders trying to enter, with the same political goals: power over luxury (including the luxury of safety), labor, and learning. When the Semites conquered the ancient city of Babylon, they took from the Sumerians not only the city itself, but the art of writing and an alphabet. When Crusaders conquered Constantinople and sacked the city in 1204, they stole gold and gems, books in Latin and Greek, and works on mathematics. Outsiders have wanted access to beauty, wealth, safety, learning, and, as Machiavelli might add, control over a walled-in population, a captive audience.[21]

Outsiders have entered cities seeking not only political control, but political freedom. The medieval serf's only hope was that "city air makes men free." One year and one day away from the land to which he was bound and the serf owed no work, had no obligations, need not give up his new bride at the lord's pleasure; he was free. Where was the magic in the city air? Why would such a custom develop? What did it mean? Perhaps the former serf simply passed into some other ruler's sphere of power. Burghers and merchants and a few powerful city dwellers vied with feudal lords for control; maybe the serf just changed jurisdictions. The Holy Roman Empire in fact had no power over the free cities, which joined in leagues to protect their interests. Yet the free city air also would have favored the lord; after a year and a day he would be freed of his obligations to look for the serf or to take him back. A serf who has been free for one year is a different person, a man with broader horizons, perhaps a troublemaker. Learning new ways makes people free.

Economic activity has historically brought strangers together in the city. Historian Henri Pirenne's classic work on the growth of cities focuses on the growth of trade.[22] Trade, a small eddy in Europe of the medieval age, grew into a whirlpool, drawing in more and more merchants and then industrialists. The origins of city populations, he argues, should be sought not "in the older population of the early fortresses, but in the immigrant population which trade brought to them."[23] Newcomers who both created and profited from the investment opportunities of new trade centers became the urban middle class of proprietors. They did not chance upon ownership, nor did they simply blossom, but purposefully entered cities as strangers, intent upon a new kind of ownership.

Where some came to own, others were drawn to labor. Factories drew hundreds, then thousands, then hundreds of thousands in search of work and the antidotes to poverty and famine. In the brief thirty years between 1770 and 1800, the population of Manchester, England, almost tripled. In the next thirty years the population tripled again. The overwhelming majority of the city's population were working-class wage earners, driven off the land and into Manchester's factories.[24]

Even before the rise of factories, workers other than peasants had to travel as strangers, wandering or journeying for love or livelihood. Many moderns see the past in sepia tint, a static image of land and homeland. Yet the European past is filled with pilgrims journeying thousands of miles, beggars making a life along endless roads, highway robbers, scholars traveling from one university to the next, artisans and tradesmen, apprentices and journeymen, then seamen, pirates, colonists, soldiers, all of whom sought fortune, all of whom entered ports and merchant towns as strangers. The history of printing and books is a history of traveling typesetters who carried their characters with them.[25] Where was a ship being outfitted? Where was there need for a shoemaker? Whose child needed a tutor? And later, where could a country soul escape the curse of country life and take up some work in a factory? Men and women have chosen city life to escape the curse of tradition and the clutches of small-town acquaintances. They have sought the relief of anonymity. Social escape makes men free.

Newcomers enter the city seeking community as well, especially in this century as a feeling of isolation has descended on many men and women and they seek new ways to find mates or a community of friends. The village outcast may be accepted or even admired in the city. The large homosexual population in San Francisco is not due to the city itself; that is, the city does not create its own estranged or marginal people. On the contrary, homosexuals choose San Francisco as newcomers joining the community they know is there.[26] That community and other urban communities and interest groups are so strong that they disprove the notion that cities are cold, uncaring crowds of atomized individuals. Recently, social scientists have more and more espoused the view that cities are neighborhoods of concern and interest.[27] Some city dwellers even find these urban communities of interest confining. Some who begin as outsiders prefer to remain outsiders.

Cities, then, consist of strangers, but not because city life estranges. All urbanites are strangers when they first enter the city. Each newcomer is a stranger long before he reaches the city gate, simply because he believes he does not belong where he is. It may be the uneasiness of a family dispute or a tragedy of historic proportions that prompts this feeling of displacement. It may be economic or psychological. In any case, the stranger is one for whom the world is not obvious, not obvious at all. It needs to be changed, to be learned.[28] While many work at whatever toil they inherited and follow tradition not knowing it as tradition, the stranger questions from a distance. The stranger is apart. You, reader, are the stranger, reading a book about your own culture and history. And while all the criticisms of city life may sound familiar, every appeal of the city must also call to you, for in each of us, now, there is some of the stranger.

This work is about one possible fate for strangers who enter into city life. All cities have strangers, but only some cities prize and encourage them, valuing variety and taking pride in their achievements. These are cosmopolitan centers. In the cosmopolitan city, glamour and tolerance go hand in hand and the project of producing a great city overshadows fear and violence. This is not a story of kindness, nor generosity, nor open-heartedness. This book does not argue that people like foreigners, recognizable or unrecognizable. Some people are by nature generous and some are meanspirited. It does not matter. Rather, in some cities a way of living and working and organizing exists which favors those who favor outsiders and stifles those who would stifle others. It works this way: not every fashionable woman with a kimono-style robe will have fond thoughts for the Japanese, but where stores are filled with kimono displays and the streets are filled with sophisticated Japanese on an international tour, who will point and laugh at a Japanese woman in a kimono? Social life takes us beyond our private dispositions—it may encourage us to keep our criticism quiet, or else to reveal our intolerant selves while keeping our kindness quiet and personal. In one setting it is the thoughtful person who wins respect; in another it is the bully. This work is about the social setting, not individuals' private dispositions. Why, in some times and some places, is variety valued and great cities of enormous accomplishment hewn out of this variety? Is it possible that in one place all the kind, open-minded people of the world are found, while in another only surly, ill-willed individuals live? No. That is not possible. And besides, a great city can be built even by petty, spiteful people.

Cosmopolitan culture is not a personal predisposition, but a shared social world. The rest of this book is an examination of the necessary ingredients of such a grand design, one ingredient at a time, each ingredient illustrated by the case of a particular cosmopolitan city. The story begins with ancient Babylon, the biblical city whose gardens and temples still evoke for us luxury, grandeur, and sin. For what is a city which we dare to call great? It is, first, a city of physical beauty, magnificent in its scale. Imagine the world's capital cities. Visitors stand in awe of the architecture, not so much for its size, but for its sense of dignity and importance. There is no single style which confers this sense of importance, nor is there a single street plan or urban design. Wide boulevards are often associated with grandeur, but small squares and narrow streets can also have significance. While the art and architecture alone could stun the outsider, it is the reason behind the stone that makes the city great. Cosmopolitan cities convey a vision, a sense of purpose or mission. The reasons behind the buildings might now seem misguided, outdated, selfish, or politically reprehensible. Yet all great cities have not only great buildings, but a sense of mission carved into stone. So Chapter I, about Babylon, is a discussion of the importance of the ideas and beliefs behind the building of a cosmopolitan city, the spirit behind the stone.

Chapter II is about Constantinople, another great city, further west, closer to us in time. Constantinople will show us how the cosmopolitan city acts as a magnet, thrives on diversity. The great city has within it a taste of the whole known world. Anything that is available at all is available in that city: foods, goods, ideas, experiences, languages. We turn to Byzantium's capital to watch it draw in outsiders and outside ways. In as unlikely a place as the golden court of a brocaded emperor we find the seeds of tolerance. Diversity sows the seeds of tolerance. Diversity is the heart of cosmopolitan culture.

Cosmopolitan culture is not hammered into streets or painted onto sidewalks. It is based on shared experience and beliefs about the world. So in order to address the less concrete side of city life, in order to move still further west and closer in time, in order to fill in historical background and foreshadow future cities, Chapter III examines the urban diaspora—the experience of Jews in Western cities. At its end we will better appreciate the context of Sigmund Freud, a famous Jew in a famous city. Freud's city, Vienna, is Chapter IV, and it illustrates the importance of the public world.

Public life is what draws strangers into the city and makes them a part. Schools, parks, museums, concerts, hospitals, libraries, all of the institutions open to everyone are open to strangers. Some cities, like Boston, have a distinguished history of private education, private libraries, and privately subscribed concerts.[29] Private institutions can achieve excellence, world renown, even some degree of diversity. Yet it is its public life that turns a city into a great world capital and a place where strangers go to make their mark.

Were it just longevity and a sense of mission and a magnitude of foreign things and peoples that were necessary, many cities could claim greatness. And yet a walk through the streets of Boston would raise doubts. Boston was a great trading city even as late as 150 years ago. Its architecture still has a sober distinction. Its harbor still has a wild beauty, although whaling ships now go out to watch, not to hunt. Boston has a history of immigration and ethnic mix. Were a visitor to stroll down Newbury Street, however, he would never guess that Boston has a large Chinese population. Were the same visitor to walk through the North End, he would see a thriving Italian community, but no hint of Boston's prominent black population, descended from one of the oldest communities of free blacks in the United States. There is no place where Boston's variety is obvious or observable; there is no place where the city of Boston belongs to everyone. There is very little public life.

What, then, of cities like Boston, that are famous without quite fitting the bill? Can we explain why they never absorbed their strangers or delighted in their newcomers? Chapter V presents not-quite-cosmopolitan cities far more grand than Boston: Paris and Tokyo never truly became havens for strangers. They struggled with the seductions of the foreigner, but were held back by the rural values in their hinterlands. These not-quite-cosmopolitan cultures usher us into the twentieth century.

New York, in Chapter VI, is the land of dreams. Due to its mission, its mixture of peoples, and its public life, the cosmopolitan center is also a center of opportunity. It is a new horizon. Each stranger sees before him the chance to leave off his outsider doubts and take up the task of making a great city and signing his name to it. In a cosmopolitan culture, strangers do not simply survive, they contribute. They contribute to the project of a great, worldly city.

But the bittersweet theme of New York is really the limit to opportunity. Cosmopolitan culture depends on opportunity limited by a strong division of labor. When labor and the economy enter the discussion, the golden dream seems not so perfect. In fact, the dream is deferred, left unrealized. Chapter VII, on the Harlem Renaissance, shows cosmopolitan culture at its best and its worst—as a dream of a thriving, vital metropolis and as a dream that cannot last.

Meaning or purpose, diversity, public life and opportunity, these are the ingredients of a cosmopolitan culture. Where these ingredients flourish, the stranger is welcomed. Where these exist, there is glitter and sparkle, beauty and grace, achievement and glory. The cosmopolitan cities are the cities of great architecture, great art, great music, the cities of great renown. It is no accident that where the stranger is welcomed, there is both tolerance and genius. Or that hope and achievement live side by side. This is an ode to all that is best and valuable in human achievement, the cosmopolitan city.

Alas, it does not last.

I

Babylon: Meaning and Purpose in a Great City

Cosmopolitan cities are cities with powerful stories to tell. They are cities with a purpose, a sense of mission, an idea. Babylon was a cosmopolitan city with a strong religious sense of purpose. Why are there cities? There are cities because there are gods. Sometimes, as in Babylon, they are religious, literal gods, but the cosmopolitan city worships some ideal, something. Babylon holds the key to a theory of cosmopolitan culture, for its story has become so powerful, its gods so important, that it has become the prototype for the cosmopolitan city. Beautiful. Seductive. Sinful.

The whore of Babylon sits waiting in a linen robe. She is perfumed. She is beautiful. She is upper-class. She is unquestionably a whore. It is not just a metaphor, this whore business; priestesses exist whose job it is to make love to those who enter the temple and in making love to pay homage to Ishtar, goddess of fertility. She now owns the dowry that would have gone to her husband, since she will never marry. Maybe she went to court for her share of her late father's estate; she has it. With the money she has bought slaves, and the slaves are named in her honor: "The-slave-of-the-beautiful-mistress-Amu"; "I-am-the-obedient-servant-of-a-kind-mistress."[1] Some wait on her, curling and oiling the long ropes of black hair that fall past her shoulders. Other slaves she sends out to work; she receives their wages. Still others learn crafts; she sets them up in trade and her income expands. She adopts heirs. She is refined and honored, the last representative of a long tradition of worship, and she is its purest form.

At other times, according to other accounts, the temples were filled not with these priestesses, but with the women of Babylon themselves.[2] Each woman living in Babylon was obliged, once in her life, to wait until a stranger would enter and pay to sleep with her. If the competition was not too stiff, the woman not too unappealing, and peace and good trade were bringing many visitors to the city, a woman could dispatch her duty to the gods in several days. But an unluckier sister might languish for months at least. Could it be years? Perhaps the duty was eventually taken up by a few special women. It is a peaceful and tempting adaptation to a problem every tribe faced—each one depended on new blood, new genes, new characteristics. Other groups plundered and raped, stole men and women or traded them. But in Babylon, when the stranger came, there was a woman waiting to tempt him.

Even before women waited for strangers, scholars say, the women of Babylon were all up for sale. Wives were sold at auction: the most desirable fetched high prices and were taken first. This money was used to buy husbands for the least desirable. In this way, the women were never in competition for husbands, but helped one another gain security. And it helped the men, too: a poor man could walk away from the auction with a less-than-perfect wife, but he would also have the means to set up a shop or purchase a field.

The Sumerians, the city's first settlers, worshiped gods of fertility and their gods were kind. Unpredictable rains and winds, like benevolent strangers, brought fertility to their valley. Wives distributed at auction, women who gave their bodies to strangers, all this was in the name of fertility. In Babylon outside influence was often considered benevolent. If a person was sick in Babylon, he could rightfully demand of each passer-by a medical opinion. The stranger's answer could be the best answer, just as fertility could best be served by absorbing the stranger.

But if you came to Babylon as an ancient Hebrew warrior, warned against giving in to other people's gods, you would find yourself sorely tried. The Babylon which welcomed strangers was also Babylon, the city of sin. The two go together. Temptation and confusion go hand in hand. Babylon has become the prototypical city filled with strangers, filled with luxury and corruption. The Bible has it written thus (but we will read between the lines). The Bible speaks of Nebuchadnezzar II, king of Babylon (known more accurately in recent scholarship as Nebuchadrezzar), who subdued Jerusalem and destroyed the temple in 586 B.C. He took the Hebrews captive and brought them to Babylon. Exile and corruption have become the city's legacy in Judeo-Christian tradition. Scholars such as James Dougherty explain that the Babylon of the Bible has become the Babylon of the Western imagination, the city of eventual destruction and retribution.[3] Christians in ancient Rome were already using the image. It was called a Babylonian captivity when from 1309 to 1377 (like the seventy years the Hebrews spent in exile) the Papacy moved to Avignon, France, and, according to many, too lavishly enjoyed the refuge. Hundreds of years later the Protestant Reformation put the final stamp of disapproval on frivolity and temptation with the name "Babylon."

If you read with awe when you read about Babylon, read slowly. If you read with contempt and shame, move fast, deliberately, with a Reformer's step and a Puritan's gaze. There is no sin in Babylon but temptation, and that is the worst.

THE GOLDEN CUP

> Babylon hath been a golden cup in the Lord's hand
> that made all the earth drunken;
> The nations have drunk of her wine,
> Therefore the nations are mad.
>
> —Jeremiah 51:7

Babylon's wealth made it a golden cup, tempting to all those who loved luxury. The docile cooperation of the rivers Tigris and Euphrates and the legendary fertility of the Mesopotamian river valley helped create a grain-producing empire so great that it financed the known world. The Greek historian Herodotus, writing around 450 B.C., was overwhelmed by Assyria, part of the Babylonian-controlled lands. Herodotus especially admired the irrigation systems used in Babylon, among the most sophisticated in the world. But his greatest praise was for the agriculture.

> As a grain-bearing country Assyria is the richest in the world. No attempt is made there to grow figs, grapes, or olives or any other

fruit trees, but so great is the fertility of the grain fields that they normally produce crops of two-hundredfold, and in an exceptional year as much as three-hundredfold. The blades of wheat and barley are at least three inches wide. As for millet and sesame, I will not say to what an astonishing size they grow, though I know well enough; but I also know that people who have not been to Babylonia have refused to believe even what I have said already about its fertility.[4]

If grain-growing and agricultural expertise alone do not spell wealth, trade them eastward for spices, fruits, game and cook them into sumptuous meals. Recipe books written in cuneiform symbols on stone tablets, deciphered by the French scholar Jean Bottéro, tell of sophisticated dishes and master chefs, of spices and stews of breathtaking variety. The Babylonians could make at least one hundred soups, three hundred types of bread, eighteen cheeses, and meats of wide choice flavored with garlic, onions, leeks, mint, juniper, mustard, coriander, or cumin. Fish, turtle, shellfish, vegetables, fruits, mushrooms, insects. These dishes not only show wide-ranging tastes, curiosity, and experimentation; they also spell wealth.[5]

If grain and oil have bought enough of these, trade them to the Syrians or further northward for iron, gold, copper, silver, bronze, for tools, for weapons, for armaments, or for clothing. Herodotus further described the wealth of Babylon in its dress.

> The dress of the Babylonians consists of a linen tunic reaching to the feet with a woollen one over it, and a short white cloak on top; they have their own fashion in shoes, which resemble the slippers one sees in Boetia. They grow their hair long, wear turbans, and perfume themselves all over; everyone owns a seal and a walking-stick specially made for him, with a device carved on the top of it, an apple or rose or lily or eagle or something of the sort; for it is not the custom to have a stick without some such ornament.[6]

Clothes were extravagantly fringed, dyed, and supplemented with much jewelry—even though styles were simple. Household necessities were ornamented: chairs, couches, and tripods for containers had the carved feet of oxen or clenched fists for support. The so-called "Luristan bronzes," bronze artifacts from around 1000 B.C., suggest an extensive bronze industry, possibly inspired or directed by Babylonians, possibly just patronized by them.[7] If all this does not spell wealth, look at the city itself, with its walls and temples and sophisticated system of drainage which allowed each inhabitant access to fresh water from one canal and a waste sluice in another. Look at the pillars of carved palm trunks, columns with distinctive capitals—and everything clay could possibly become.

And Babylon was full of gardens. The "Hanging Gardens" did not really hang, but arched and rose in steps, recreating the wooded mountains of the king's wife's homeland, Media. Stones signified mountains and on them the king had trees planted. The garden, continually fed fresh water pumped from the Euphrates, was the wonder of visitors.[8] Its wonder was not only beauty, although it was beautiful. Engineering and design added to the garden's glory. Now can we appreciate its longevity as well—it is one of the few ancient monuments seen by twentieth-century archaeologists. Between 1899 and 1917 a German expedition of archaeologists headed by Robert Koldewey saw evidence of the gardens described by historians and geographers in 200 B.C., 100 B.C., and A.D. 20.

Around the city was a moat. Then walls. The Ishtar Gate, the city's main gate of entry, named for the goddess, opened into a broad, walled road, wide enough for carts, the walls high enough to obscure either side, and this road led into the city. The walls along this road were covered in glazed clay tiles of hues so brilliant that they still shine; glazed tiles have been recovered and walls reconstructed. Brown lions on a blazing blue background and life-sized foreigners bearing tribute to the king guarded these walls.[9] Imagine the awesome color and shape, the dyes, glazes, paints. The ashes and dust and crumbling clay which we think of as biblical are only reflections of our own dry disillusionment. Once Babylon was a bright, colorful industrial city of technical achievement and artistic accomplishment.

All of Babylon's beauty and wealth could be traded on an open market where ownership was not limited to the few and even a slave could barter and bargain. Priests and the temple were privileged, and the empire was funded and fortified. But substantial private property was held by great landowners, who hired tenant laborers, and by great banking families, like the Egibi, whose power lasted for hundreds of years. Any craftsperson could sell his wares. The temptation of the senses led to the temptation of ownership. And more. To the temptation of opportunity. The historian A. Leo Oppenheim has pointed to ancient texts as a source of information about Babylon's economy. As he says, these texts reveal

> a remarkable degree of economic mobility: poor people expect to become rich; the rich are afraid of becoming poor; both dread interference from the palace.[10]

One thing that contributed to Babylon's wealth (and later disrepute) was the fact that capital was a commodity for which interest was charged. An old letter pleads with its recipient: "Give [in the meantime] the 140 shekels which are still outstanding from your own money but do not charge interest between us—we are both gentlemen!"[11] In Babylon the charging of interest was a way to expand resources. The element of time increased the value of goods, allowed traders to accumulate wealth beyond simple barter, and promoted investment in bigger farms and bigger construction projects.

Finally, there were taxes in Babylon, and that also increased the city's wealth. Herodotus admired the fact that tribute was so complete and so completely enabled the king to go to war.

> I will give several indications of the wealth and resources of Babylon, but the following is a specially striking one. Apart from normal tribute, the whole . . . empire is divided into regions for the purpose of furnishing supplies for the king and his army, and for four months out of the twelve the supplies come from Babylonian territory, the whole of the rest of Asia being responsible for the remaining eight. This shows that the resources of Assyria are a third part of the resources of Asia as a whole. . . . The governorship

. . . of Assyria is by far the most coveted of all their provincial posts.
. . . Tritantaechmes, the son of Artabazus, who held it from the
king, received an artaba of silver every day—the artaba is a Persian
dry measure of about five bushels. . . .[12]

This golden cup, Babylon, was the capital city of an empire whose
boundaries changed but whose laws stayed surprisingly constant. Different dynasties ruled harshly or compassionately by their own convention.
But through all the changes in leadership, the tradition of law, written
law, remains steady. Two thousand years before the birth of Christ, King
Hammurabi, sixth king of the first dynasty of the empire of Babylon, had
carved in clay a code of laws concerning life, property, and conduct.
Hammurabi's laws were not the first written laws in existence and the
king himself is now believed to have been a mediocre code maker. No
matter how wise the lawgiver, what matters is the law. Babylon was a
kingdom where laws took precedence over men, where slander or un-
proven accusations were punished and crimes met appropriate punishments. "If a man destroyed the eye of a nobleman," the law said, "they
shall destroy his eye. If he has broken another's bone, they shall break
his bone."[13]

There is a theory, a simple, compelling theory, that people assimilate
what is to their advantage and always move toward a better life.[14] To
the extent that codified law ensured a better life, it is not surprising that
peoples migrating into Babylon took it up and enjoyed it. Just as Babylon's gardens made the life of the wealthy sweet, justice made the life
of the disadvantaged bearable. Law, even law, with its unbending rules,
stiff punishments, and formulaic phrases, can be a temptation.

Add to this poetry, music, scholarship, medicine and then try to
calculate cause and effect. Did a thriving economy make leisure, love
letters, bank records, and scholarship possible? Was it the advent of
geometry and bills of sale that made large-scale farming profitable? Did
a stable legal system ensure the trust that would make business possible?
Or, as Oppenheim suggests, did business require law, writing, and educated traders as well as new wares, such as medicines, and new methods,
such as capital loans?[15] Finally, did all of these things tempt newcomers,

or did the constant stream of newcomers revivify the city—was it cosmopolitan before them or cosmopolitan after? The answer to this question is both. The fate of the nations which drank from Babylon's golden cup, their movement toward a better life, shows that they both profited from and created the first cosmopolitan center.

THE PEOPLES OF BABYLON

Babylon's resources allowed the city to expand and expend on luxury, but wealth alone does not make a cosmopolitan center. The city's diversity of peoples contributed to its sophistication. Early Babylon was a blend of Sumerian and Semitic cultures.[16] The Sumerians were slowly forced back by the Akkadians, finally disappearing through assimilation and intermarriage; they were unknown to history until one hundred years ago, when clay documents were unearthed which revealed they had come from the Persian Gulf to settle in Babil, a place whose name might have existed even before them. But then, the origin of the name is not certain.[17]

The Sumerians were not empire builders. Maybe for that reason, maybe in spite of it, their world has left a powerful image. Their treatment of women, their literature, and their custom of adoption seem to reflect refinement and care. They did not found dynasties, but they built the base of a cosmopolitan center. The high social estimation of women later on diminished, fading into a shadow of what it had been; but the value of love and the importance of the goddess of fertility long outlived its Sumerian founders.

A Sumerian proverb said, "He that supports no wife, he that supports no son, does not support himself."[18] At first, that was taken to refer to the fact that Sumerian men believed women to be indispensable and powerful. Women argued in court, bought and sold property, inherited as much as men did. Later versions of the proverb look more favorably on bachelorhood; over the thousands of years of Babylon, as the beliefs of other people grew dominant, narrower views of women prevailed. With time, the equitable wife auction disappeared. Yet belief in love pervaded Babylonian life, and women, who were often educated and literate, retained respect, if not power. This personal letter was probably read privately by the woman who received it.

> To the lady Kasbeya thus says Gimil-Merodach: May the sun-god and Merodach for my sake grant thee everlasting life! I am writing to inquire after your health; please send me news of it. I am living at Babylon, but have not seen you, which troubles me greatly. Send me news of your coming to me, so that I may be happy. Come in the month of Marchesvan (October). May you live for ever for my sake![19]

No modern reader could remain untouched. Then again, love letters may always sound modern.

More wonderful still is the writing itself. The Sumerians had given the world literacy. And much later, long after the Semitic tribes of the West, particularly the Akkadians, wrote in their own languages (Akkadian or Aramaic), they maintained Sumerian as the language of erudition; scholars have compared it to the Latin of the Middle Ages. Semitic words for "palace" and "city" come from Sumerian; there were none before.[20] Sumerians were the first literate city dwellers. They wrote poems, essays, and debates as well as legal documents and school texts. Their proverbs, many giving voices to objects or dumb animals, sound familiar to the modern ear. Sumerian literature, in its fables, proverbs, stories, and, above all, in its written form, gave birth indirectly and slowly to many of the West's oldest traditions.

Aesop could have been the name the Greeks attached to some proverbs and fables which had their origin in Babylon. Meanwhile, the Babylonians of the fifth and sixth centuries had inherited them from the Sumerians. Aesop, the fictitious storyteller, is interesting in his own right for other reasons. The Greeks described him as dark, misshapen, and, above all, a slave. They were perfectly justified in describing his "Eastern" nature, for only in the Near East, not in aristocratic Greece, could a clever man of humble origins be promoted in the government as a wise man.[21] Opportunity was greater in the cosmopolitan East.

The Sumerians wrote an unusual form of poem or essay which may reveal something of their character. This was a kind of contest or debate.[22] In "The Dispute Between Summer and Winter," the two seasons brag about their merits. "The Dispute Between the Farmer and the Shepherd" sounds very much like Cain and Abel's dispute over who gave a greater sacrifice in God's eyes, or Jacob and Esau's alternate claims to inheritance. And indeed the older Sumerian version may have influenced the writers of the Old Testament.

One archaeologist analyzes these essays as proof of the competitiveness and drive for superiority among the Sumerians. Long years of formal education demanded intense competition. Their culture was contentious and aggressive and so was their law and legality. Could the Sumerians have been driven to their advances in the arts and letters, in law and science, and in the economy by an American-type ambition? According to this archaeologist, that is a more likely explanation than simple intellectual curiousity.[23]

If these refined, articulate Sumerians did harbor aggressiveness and competitiveness, they successfully controlled them. One example of this is the Sumerians' broadly applied, often-used system of adoption. Individuals could include in their families almost anyone at almost any time. This unusual practice created a legal way to bring an outsider closer to the center. Individuals could adopt slaves, friends, orphans, debtors. The laws behind this practice are complicated, as the code of Hammurabi, a Semitic king, shows.

If a seignior adopted a boy in his own name and has reared him, that foster child may never be reclaimed.

If a seignior, upon adopting a boy, seeks out his father and mother when he has taken him, that foster child may return to his father's house.

If a seignior, who adopted a boy and reared him, set up a family of his own, has later acquired children and so has made up [his] mind to cut off the foster child, that son shall not go off empty-handed: his foster father shall give him from his goods his one-third patrimony and then he shall go off, since he may not give him any of the field, orchard or house.

If the adopted son of a chamberlain or the adopted son of a

votary has said to his foster father or his foster mother, "You are not my father," "You are not my mother," they shall cut out his tongue.

If the adopted son of a chamberlain or the adopted son of a votary found out his parentage and came to hate his foster father and his foster mother and so has gone off to his paternal home, they shall pluck out his eye.[24]

One result of the adoption policy was the chance for betterment and mobility. Artisans taught their trade to adopted sons who, according to law, could never be reclaimed. But at the same time, adoption kept the Sumerians, who originated these ideas, from remaining a distinct ethnic community. The system of adoption gave the privileges of citizenship to many foreigners, allowing them to sign contracts and conduct business. Babylon, the commercial community, gained by avoiding exclusivity on the grounds of race and nationality. Babylon, the cosmopolitan center, grew in diversity.[25]

When the Semitic Akkadians came into power around 2000 B.C., they expanded Babylon to imperial proportions while taking on the urban ways of the Sumerians. Akkadian became the vernacular, but Sumerian was still used for classical writing. Aramaic was also a popular language; literacy and linguistic ability remained important. The Rab-shakeh, an Assyrian official, knew Sumerian, used Aramaic when called upon to do so, and knew Hebrew so that he could address the subjects of Jerusalem. Yet he was a simple bureaucrat, neither a scribe nor a scholar.[26] The Akkadian language added to Babylonian literature a mass of private letters and business contracts and creative literature which reveals pessimism and world-weariness. The new pessimism was itself a product of wealth and empire. The Akkadians expanded the world, but as their vision of their gods became more complex, their actions seemed to lose meaning. It is the sad Akkadian voice that influenced the Judeo-Christian voice of pessimism in Ecclesiastes.[27] In the Akkadian "Pessimistic Dialogue Between Master and Servant," the lord decides he will ride, and the servant agrees. Then the lord decides it is futile. Yes, the servant agrees, riding is futile and so is not riding. Building is pointless, as is not building; enjoyment, contemplation, largesse as well as greed, all are futile.[28] *The Epic of Gilgamesh*, an Akkadian literary masterpiece from before 1000 B.C., is heroic, but it does not recount triumph. The hero fails in his attempt to grasp the key to immortality and his friend is killed. Gilgamesh wonders why he has toiled so hard. The full weight of disillusionment falls in these familiar sounds:

> Who, my friend, can scale heaven?
> Only the gods live forever under the sun.
> As for mankind, numbered are their days;
> Whatever they achieve is but the wind![29]

Empire building can be a sad business.

If the empire's foundation was Semitic and Sumerian, its legal and economic life was filled with many other peoples. They came for trade, grazing, and general fortune seeking, as warriors or as captives. We know that in one district, where the Amorites settled, natives or foreigners were on equal footing—either could hold land, and both faced the same judge and the same law. There seems little reason to believe the Amorites were restricted in where they were allowed to settle. A foreigner had as much right as anyone to buy, sell, or bequeath pieces of Babylon. Foreigners held military appointments, witnessed deeds. One deed was signed Yavanni—"the Greek."[30] The head of a large commercial family was called "the Egyptian." Greeks lived in Babylon during the sixth and fifth centuries B.C., learning or practicing crafts, especially the art of glazed tiles. But they were employed equally as doctors and as seamen.[31] Proof that peoples migrated to Babylon might be inferred from the fact that gods were said to migrate to Babylon, just as gods were said to adopt children. In one story the Syrian god Hadad, or Rimmon, goes to Babylon in order to watch over the Amorites.[32] An unusual essay, written in 1898, the heyday of ethnic self-promotion, claims that the Celts had a strong influence on the ancient Near East.[33] Influence or not, there is at least the possibility that a tablet with Celtic writing outlining some matrimonial deal was delivered to Babylon. And then, of course, there were slaves.

As time went on, there was more demand for foreign slaves. We can make guesses why—as Babylon filled with more peoples, property owners were more open to foreigners, or they wanted translators, or it was chic. Yet no single group emerged as a recognizable slave class. Sixty percent of male slaves' names appear for free men as well. Only 7 percent of the names were not Akkadian. Owners saw no stigma, in other words, in having a slave who had changed his name to resemble the name of his master. While many more women's names belonged only to slaves, no stigma was attached to them—freed slaves did not shed their old names.[34] Some slaves were foreign, but some slaves were the same nationality as their masters, and the laws did not distinguish slaves by race or origin. The rank of slaves was often higher, and the protection greater, than that of free laborers. Women slaves kept their children with them. Slaves were not used in large-scale farming. Even the imperial work crews constructing temples and monuments were for the most part hired laborers. In an empire where life expectancy was between seventy and a hundred years, slaves also lived to an old age, often between sixty and eighty.[35] If injured, they were compensated. Some people became enslaved due to debt, most due to conquest. None were enslaved due to nationality. War had its losers and conquest its victims, and defeat, not the accidents of birth, made slaves of ancient men.

The assimilation of the Chaldeans was quietest and most complete. They entered Babylon as foreigners and some among them became monarchs. They say Nebuchadnezzar, Babylon's greatest ruler, was a Chaldean. Around 850 B.C. the Chaldeans, attacked by Assyria, moved for refuge and for prosperity. They took Babylonian names. As one historian says of this assimilation:

> Though the Chaldaeans kept their tribal structure, in other ways they adopted themselves to Babylonian life, settling down in cities, planting date-palm orchards, taking Babylonian names (few native Chaldaean names are attested) and assuming an active role in the government of Babylonia. . . .[36]

It sounds so easy. Assuming an active role in government. Settling down in cities. Did no one object? How did they do it? First, they contributed highly valued skills. The Chaldeans were noted for their problem-solving ability and their advances in astronomy, two fields important to the Sumerian-Akkadian tradition. Indeed, they excelled in accepting Babylonian values and then surpassing them. The Chaldeans calculated the diameter of the moon so accurately that they were still undisputed in the eighteenth century. The arithmetic which Greece learned from Babylon was Chaldean arithmetic.[37] Berosus, the great Babylonian historian, was Chaldean. All of this took place in an adopted language, in a foreign city.

We can say that Babylon was rich or powerful or well-placed geographically or militarily. We can even locate the ways in which foreigners were or were not included in city life. We can conclude that all of its peoples were pawns in a capricious history, responding to their own greed or fear, unaware that their ashes and dust would interest us. But this is not right: it is no accident that we have heard of Babylon. The people of Babylon wanted it to be great. It was their sense of purpose which made them incorporate strangers. After all, it is the stranger who may carry the tale.

BUILD YE HOUSES AND DWELL IN THEM: RELIGIOUS PURPOSE FOR BABYLON

"Now, O lord, thou who hast caused our deliverance,
what shall be our homage to thee?
Let us build a shrine whose name shall be called
'Lo-a-chamber-for-our-nightly-rest': let us repose in it!"

. . . when Marduk heard this,
Brightly glowed his features, like the day:
"Like that of lofty Babylon, whose building you have requested
Let its brickwork be fashioned . . ."

. . . "This is Babylon, the place that is your home!
Make memory in its precincts, occupy its broad places."

The great gods took their seats,
they set up festive drink, sat down to a banquet.
—from *Enuma elis*,
the Babylonian creation epic[38]

On the fourth day of each New Year's festival, when these words were recited, the citizens of Babylon were reminded that their city was built to house the gods and that it especially delighted Marduk, first among them. The city was founded to embody a mission and a consistent theme: the gods loved Babylon because it was their home. How else explain the fertile fields, the wealth, the abundance of festive drink and banquet delicacies? An eighth-century-B.C. literary text giving "Advice to a Prince" detailed the special privileges to be afforded cities, and, above all, Babylon. The city of Babylon at the time paid no tax to the empire whatsoever. It was a holy center and was therefore left alone. The empire could reclaim none of the city's private fields or animals, nor could it demand forced labor of its people. All of this on the grounds that it was a special, sanctified place.[39]

It doesn't matter that powerful private landowners might have prompted these rules or that the wealth of the city might have benefited the empire so much that taxes were unnecessary. All that matters is that the city had a reason to exist and, what is more, a reason to be great. Remember, there are cities because there are gods. Even an early Sumerian account of a great flood which does not mention Babylon includes an explanation that individual cities were founded as cult centers to various gods. It is no wonder that the kingdom built on the roots of Sumerian culture found its justification in the glory of the gods.

No wonder at all. Ancient peoples made few divisions between different spheres of life. Religion infused daily life; it was daily life. It is of no use asking if a Babylonian was a true believer or a skeptic. It would be like asking if you or I believed in air or better yet, in trees, in soil. What would such a question mean? You would look puzzled; you might shrug. Trees? They exist. What fool would say they don't? And if I said, no, no, I don't believe in them, would I stand in the sun while all my friends enjoyed the shade? Or would I, too, be in the shade, unable to explain myself? Babylon was explained by the best, the only explanation of its age.

Nowadays the rule of religion grows smaller and smaller. It is housed in a special building, confined to a given day, and sifted out from more worldly concerns: politics, law, gardening, cooking. How many moderns think of their god each time they flick a light switch, run a faucet, make love, go to work? And yet at one time the giving of light, of water, fertility, and the necessity of labor were intrinsically part of religion. Max Weber, the German social theorist, has called the slow change between then and now the "disenchantment" of the world. More tasks have become less tied to religion and the supernatural as life has become more ordered and organized, more rational—as one act has become associated with its one result, one means with its one end. And what makes life more rational? A long process of change beginning with the change from many gods to one god—the one god who is not present in each act, or behind each shadow, but abstract and all-knowing.[40]

By the the Neo-Babylonian period, after power was seized in 625 B.C. by the Chaldeans and Nabopolassar began a newly powerful empire, the city's sense of purpose had subtly changed. For now, in addition to being a religious center, Babylon had a historical call to greatness; many cried for the restoration of its former glory. Babylon also became an expression of its rulers' personal power and glory. The long-reigning Neo-Babylonian kings Nabopolassar (625–605 B.C.), Nebuchadnezzar (605–562 B.C.), and Nabonidus (556–539 B.C.) made a bid for immortality through building and conquest, and they justified this by pointing to Babylon's greatness. Nabopolassar inscribed the monuments he erected with an explanation of his inspiration.

I, Nabopolassar, king of Babylon, to whom Nabu and Marduk stretch out the hand, have established Imgur-Enlil, the great wall of Babylon which in my time had collapsed and fallen at an angle on the ancient basis of its foundations, with the workmen levied from my land, I have rebuilt it and surrounded Babylon with it in the direction of the four winds. I have raised its summit as in former days. O Wall, speak favourably to Marduk, my lord.

I, Nabopolassar, king of Babylon, to whom Nabu and Marduk stretch out the hand, have inspected the old foundations of Imgur Enlil, the great wall of Babylon, from the bank of the Arachtum Canal on the upper side of Ishtar Gate to the lower side of Uras Gate, and I have rebuilt it on the same pattern for Marduk, my lord. O, Wall, speak favourably to Marduk.[41]

Marduk has taken precedence in these inscriptions—he is the single one to whom the wall must speak. Of what must the wall speak? Of Nabopolassar, the king, Nabopolassar in his glory, Nabopolassar, who wants his empire remembered. Nebuchadnezzar, too, hoped for immortality, though he sought it in more earthly greatness.

On a wall made of bricks towards the North, my heart instructed me to build a palace to protect Babylon. So I built there a palace of bricks and plaster. . . . I built a pillared hall, an earth levelling in the direction of Sppar in the form of dry land, and made its foundation deep in the ground. Huge trunks of cedar wood which I placed in the ceilings. Double door of cedar wood engraved with copper, with their hinges and holders made of bronze and set them in the entrances. That building I called Nebuchadnezzar's life. I hope it will last long like the glory of Esagila.[42]

The Neo-Babylonian period was the most distinguished period for architecture in Babylon. Public works, sanctuaries, city walls, gates, palaces, canals were built or repaired. Staircases along the river allowed descent along the quays, much like today's Paris. The Etemenanki enclosure, or main ziggurat temple (the wedding-cake-shaped temple), was rebuilt on old foundations. Nebuchadnezzar's gardens and palaces had no rivals.

For these great kings the mission of personal glory was not inconsistent with the glory of the gods. And both were consistent with the growing power of the city of Babylon—the home of gods and of kings. As for the citizens, they traditionally believed that the kings understood the way to the gods' honor. And who could deny Babylon's greatness? Was that not justification enough? Babylon had a founding myth and a sense of mission. Who could deny tradition and the glory of the gods? Only a prophet.

In the days of Nebuchadnezzar the nations swayed between war and servitude; alliance meant submission, betrayal meant death. The Assyrians, uneasy allies to Babylon, threatened Judah, which sought protection from Babylon. When the moment seemed propitious, the people of Judah tried allying with Egypt against Babylon, or as it is written, the Chaldeans. The Chaldeans had become so integrated into Babylonian life that Babylon was known by their name. When Jehoiakim rebelled, the people of Judah found themselves in battle against the Babylonians.

> In his days Nebuchadnezzar king of Babylon came up and Jehoiakim became his servant three years; then he turned and rebelled against him. And the Lord sent against him bands of the Chaldaeans. . . .
>
> —Second Kings 24:1–2

Judah was rife with dissension and weakened from disputes over succession. The days of the great kings, Saul and David and Solomon, had dissipated to days of squabbling and laxity. The alliances that they sought with stronger states misfired, and their independence was tenuous and short-lived. Once Nebuchadnezzar crushed the Egyptians, Judah and its city Jerusalem were directly besieged by Babylon. When Nebuchadnezzar's armies entered the city, they took its riches and made captives of its people, bringing to Babylon yet another nation of foreigners.

> And he carried away all Jerusalem, and all the princes, and all the mighty men of valour, even ten thousand captives, and all the craftsmen and the smiths; none remained, save the poorest sort of the people of the land.
>
> —Second Kings 24:14

It was during this time of confused and miscalculated actions that the prophet Jeremiah preached the words that he believed to be the true way of the Lord (against all the false prophets who spoke the opposing view). Jeremiah was the son of the high priest Hilkiah, and came from a pious, well-educated family near Jerusalem.[43] He was no blind leper, frenzied with religious fervor, drooling over cryptic phrases, proselytizing the deaf and those who could not walk away. Nor did he wave and glad-hand, wearing madras pants and a team-player grin. He was learned and exact as he dictated to his scribe Baruch, who read his words aloud. His message was to Judah, but it helped the people of Judah see Babylon. They came to see in Babylon the instrument of God; the city became the meaning of their lives.

We face the same dilemma looking back that the people of Judah did looking ahead: Who is a prophet? Is he one whose words become true or one who voices truths already known?[44] Does he reveal the obscure or insist on the obvious? Is it really possible that everyone but Jeremiah wanted to stay and defend the doomed city of Jerusalem and surely die rather than go to Babylon? Or did Jeremiah dictate with an eye for politics, repudiating those who stayed behind so that the future would belong to those in Babylon? He was right. The future did belong to those in Babylon. Some believe that the words of Jeremiah and much of the Bible were written in Babylon. The Bible speaks so strongly against those who remained in Judah rather than go into exile that many scholars believe it was written by those who went to Babylon and expressed their feelings. The religion of those in exile became the dominant form of Judaism. Jewish rituals and laws and priorities may have all developed while the people of Judah were in exile.[45]

In short, exile demanded some changes in religious practice that were later retained. One important change was a text strongly influenced by Babylonian literary tradition. In retrospect, the Jews, or at least Jeremiah, saw in Babylon not only the instrument of God, but the opportunity to consolidate their religious interests. So they had reason to accept Babylon just as so many other foreign tribes had entered and assimilated to their advantage. But if Babylon is so powerful in its influence on Judah, why is it cursed as wicked and evil?

The words of Jeremiah carry a double message. First he counsels the Jews to cooperate, to go to Babylon and, what is more, to enjoy life there.

> Thus saith the Lord of hosts, the God of Israel, unto all the captivity, whom I have caused to be carried away captive from Jerusalem unto Babylon:
>
> Build ye houses, and dwell in them, and plant gardens, and eat the fruit of them; take ye wives, and beget sons and daughters; and take wives for your sons, and give your daughters to husbands, that they may bear sons and daughters; and multiply ye there, and be not diminished. And seek the peace of the city whither I have caused you to be carried away captive, and pray unto the Lord for it: for in the peace thereof shall ye have peace.
>
> —Jeremiah 29:4–7

As counsel, this is wise, but as fact (since many believe it was written in Babylon with the advantage of hindsight), it is impeccable. The Jews enjoyed the same luxury and prosperity in Babylon other peoples there did. They could own property, indulge in sensual, spiritual, and familial pleasures, and live in peace. It was a golden captivity. They were neither enslaved nor forced to labor. Nebuchadnezzar wanted craftsmen, especially in this period of building and expansion. Jeremiah was wise to tell his people to enjoy a new world of riches and culture. If Jeremiah's words were written after the fact, their counsel really explains the lessons the Jews learned in exile: it is best to enjoy prosperity and domestic happiness, to have a wife and legitimate heirs; a life of temporary encampment, broken standards, and illegitimate children will lead to ruin. There is a temptation in feeling temporary, that the rules do not apply today since tomorrow we will be gone. In love this causes pain. In life this leads to regret. So Jeremiah counseled his people in favor of responsibility.

Yet the enjoyment of exile has a price, and this is the second message. The reason it is all right to stay in Babylon is that this city is the instrument of God and, as the instrument of God, it will be punished and fall. Thus is founded a paradox of diaspora life: the only reason one may enjoy assimilated life is that it is God's will, but recognition that it is God's will means recognition that this place is corrupt, wanting, and destined to fall. Jews may enjoy, but they must criticize at the same time.[46] Enjoyment without guilt is a life without meaning; participation without social criticism is empty—it would be Jeremiah without jeremiads, blind and obedient captivity. Criticism without participation, however, is life without joy.

Ambivalence is the unique contribution of the Jews to Babylon, the city whose purpose was both to succeed and to fail, where joy so closely clung to sorrow. The psalm sings of weeping, but they are tears of ambivalence.

> By the rivers of Babylon,
> There we sat down, yea, we wept,
> When we remembered Zion.
> Upon the willows in the midst thereof
> We hanged up our harps.
> For there they that led us captive
> asked of us words of song,
> And our tormentors asked of us mirth:
> "Sing us one of the songs of Zion."
>
> How shall we sing the Lord's song
> In a foreign land?
> If I forget thee, O Jerusalem,
> Let my right hand forget her cunning.
> Let my tongue cleave to the roof of my mouth.
> If I remember thee not;
> If I set not Jerusalem
> Above my chiefest joy.
>
> —Psalm 137:1–6

The greatest wickedness and evil of a cosmopolitan center is the temptation to enjoy and to forget.

For some the god Bel, for some Marduk, for others the Hebrew God gave Babylon meaning. The inhabitants of the city believed the city had a purpose, and in believing in the purpose they cooperated in the creation of a great cosmopolitan center. No matter if the purpose had a tragic touch. There was a reason for wealth, a reason for beauty, a reason to take in strangers with special skills, a reason to increase the population, a reason to teach and study and write. No matter if the purpose was the ill-fated and vain hope of immortality. Vanity is something in which all peoples can participate.

THE BOOK OF DANIEL: STORY OF A STRANGER

Of all of the historical sources we have, the Bible is the most accurate, next to cuneiform texts.[47] One scholar summarizes, "The Book of Daniel presents an authentic picture of Babylon at the height of its glory."[48] But this notion is odd. We imagine the Greek historians to be geometric and exact in logic, piercingly perceptive in imagination. But the writers of the Bible? Poetic shepherds, inspired by God, perhaps, but with little grip on reality. In fact, though, what is called history is often poetry: poetry is called prose; fiction, fact. And so one cannot judge a book by its intent. The Book of Daniel, scholars now believe, was intended as a comment on the Jewish struggles against Rome, not Babylon, and was written around 168 B.C.[49] The visions and dreams that foretold the fall of the mighty were meant to exhort Jewish resistance at that time. The dreams and visions, in language exotic and surreal, have been interpreted and interpreted. Our reading is a simpler one.

The story of Daniel is the story of a foreigner in Babylon. When we follow Daniel and the others taken captive with him, life is breathed into the rules and laws and documents. We see how the laws worked, and we see Babylon as a cosmopolitan center. Daniel and three other Jewish aristocratic children are adopted by King Nebuchadnezzar. The king intends to educate them and prepare them for imperial service and so he gives them appropriately Babylonian names. Why does he do this? Doesn't he fear that foreigners, no matter how young, cannot be trusted and, especially if they are educated, will betray Babylon? But the king believes they are less of a threat if incorporated into his palace. After all, adopted children who are trained cannot be reclaimed, and if they denounce their adopted parents, they may be put to death, as they will if they seek out their true parents and go to them. (When in the story the youths refuse the king's food, they may be trying to resist the temptation to forget they are different. Or perhaps they are unaccustomed to it and don't like it. Or perhaps it is a way of denouncing their adopted father without saying it aloud and being punished.) And more importantly, royal blood means more than foreign birth. If Daniel and his friends are attractive, if they are wise, if they are skillful, then they are needed. So the outsider becomes the insider if he has something to contribute.

Daniel's skill at dream interpretation is unsurpassed, he is wise, and he is necessary to kings. In short, he is the master of one of the Chaldeans' most treasured values, the interpretation of signs. Although he entered Babylon unable even to speak the language, he rises to prominence. Why? Obviously, the story implies, because he is clever and loved by God. But could it be that as an outsider he has grasped what is most important to the Chaldeans and has chosen to excel precisely at that? It is possible, since Daniel interprets his first dream out of necessity, to save his life and the lives of the kingdom's wise men. Could it be that he is just a brilliant student who has outdone his Chaldean teachers? The children he came with also rose to prominence, learning to do their tasks perfectly. Could all foreign children taken captive have excelled?

The outsider, like Daniel, has an advantage. The first skill he acquires is translation. Not only must he learn a new language, but he must always ask himself, How does the world I know resemble or not resemble the one where I find myself? How can I translate my experience elsewhere to mean something here? If he is young, and clever, this skill never leaves him. He translates what the teacher says again and again until he understands it perfectly, always traveling back and forth between the known and the unknown. And if he is lucky and has entered a place at least moderately tolerant, he can use his skill as interpreter—as a writer, an editor, a teacher, an administrator—as anything that is a go-between, interpreting signs and explaining their significance. Daniel was an interpreter of dreams.

Yet there are always jealous voices speaking against Daniel and his companions. Their critics within the palace make them undergo trials. Each time they are criticized, it is on the subject of their foreign origins, even though some of the criticisms derive from jealousy of the king's favor, or of their high position, or from simple competitiveness. Chaldean enemies lay traps, demanding the king enact laws with which they know the Jews cannot comply. In short, the Jews are never Chaldean—or Median or Persian—enough. And for all of their power and position, they have not passed the necessity of life-endangering trials. So to threaten him and force him to doubt his God, Daniel is put in the lion's den. The fact of Daniel's religion was pulled out as a last resort, not against his people, but against him personally.

> Then the presidents and the satraps sought to find occasion against Daniel as touching the kingdom. But they could find no occasion nor fault; for as much as he was faithful, neither was there any error or fault found in him. Then said these men: "We shall not find any occasion against this Daniel, except we find it against him in the matter of the law of his God."
>
> —Daniel 6:4–5

The satraps and presidents had to manufacture a new statute in order to challenge Daniel; he was assimilated and obeyed all of the existing laws. The events imply that had Daniel's position been different or had he not inspired such jealousy, he would have faced few obstacles as one of the people of Judah.

The Book of Daniel does not solve the riddle of assimilation, but it does demonstrate the extent to which a foreigner could penetrate Babylonian society. The temptations of power and honor, as well as riches, made Daniel into a model Chaldean wise man, although as a biblical hero he was bound to temper those with ambivalence and undergo trials to ensure that he did not enjoy Babylon too much. For the message of the Book of Daniel is still that Babylon will fall. The writing on the wall, threatening Nebuchadnezzar's successor, King Belshazzar, refers to his coming demise:

> Mene, mene, tekel, upharsin . . .
> Mene, God hath numbered thy kingdom and brought it to an end.

Tekel, thou art weighed in the balances, and art found wanting.

Peres, thy kingdom is divided, and given to the Medes and Persians.

—Daniel 5:25–28

Darius, a Mede, replaces Belshazzar and is in return replaced by Cyrus, a Persian. Babylon fell and was no longer the instrument for punishing Israel, but instead was punished by others. The setting for the Book of Daniel is Shinar, the name from Genesis for the place of the now-destroyed Tower of Babel. Thus wickedness and evil are the backdrop for Daniel's temptation.[50]

Babel, babble, Babil, Babyl. Confusion and chaos are associated with the mixing of many peoples. The Tower of Babel in the land of Shinar was probably the temple of Etemananki in Babylon, built by Ur-Nammu (who built the ziggurat in Ur before 2000 B.C.) and restored by Nebuchadnezzar. The temple was a ziggurat within a walled sacred precinct whose walls were fifteen yards thick.[51] Jerome (A.D. 347–420), in his translation of and commentary on the Bible, explained that the name Babylon was derived from the word for "confusion" and the meaning grew out of the fact that so many peoples were living there.[52] So Jerome extrapolated from the Tower of Babel, with confusion as divine retribution, to Babylon, the city of many peoples, and concluded that the chaos of many peoples was either a punishment or wrong in God's eyes.

Jerome saw that the fall of the Tower of Babel in a mythical past and the fall of Babylon to Cyrus the Persian in the fifth century B.C. were due to the same weakness—vanity—and came to the same end. While the city of Babylon was being attacked at its outskirts, a vain festival went on undisturbed within its precincts. Belshazzar, the Chaldean, presided in the city and Nabonidus, his father-in-law/co-ruler, protected the distant reaches of the empire.[53] The closest Belshazzar came to destruction was the writing on the wall which interrupted his feast: Mene, mene, tekel, upharsin. He preferred the study of planets and the contemplation of interesting questions to political action and defense of his empire.[54]

The destruction of Babylon and the fall of the Tower of Babel share a common message: cooperation cannot be defeated, while division is destructive. In Babel, cooperation was strong enough to threaten God.

> And the Lord said: "Behold, they are one people, and they have all one language; and this is what they begin to do; and now nothing will be withholden from them, which they suppose to do."
>
> —Genesis 11:6

But in Babylon lack of cooperation led to defeat. Not only does the Book of Daniel tell of palace intrigue and divisions, but defeat and division are synonymous: "Peres, thy kingdom is divided and given to the Medes and Persians" (Daniel 5:28). Both Babel and Babylon were ultimately divided, but both began as cities of cooperation. Both cities were destroyed and, according to Jerome, both were cities of sin. And so Western tradition has come to associate cooperation with sin and diversity with temptation.

CONCLUSIONS: THE LEGACY OF BABYLON

Cosmopolitan culture always requires, as it did in the first cosmopolitan center, a sense of purpose on the part of its people. The glory of a god, the greatness of a dynasty, the luxury of truly knowing how to live, the desire for power, money, beauty, goodness: any of these can provide a purpose. Bel and Marduk and Jahweh gave Babylon meaning for its inhabitants. So did Nebuchadnezzar's thirst for immortality. We are not sure why he rebuilt the Etemananki ziggurat or built new walls and monuments, but whatever the reason, it was part of his understanding of the purpose of the city. We would like to call it a sense of history and claim that without a sense of where they've been and where they're going, people have no purpose or mission and little justification for their actions. But that is unfair; that Nebuchadnezzar wanted his works to outlive him does not necessarily show that he had a feeling for his place in a broad context of time. Let us be satisfied if it showed an awareness of who he was, what kind of empire he ruled.

This awareness of a purpose is one of the driving powers behind empires. Why build great buildings? Why weave beautiful cloth or delight in new songs? There must always be a reason. And great buildings need craftsmen, cloth needs weavers, songs need singers. Whether foreign peoples are lured, cajoled, enslaved, or contracted, they enter the city because the city has a mission, just as the inhabitants of the city draw them in for a purpose.

Can a cosmopolitan center exist without a purpose? No. Places exist without one, just because they always have. A stranger or two might drift in and then out or they might stay. But drift accounts for very little in the movement of people. Drift is not enough to foster a place that values variety. Imagine a small-minded small-town sheriff in the Old West of the American frontier. "We don't like your kind here. I reckon you'll be out of here by daybreak." On the other hand, a city can be forced into a cosmopolitan frame. If, due to outside reasons, purges, threats, or wars, many groups enter and stay, self-awareness is forced upon the city. Who were we before? people begin to ask. Who are we now that these others are here? Why are we here together?

The inhabitants of Babylon created answers to these questions. If more and more tribes came to settle in the fertile valley, then they were the people who together worshipped fertility. If they found themselves on Sumerian ruins, then they were the people who had inherited the Sumerian city, its language, its buildings. And self-awareness is needed for tolerance, any kind of tolerance. Inclusion needs something in which to include people. And understanding requires knowledge of difference. The more relative the self-awareness is, the more open-minded. The Sumerians and then Akkadians described themselves as "the black-headed ones," referring to the color of their hair. The very description leaves room for other groups—why not brown-, red-, yellow-, white-, gray-headed ones? The words themselves are relative and descriptive and demonstrate a knowledge that other people are different. Groups that might know themselves as "the Human Beings," or "the Perfect Creatures" leave little room for others. The way one conceives of one's own purpose is the key to the way one treats others.

A sense of purpose is no guarantee that the purpose is cooperative and not all senses of mission lead to tolerance. Obviously, empires have been founded that oppress others, scorn outsiders, and intimidate strangers. The very purpose itself may be destructive. The white rule of apartheid in South Africa originated with a mission, but it was a mission of exclusion and hatred. So while many tribes and peoples live in South Africa, it is more a group of encampments than a cosmopolitan country. A sense of purpose is necessary, but not sufficient, to create a setting that thrives on diversity.

Babylon shows us the necessity of a sense of purpose, but no more. Imagine a Babylon without gods or greatness proclaimed in exaggerated hymns of self-praise. Imagine a Babylon without public works and spectacular gardens, without astronomy and the drive to interpret signs, without temples and temple prostitutes and extravagant feasts.

> . . . Babylon shall become heaps,
> A dwelling-place for jackals,
> An astonishment, and a housing,
> Without inhabitant.
> —Jeremiah 51:37

> Her cities are become a desolation,
> A dry land and a desert,
> A land wherein no man dwelleth,
> Neither doth any son of man pass thereby.
>
> And I will punish Bel in Babylon,
> And I will bring forth out of his mouth
>   that which he hath swallowed up,
> And the nations shall not flow any more
>   unto him;
> Yea, the wall of Babylon shall fall.
> —Jeremiah 51:43–44

So the story of Babylon became part of our story, with far-reaching consequences for Western culture and even, in the West's attempts to dominate, for other parts of the world. No story is complete without the tale of how the teller came to know it. And in this case the history of the story is the history of a posture toward cosmopolitan life. So our last thoughts will concern the importance of the idea of Babylon and how it has come to influence our idea of cities.

The Book of Daniel was of special interest to the biblical scholar Jerome, who was educated in Rome, well traveled, and well respected. Most important to the growing church was his translation of the Old and New Testaments from Greek into Latin, the so-called Vulgate Bible. In his lengthy commentary to the Book of Daniel, Jerome argued that the book was actually written in the sixth century B.C. and was a book of prophecy which predicted Babylon's decline. Jerome's view became orthodoxy.[55] Almost one hundred years before Jerome wrote, a Neoplatonist philosopher named Porphyry had already suggested that the book was written in 168 B.C., after Babylon's fall, and that the visions actually reflected events entirely outside of Babylon. But Jerome's view was widely held.[56] Consequently, the traditional view of Babylon was that its destiny was foretold and its wickedness punished.

Why was this view so important to Jerome? As a writer and translator, he might have had an interest in believing his work was based on more "authentic" sources. As a Roman citizen, however, his interests might have been even stronger. If the Book of Daniel was written in 168 B.C., it would have really referred to the Roman treatment of the Jews, an event entirely outside Babylon. Then Jerome would have been in the awkward position of criticizing the empire which had raised him, an empire which he was happy to see was becoming increasingly lenient toward Christianity. More importantly, though, the Rome of Jerome's time, the fourth century A.D., was in decline. While Jerome may have been loath to believe that Daniel's visions foretold the destruction of his own home, he might indeed have been sympathetic to the view that a city of many peoples is an abomination in the eyes of God. Frightened by barbarians, and an uncertain future, Jerome might have been more attracted by the idea of diversity punished than of diversity rewarded. So Jerome's Babylon is a Babylon duly punished.

Hundreds of years later, in the late fifteenth century, Jerome's work was of special interest to Erasmus, the famous Dutch theologian and scholar engaged in rediscovering the primary church sources and the

works of antiquity. Erasmus created a new edition of all the writings of
Jerome, reinserting the Greek passages and translating the whole with
unusual care for the original.[57]

While Erasmus' own work was in a polished Latin, he was unknowingly
involved in the events that led to the decline of the Catholic world and
the rise of the vernacular and the Reformation. When Erasmus wrote,
the newly founded book-publishing industry preferred Latin. But soon
after, printing turned to the vernacular languages of Europe to increase
readership and bring in more business.[58] Erasmus believed that the
classics and Christianity could be reconciled, but the classical texts
which he put in the hands of readers encouraged criticism of the church.
And indeed, Luther, one of the first Protestant theologians, saw in him
a potential ally, someone who defended the common reading of original
texts.[59] Erasmus, the European Latinist, gave rise to Luther, the German Reformer.

Once again the story of Babylon as a story of wickedness was relevant,
but this time Babylon was the Holy Roman Empire, the Catholic world
of too many luxuries, too many peoples, too many laws. Although the
history is long and slow, it is direct—the path that led to the Reformation and Puritan condemnation of Babylon also led to the vernacular,
the nation-state, and a mandate against diversity.[60] Nationalism is the
enemy of cosmopolitanism. Protestant reform was the enemy of cosmopolitanism. Both are part of our culture. Both are predicated upon
the wickedness of Babylon. The golden cup, empty; the drunken stupor,
over.

> Babylon hath been a golden cup in the Lord's hand,
> That made all the earth drunken;
> The nations have drunk of her wine,
> Therefore the nations are mad.
> Babylon is suddenly fallen and destroyed,
> Wail for her;
> Take balm for her pain,
> If so be she may be healed.

We would have healed Babylon,
  but she is not healed;
Forsake her, and let us go every
  one into his own country. . . .
  —Jeremiah 51:7–9

II

Constantinople: Diversity and the Origins of Tolerance

It is the perverse intention of this chapter to prove that Constantinople, capital of the Byzantine Empire, had no particularly tolerant bent. In fact, the city was hostile to outsiders and its citizens upheld an ideal of narrow orthodoxy. But political and economic fact and necessity brought together peoples from three continents and they coexisted because they had no choice. Eventually, they began to adopt manners and customs from one another, and they rose to prominence in a society which seems to have been open to at least the most talented outsiders. In other words, diversity creates tolerance and not vice versa. First, different peoples must find themselves in the same place.

SAILING TO BYZANTIUM

I

That is no country for old men. The young
In one another's arms, birds in the trees
—Those dying generations—at their song,
The salmon-falls, the mackerel-crowded seas,
Fish, flesh or fowl, commend all summer long
Whatever is begotten, born and dies.
Caught in that sensual music all neglect
Monuments of unageing intellect.

II

An aged man is but a paltry thing,
A tattered coat upon a stick, unless
Soul clap its hands and sing, and louder sing
For every tatter in its mortal dress,
Nor is there singing school but studying

Monuments of its own magnificence;
And therefore I have sailed the seas and come
To the holy city of Byzantium.

III

O sages standing in God's holy fire
As in the gold mosaic of a wall,
Come from the holy fire, perne in a gyre,
And be the singing-masters of my soul.
Consume my heart away; sick with desire
And fastened to a dying animal
It knows not what it is; and gather me
Into the artifice of eternity.

IV

Once out of nature I shall never take
My bodily form from any natural thing,
But such a form as Grecian goldsmiths make
Of hammered gold and gold enamelling
To keep a drowsy Emperor awake;
Or set upon a golden bough to sing
To lords and ladies of Byzantium
Of what is past, or passing, or to come.[1]

Centuries before Yeats, when Ireland and England and the outer reaches of the Roman Empire were in the hands of barbarians, northern Europeans dressed in skins, hunted, fished, plundered, fought, and died. Fish, flesh, and fowl shared a world of birth and death and natural danger. Different tribes moved in waves from north to south. But at the eastern edge of the Mediterranean there remained what had been the eastern part of the Roman Empire. It remained an empire and guarded the monuments of ancient Greece and Rome. That was Byzantium. In 667 B.C. a Greek trader named Byzas founded a city on the tip of land between the Bosporus, which leads to the Black Sea, and the Sea of Marmara, which leads to the Mediterranean, where Europe and Asia come face to face. When in A.D. 330 the Roman emperor Constantine moved his capital to the East, where his empire would be safest from the invading barbarians, he chose Byzas' city, and renamed it Constantinople. Constantine's new Christian empire lasted until 1453, when it fell to the Islamic Ottoman Turks. For over one thousand years the precepts of geometry, astronomy, the grammar of classical Greek; the artistry of silk making, dyeing, and weaving; the public works of Rome; the political ideals of Greece; and the poetry, orations, the sculptures, and the lessons of architecture lived on. To the north the European sang epics of love, birth, and death, and little more.

By A.D. 330 the Roman Empire had become emaciated and torn. Constant wars demanded increased revenue. Public roads and bridges fell into disrepair for want of funds, while small farmers, driven under by impossible taxes, became impoverished workers on others' estates. The few remaining Romans tended to repudiate the religion of the empire and to adopt Christianity. And the demand for more and more soldiers led to more and more barbarian mercenaries fighting on foreign fronts. All of this clouded the meaning of Roman citizenship. The soul of Rome, its meaning, had been lost, and the empire was slowly decaying. Constantine founded in the East what he believed to be not only a stronghold, but a refuge for civilization, a holy city.

The Byzantine Empire was a Christian empire. Christianity in part inspired the charitable works, public orphanages, and hospitals which the emperors had built, as well as the basilicas and chapels. Cyril, a learned monk who was charged with spreading the word of Christ among the Slavic peoples, adapted the Greek letters to accommodate Slavic sounds and created a new alphabet that was named after him, Cyrillic. Christianity also inspired the gilt-edged images of sages and saints, the icons blazing in gold paint or gold mosaic. Spirit and substance were meant to meet in these holy images. While the golden halos of the mosaics that now remain in the Hagia Sophia are still bright and glorious, it is the eyes of the saints that are most powerful. They are cool and steady and innocent, yet they have a depth that is penetrating and wise. The Byzantine Empire, with Constantinople as what Dean A. Miller has called its own "city-icon," created beauty to far outlast even its own religious devotion. Miller, a scholar writing on the imperial city, has explained that the city itself was an icon, an object of devotion, which represented the whole empire.² The city's beauty demonstrated the empire's glory.

Through art and artifice, the Byzantines lifted man out of nature and gave him lasting beauty. The long faces and exaggerated gestures of the iconic figures, the flat images, may seem unnatural to us now. We call things Byzantine when they are complex, too intricate, too wrought or filled with intrigue. Yet that is what Byzantium celebrated, not nature but nature as man fashioned it, gold and silver spun into thread and embroidered on purple silk, mechanical devices to add to the throne's glory. Man's natural life may be short, but his art can preserve the past, heighten the present, and foretell the future, when Christ will come again and life will be eternal. Past, passing, or to come. So William Butler Yeats' poem speaks of Byzantium not only as a place of extreme beauty, of rarefied intellect, of holy passion, of artifice, but also of timelessness and agelessness—the world after this life.

Yeats' poem is not lacking in historical irony. When his Norman ancestors did sail to Byzantium, sacking the city in the First Crusade of A.D. 1096–1099, it was not for spiritual renewal. Under the guise of aiding fellow Christians, Norman armies sought loot, land, and titles and they attacked the empire. Yeats' Byzantium, the empire of gold and longing, may not be the Byzantium that really was, the Byzantium elucidated by modern scholars. Yet we need Yeats. How else can we begin to unravel the paradox of an empire at once stilted and adaptive, conservative and expansive, exclusive and open? An orthodox culture of aesthetes which is also a bustling metropolis filled with many peoples, many of them outsiders?

The golden city on the Bosporus was the center of an empire and it stood for empire. The city was founded on the site of the ancient city of Byzas when Diocletian split the Roman Empire, and this new Rome, too, had seven hills. The statuary, the palace, the circus, the monuments, the imperial palace could barely do justice to its setting: near the fertile fields of Anatolia, the natural resources of the northern lands and the sea, yet far from the dangers descending on the Western Empire.

It was Constantine who beautified the city and made it the center of Christendom. Under Constantine it became the center of the world, courted by visiting ambassadors awed by the spectacle of its imperial court. Traders filled its great ports. Under Constantine it was also a Hellenic empire, Greek-speaking, with Greek scholars and artists. But it was not a haven of tolerance.

By the eleventh century the city blossomed into a golden age. No city in the empire was autonomous, if autonomy meant freedom from the control of Constantinople. All institutions, church and government, were centered in this metropolis, center of Christendom and empire. The most important trade reached Constantinople; the most important dictates of church, state, and culture emanated from the city. By the time the Comneni ruled in the eleventh century, Roman togas had been replaced with coats of brocade; the men were bearded and turbaned, the women were made-up, everyone costumed in one of the fashions of the day. Even the restriction on the wearing of the purple, the royal color, was becoming lax by then. Anyone might be from any quarter, any family. The fashion was to look foreign.[3] It had become a diverse, cosmopolitan city. It was an empire—a world of a thousand peoples somehow organized, living together.

The city was administered by an official appointed by the emperor, a prefect, but a special one with enormous power. He was the most powerful of the eunuch-bureaucrats, the administrators chosen for their selfless service to the empire without regard for personal gain or gain for their descendants. He ordered all supplies for the city, determined markets and taxation, population movements and municipal protection, except when these were determined by the emperor, to whom he was directly responsible. Constantinople, like the empire of which it was center, depended upon a controlled economy and centralized planning. The emperor, from his palace, could walk down the street of the most exclusive shops and see with his own eyes the enactment of his laws on the cloth trade, on uniformity of measurement, the use of money. Settlements of foreign traders were subject to imperial regulation. Only much later, during the thirteenth century, the emperor's power was whittled down and whole parts of the city, the foreign parts, became prosperous and powerful.

The circus grounds were directly adjacent to the emperor's palace. And the struggles of the circus teams, the blues and greens, were important to him, whether or not he attended. It was here that popular sentiment was expressed, as well as in front of the churches or in the streets themselves. The emperor's people were loyal to church and church orthodoxy, and he had best be aware of bad feeling and possible church-led revolt.

Constantinople was filled with devout worshipers from Anatolia, the region outside the city. It had populations of Slavs, Armenians, Greeks, Jews, and Venetians. Migration into the city, like migration into the empire, was controlled, yet the city's ranks swelled with newly made aristocrats, ecclesiasts, and foreign merchants. Despite regulations on migration, the city was becoming more and more diverse. That diversity might have seemed to make heresy or revolt more likely. Yet for all its complexity, its diversity, its glory, its power or riches, Constantinople was no political powder keg. It was the seat of orthodoxy.

UNAGING INTELLECT

Byzantine intolerance was part of a cultural tradition and thrived in the world of symbol. In the world of symbol, good and bad, right and wrong take shape, and from it acts derive their meaning. The empire maintained its identity by using symbols to distinguish itself from "the others," or the barbarians. One of the most important ways this was accomplished was through Greek scholarship and intellectual life. The three tenets of Byzantine civilization, Paideia, Basilia, Ecclesia, or Education, Empire, Church, were ideals of rigor and obedience, not tolerance. The first of these, Paideia, taught the educated class of the capital to despise the foreigner and the boor. Most emperors slighted the talents of gifted Slavs or Franks, since education meant Greek education.[4]

Education was respected, widespread, available to both men and women, and was a necessity for advancement in government or distinction in society. It was based on classical Greek studies. Latin chairs at the University of Constantinople (formally founded by Theodosius II in 425) gradually disappeared as the Western half of the Roman Empire was lost. Greek scholarship became more and more central to education.

Primary instruction, whether in private or public schools or from individual tutors, consisted of learning to read, write, and analyze ancient Greek texts. The spoken language gradually evolved into a commonly used vernacular, the koine, made up of many local dialects from the ancient world and the ancestor to modern Greek. Yet educated Byzantines wrote in Attic Greek, the language of Thucydides.[5] Scholarship was dominated by the purists' insistence on the classics. Scholars devoted their time to dictionaries, grammars, encyclopedias, and commentaries—the tools of an educated but not critical or independent-minded people.[6]

Devotion to rhetoric meant obedience to rules of classical Hellenic form. In the writing of the time allusions and quotations from Homer were not attributed to him, because they were recognizable, as Shakespearean lines might be recognizable today—a sign of a uniformly shared culture, at least among the educated, and many were educated. At best this literary conservatism preserved important literary works. At worst it produced unnatural prose and a people educated to revere the past, possibly to the neglect of the present.

Not the form alone, but the content of Byzantine scholarship emphasized uniformity and orthodoxy. Great works in history and theology stood alongside studies in philosophy and mathematics. Anna Comnena, daughter of one of Byzantium's great emperors, studied the trivium and quadrivium, the standard medieval curriculum of Greek and Latin, math, music, and science.[7] It is difficult to determine whether or not Byzantine scholars added to or simply preserved insights in math and science. Reluctance to use Arabic numerals, some scholars argue, held back Byzantine mathematics. Cumbersome Roman numerals without a zero, they claim, could be favored only by arrogance, not intellect.[8] Within rigid forms and strictures, they worked in small spaces, but used them well. It is more interesting to see what the Byzantines did not study.

The voluminous works produced in Constantinople as tributes to God and the Greeks are strangely incomplete compared to the works of other times and places. They contain no travel literature. That is, no writer described foreign peoples or customs, foreign lands or their geography.[9] Byzantine historians gloried in their Greek tradition. Nicetas Choniates called history "the finest invention of the Greeks," and authors such as Leo the Deacon or Anna Comnena, public figures who wrote and studied history, demonstrated that history had widespread appeal as part of public life.[10] Yet the Greek tradition of geography, of description of foreign peoples, is totally absent. There is only one Byzantine historian who wrote about foreign peoples and travels; by contrast, the Arabs, near neighbors, especially the Ottomans, kept extensive ethnograpic notes to help understand their widely spreading empire.

What can this mean? Byzantine knowledge of geography was good—there is evidence that information on prevailing currents and winds was available;[11] Alexius I had a map made of the Adriatic with winds and currents noted. It would be extraordinary if the Byzantines did not travel; they certainly did. But for them other peoples were simply not a subject for educated reflection. Aside from Greek, the dwindling Latin, and a little Hebrew, languages were generally not studied. Interpreters must have been available, and speakers of foreign tongues were unquestionably present, but for the most part barbarian languages went unstudied and polyglots were few. Authors even apologized when they inserted foreign names into their texts.[12] Indeed, the most successful students were not those who were most aware of their world, but those most Hellenized. And success in studies could lead to high positions in the imperial administration, wealth, and power, especially for eunuchs. Hellenic orthodoxy was a deeply entrenched value, reinforced with very real rewards, shared among those who made the laws, wrote the books, and taught the young. Tolerance for diverse peoples was not taught in schools; other peoples were not even a subject of curiosity.

Is the paradox almost grating? The empire recognized as the capital of European civilization, reaching thousands of miles, showed no apparent respect for diversity. But then if we think back to the United States at the start of our own century, schoolbooks did not acknowledge the Chinese contribution to American railroads or describe the life and conquest of Native Americans. And yet at that time immigrants were entering the United States. Like the Chinese and earlier immigrants, they did not enter a land of tolerance. It isn't tolerance that creates diversity. As for languages, look at American education's record on foreign languages. What percentage of non-Hispanics know Spanish in our country? Language and regional specialists are sometimes not even consulted on foreign policy. As in our own country, the Byzantine empire's highest positions were filled with those who least understood or valued diversity. The keepers of the symbols held on with a tight grip.

LORDS AND LADIES OF BYZANTIUM

Scholarship maintained its Hellenic orthodoxy until Hellenic culture was taken West. And just as education encouraged orthodoxy and a disdain for foreigners, so did court custom and the life of the aristocracy. Wherever ceremony was kept and simple acts were accorded great significance, diversity was scorned.

Ceremony was the mainstay of Byzantine diplomacy. It was so important that the Book of Ceremony *(De ceremoniis aulae Byzantinae)* was compiled personally by the emperor Constantine VII Porphyrogenitus, who reigned from 913 to 919 and from 944 to 959. (The name Porphyrogenitus is itself witness to the importance of pomp and ceremony among the aristocracy. It means "born in the purple." Purple was the color of royalty, both metaphorically and literally—the palace room for royal births was purple.) Ceremony created an ordered pageant in which the emperor, in solemnity and dignity, demonstrated his power. It ordered coronations, imperial marriages, and funerals, festivals of the church and the reception of ambassadors.

As the *De ceremoniis'* introduction explains:

To neglect . . . ceremony, and to sentence it as it were to death, is to be left with a view of the empire devoid of ornament and deprived of beauty. If the body of a man were not gracefully formed, and if its members were casually arranged and inharmoniously disposed, one would say that the result was chaos and disorder. The same is true of the institution of empire: if it be not guided and governed by order, it will in no wise differ from vulgar deportment in a private person.[13]

Beauty and imperial stature naturally occurred together, believed the Byzantines. When an emperor sought a wife, scouts were sent to all parts of the empire to bring back the most beautiful women in the world. One empress, chosen from a bride show, was Theodora, a noted beauty who experimented with and invented creams and make-ups that preserved her good looks far into her dotage. (The poet Cassia was passed over, a tale tells, for her wit was too quick. The emperor looked upon her and remarked, what a shame that all the evil in the world resulted from woman, alluding to Eve in Eden. Cassia responded that all the good also resulted from woman, alluding to the Virgin Mary. Whether such a defense of woman would have been more acceptable in another setting is open to question.)

Beauty was imperial and was the foundation of ceremony. And the Byzantines used both to express their disdain for foreigners. A critical weapon in foreign affairs was the ceremony that put foreign ambassadors to shame, demonstrated their insignificance, and gave them tales to tell at home. (Two other weapons were trade and warfare, trade more than warfare. Byzantine policy often relied upon payment of various kinds, again demonstrating power through wealth.)

A tree made of brass, but gilded over, stood before the emperor's throne: the boughs were full of birds of different kinds, also made of brass and also gilt, which sang in a chorus of different bird-songs according to their kind. The emperor's throne was constructed with such skill that at one time it was level with the ground, at another it was raised above it, and then, in a moment, it hung up aloft. It was guarded, as it were, by lions of immense size—one could not be sure whether they were made of brass or wood but they were certainly covered with gold on the surface—which opening their mouths and moving their tongues roared aloud and shook the ground with their tails. Here I was brought into the presence of the emperor, supported on the shoulders of two eunuchs: the lions roared at my coming, and the birds twittered according to their kind: thrice I performed the act of adoration, prone at full length on the ground; then I raised my head and lo, the emperor, whom

I had just seen seated almost on the level of the ground, now appeared to my eyes dressed in different robes, almost level with the ceiling of the palace.[14]

These words, written by Liudprand of Cremona, a monk on a political mission from the Holy Roman Empire, remind us of nothing more than the intensity of live theater. Sets move, sound effects startle, costumes dazzle, and the action is blocked and choreographed for maximum effect.

Ceremonies such as this one tell us much about Byzantine power in relation to the peoples who visited. Ceremony was always a statement of disdain for foreigners; only the political circumstances around the ceremonies differed. Liudprand's reception at Constantinople was just like that of the Russian princess Olga; only she reacted with pleasure rather than disgust.

Liudprand of Cremona was forced to wait in Constantinople, promised audience with the emperor, but kept waiting for weeks on end, homesick for his Frankish land. Olga, too, was kept waiting, according to the *Russian Primary Chronicle,* an early Russian history compiled and edited many years after Olga's visit. Olga, too, was annoyed at how long she had to wait to see the Byzantine emperor.

Olga made answer to the envoys that if the Emperor would spend as long a time with her in the Pachayna as she had remained on the Bosporus, she would grant his request. With those words, she dismissed the envoys.[15]

While Liudprand represented a ruler and Olga was herself a ruler, both were judged by similar standards. Olga recommended herself immediately by being "very fair of countenance and wise as well."[16] Liudprand's physical appearance was also judged by the Byzantines: he was a mere "Frankish bishop" who refused to wear a bonnet and appeared uncomely by Byzantine standards.[17] His worst fault, however, was his lack of wit, his flagrant "show of indignation" that had him thrown in the servants' quarters.[18]

Both Liudprand and Olga discussed Christianity with their Constantinople hosts. The *Chronicle* says that Olga was blessed and baptized while in the city.

> When Olga was enlightened, she rejoiced in soul and body. The Patriarch, who instructed her in the faith, said to her "Blessed are thou among the women of Rus', for thou hast loved the light, and quit the darkness. . . ." He taught her the doctrine of the Church . . . she eagerly drank in his teachings. . . .[19]

The Byzantines attempted to teach and convert Liudprand, too. Liudprand, though, already a bishop, wanted no teaching and was insulted.

> The Patriarch with several other bishops was present, and before them he propounded to me many questions concerning the Holy Scriptures, which, under the inspiration of the sacred spirit, I elegantly answered. Finally, wishing to make merry over [Otto, the Holy Roman Emperor whom Liudprand represented], he asked what synods we recognized. . . . "Ha, ha," said he, "you have forgotten to mention Saxony. . . ."[20]

The glory of Byzantium was meant to be impressed on all foreign visitors, both the representative of a powerful kingdom and the ruler of a small nation. And so both Liudprand and Olga were showered in gifts—Olga, for her charms, according to the *Chronicle;* Liudprand, to impress him with the emperor's riches.

> But my indignation was appeased by a handsome present! The sacred emperor sent me one of his most delicate dishes, a fat goat, of which he himself had partaken.[21]

Liudprand's retinue received silks as well; so did the Russian ambassadors. Yet while the Franks were unimpressed with gifts, the Russians sang praises. They had both witnessed the same ceremony, but their reactions reflect the power of, and differences between, their homelands. Through Byzantine eyes the empire was constant. Nuances of power, measured by seating at ceremonial repasts or placement in processions, were the only concessions to the outsiders. As for the outsiders themselves, that is a different story.

Liudprand, who represented a relatively powerful kingdom, believed he was treated badly, and he felt free to report that in his account. But his description was negative because political conditions merited it; diplomatic disagreements made him see offers of gifts as weak appeasements. Olga, on the other hand, was treated well, according to Russian sources; but this is itself a comment on Russia's status relative to Byzantium.

And after all, the *Russian Primary Chronicle* has a political purpose. However the Constantinople court really was, the Russians had to stress the potential alliance, while Frankish glory did not depend on the honors paid them by the Byzantines. Liudprand was free to be suitably insulted, to see behind the ceremony to the disdain for outsiders it implied. Liudprand reported to Otto that which he experienced in order to provide information; at the same time, it was his duty to praise him. The *Chronicle*, written in hindsight, fit Olga's visit into a larger picture of Russian emergence and growing glory. This is a religious history, one that justifies Eastern Orthodoxy. The *Chronicle*, recording Olga's baptism by the Byzantines, although it is disputed by other sources, gives support to the idea that Christianity was carried directly from Rome to Byzantium to Russia—Moscow was the Third Rome.

And the Byzantines? They knew well they were mistreating a powerful leader like Otto by mistreating his representative. Liudprand was virtually imprisoned, forced to sleep in a dank cell, taunted. Both Liudprand and Olga were given insignificant seats at meals, humiliated by the lords and ladies of the empire. As for the beauty of silk, the luxury of fatted goats, these were weapons, they were part of a show of strength.

Beauty as a weapon and charm as power were also used within the royal court. The nobility were the actors, the families descended from ancient Roman senators, families gaining power as they gained property, families rewarded for service to the throne. As time went on, this aristocracy became increasingly powerful; more and more offices could be bought.

Imperial power needed an aristocracy—for marriage partners, for partners in holding power, and as a reflection of the emperor's greatness.

The empire controlled its aristocracy by giving much of imperial administration over to a professional bureaucracy, at the same time inculcating among the nobility the idea of service to the empire and emphasizing distinctions (and competition) between ranks, particularly in sumptuary laws. (Only certain ranks could wear certain robes, sit at table with the emperor, or own certain luxuries.) Despite its attempts at control, the throne faced constant tension with the city's great families, many of whom had town houses, but whose power lay in their increasing country holdings. Enemies, and sometimes friends, were constantly looking for information to present to the emperor as evidence that he had been betrayed. Cecaumenus, the descendant of a military family, advised in the eleventh century that the nobility should exhibit unswerving loyalty to the emperor and remain as quiet and isolated as possible. Even a friend, if not a spy, he thought, could destroy domestic happiness. While the nobility in Constantinople held dinner parties and were not loath to demonstrate their wealth, Cecaumenus cautioned against it. "Guests," he says, "merely criticize one's housekeeping and attempt to seduce one's wife."[22]

There seemed to be intrigue everywhere—even among the women. Women, in both the palace and the private houses of the aristocracy, were secluded in gynaecea, or women's quarters. Unmarried girls were more totally secluded; married women moved with some freedom. Men were not permitted in the women's quarters, and as a result, these parts of the palace and of private mansions became havens for intrigue and betrayal; women often guarded political dissidents in hiding and hosted their secret meetings. Aristocratic Constantinople was altogether a web of public and private places. Since so much of life was dictated by ceremony, privacy was a precious commodity. Pomp on a massive scale almost demands intimate escape. So Cecaumenus' warning was a warning not to make one's home public. In public women were objects; in private, goddesses. Thus the spirit of the household echoed the spirit of the city—beauty was prized, but it had to be guarded. Glorious ceremonies and court life must always be bought for a price: jealousy and distrust. Outsiders turn one's deities into dust.

SAGES IN GOD'S HOLY FIRE

Religious orthodoxy was another way the Byzantines insisted on uniformity. The paradox of the Byzantine Church is not that salvation was all-important; there is no mystery there, for the search for salvation or meaning is universal. But rather, why in a world of wealth and power and beauty, of relative ease and enlightenment, did people believe this world to be a shadow and the only world of importance to be the next? In theory, at least, this world was insignificant, and indeed theological debate over minute doctrinal details often took precedence over discussions of mundane secular policy. Sermons and sermonizing were so popular and respected that emperors and ministers wrote and delivered sermons more often than treatises on government. The Byzantine Empire was in this way closely related to Christian medieval Europe. Throughout Europe there were no politics without God, at least not until the sixteenth century, when Machiavelli shocked Italy and all of Europe by describing princely decision making as totally secular. Until then the Christian community believed all actions to be oriented toward the next world and all kings to be divinely touched.[23] All of time, from the hours of prayer to the days of feasts and seasons of planting, fit within three reference points: the Creation; Christ's advent on earth and Crucifixion; and the Second Coming, or Judgment Day. All of the riches of Constantinople, all the plans and events, were shadow, representations of divinity and of the divine clock.

And representation is the key to orthodoxy and the reason heresy could not be tolerated. The Byzantine Catholic Church had at its core the idea of representation and the related idea of mediation. Jesus Christ was a mediator. He came to earth to take upon himself the sufferings of mankind to ensure its salvation; that is, he spoke to God on man's behalf. Jesus' disciples spread his word, as priests and bishops and other ecclesiastics spread the word, mediating between mankind in general and Jesus the Saviour. Saints and sages, who are pure and have the halo of eternal life, represent the heavenly light while they are on earth and, once in heaven, speak to the Lord on behalf of mankind. The emperor himself is the image of Christ and, like Christ, is God's representative on earth; just as God presides over an orderly and obedient world, the vicar, his earthly model, presides over the empire.[24] Men and women have always needed help in their search for salvation, a voice that would aid them in speaking to God. "Come be the singing-masters of my soul," Yeats says, and his words have power because we understand what it means to need help in expressing our deepest hopes. His words characterize Byzantium, a world of representations and mediation.

Byzantine Christianity opposed groups and beliefs which threatened its delicate system of images and representations. But as public pomp breeds a desire for privacy, official religions breed heresies—at the very least by calling them such. These heresies may sound esoteric and the differences between them may grow dim in modern minds. Yet however similar or strange they seem now, they were all perceived as threats to God's representatives on earth and to salvation for the citizens of the Christian empire.

The official religion was agreed upon by seven ecumenical councils between the fourth and eighth centuries, beginning with the Nicene Creed, enunciated in 325 at the Nicene Council. These first seven ecumenical councils were convoked by neither the pope nor patriarchs, but by Byzantine emperors. They were councils of bishops which defined the faith; the emperors then signed the decisions and proclaimed them law. St. John of Damascus or John Damascene (died 749) compiled an account of all heresies and refutations, a sort of textbook of orthodoxy.[25] All else, all other interpretations, were heresy. The Arian heresy denied the full divinity of Christ. The Nestorian heresy divided the nature of Christ in two, human and divine. Either of these views could harm the idea of mediation for man, the first because Christ needed to be divine to speak to God, the second because if a part of Christ were fully human, then his mother, patroness of Constantinople, could not be called the Mother of God, and Mary, possibly the greatest voice who ever intervened for humanity, would be denigrated. Orthodoxy was a tightrope: Christ's being was of two indivisible natures; to suggest that he was of one nature, either human or divine, threatened the whole Byzantine order.

The extreme heresy was to argue that Christ's divinity could not be represented at all. The Iconoclasts of the eighth and ninth centuries considered icons not as images but as idols, and they destroyed icons and whole churches in their anger.

Still other variations in doctrine or belief fell outside the bounds of orthodoxy. Remnants of paganism threatened the church. Too sincere a love of Aristotle was suspect. So was the vestige of Manicheanism that inspired the Paulicians and then the Bogomils, groups which held that all things of the flesh, including labor, obedience to government, and procreation, were wicked. That meant that the church itself was under attack.

Mysticism also presented a danger to orthodoxy since it relied on direct, unmediated religious experience. Monks were also a problem: the question of whether or not they could receive the holy light directly developed into a significant controversy. Monks and monasteries occupied a prominent place in Byzantine life: they operated hospitals and charities as well as leading the holiest of religious lives. Living as a monk or a recluse was sometimes seen as a legitimate unmediated path to God. But it still posed a threat to the world of state-run churches and church ceremony.

Just as orthodoxy breeds heresies, Byzantine heresies are themselves evidence of an agreed-upon orthodoxy. There is little in the theology of Byzantine Constantinople that allowed for difference, encouraged tolerance, or even supported quiet neutrality. Byzantine missionaries tried, most often successfully, to Christianize new territories. And even here the cases of failure demonstrate most clearly the significance of the missionary's calling: Bogomilism and Iconoclasm both began in the provinces and wound their way into the capital. The missionary was the emperor's front line.

Not only was the emperor directly involved with theological debates, but he was the enforcer of a policy of orthodoxy. Emperors called frequent conferences with bishops and rabbis on the subject of conversion; they were especially concerned about Moslems and Jews, viewing the conversion of Jews as a special duty. The emperor had the power of the death sentence, against one heathen, against a group, or against many. All heresies were crimes against the empire, prosecuted by the emperor. Some say that only the most influential heretics were singled out for persecution. Barlaam, a Calabrian monk educated in Rome, was condemned in 1341 for his sharp criticism of the mysticism of the monks at Mount Athos. His attacks themselves, though, were second in importance to the particular monks he insulted, who were respected and influential. His criticisms might have been overlooked had they been aimed a little lower. Or perhaps his criticisms were not as important as the fact that he was not of Byzantine origin. Religion could be an adequate excuse to persecute a foreigner.[26] At a still earlier time all Manicheans who refused to deny their faith were gathered on ships that were then set on fire, not even buried in Byzantine soil.[27] Foreigners with different religious views were suspect; suspicious religious views automatically made one a foreigner.

The emperor also made war on heretics, pagans, and the godless, but political and religious wars were not easily distinguished even in accounts from that time. Anna Comnena writes of the campaigns of her father, the emperor Alexius I, around Philippopolis, to the northwest of Constantinople:

> Once upon a time, it seems, Philoppopolis must have been a large and beautiful city . . . but . . . it was reduced to the condition in which we saw it during my father's reign. . . . It had certain disadvantages; among them was the fact that many heretics lived there. Armenians had taken over the place and also the so-called Bogomils. . . . Apart from them there were in the city the Paulicians; an utterly godless sect were the Manichaeans.[28]

The Manicheans lived in the Byzantine region only because an emperor, John Tzimisces (969–976), had enslaved them in the East, using them to defend the Western Empire. As soon as an opportunity arose, they fought for political independence.

> Philippopolis was a meeting-place, so to speak, of all polluted waters. . . . And if the immigrants differed from the Manichaeans in doctrine, they agreed to join in their rebellious activities. Nevertheless my father pitted against them his long experience of soldiering. Some were taken without a fight; others were enslaved by force of arms.[29]

So Alexius was there to put down a border rebellion, to expand imperial territory, and also to fight heresy. He soldiered. And he also preached.

. . . the secondary object of the expedition became more important: he turned away the Manichaeans from their religion with its bitterness and filled them with the sweet doctrines of our church. From early morning till afternoon or evening, sometimes till the second or third watch of the night, he invited them to visit him and he instructed them in the orthodox faith, refuting their corrupt heresy.[30]

It is impossible to tell if these heretics were baptized from fear or from awe. Was it the battle that convinced them? Or was it the sight of an emperor who, in the middle of battle, preached words of peace? Or the words themselves? Both dignity and power seemed to be on the side of orthodoxy.

THE POWER OF SYMBOLS

What would it be like to walk through Constantinople? If you were Orthodox, you might not even notice all the mosaics and every basilica. You would hardly hear the bells, although they would speak to some part of your memory, the part that directs your steps to mass. You would await with anticipation your own saint's day, but might endure with neglect bordering on hostility the feasts for saints for whom you had no affection, scarcely admitting to yourself that you never beseeched (didn't really like) the saint. The holy men and priests who passed might hush your voice momentarily, as if you were in church. And in church the walls and windows would speak in a beautiful, sonorous voice. Even with your eyes closed you could see, on your right, the emperor Nicephorus, in the purple, haloed, between St. John Chrysostom, humble and bent, and the Archangel Michael. Or overhead the stern Christ Pantocrator, his mouth turned down into a thick beard, his brow furrowed. The pictures would speak to you and you to them. In sadness or in loneliness you would seek out the understanding eyes or the sad cheek. They would remind you of your past and reassure you about your future.

Now what if you were not Orthodox? Of course, this would not be your world. The calendar, the whole year, each day would be organized around events that meant little to you. The bells would ring for mass—you would not go. You would have no patron saint. Even if your name was taken from that of a saint, you would not celebrate her feast. The loving eyes of Maria Theotokos, Mother of God, would promise peace for others but none for you. As you passed priests and nuns and monks and theologians, you would not aspire to be like them. Or would you? Every building and every mosaic, every relic and reliquary, all the beauty, all the dignity has one message: you are different.

And the stronger statement is this: you do not belong. All this would be said without a word, all done with symbol. Intolerance is strong where the power of symbols is strong. But how can this be intolerance? Of course, the Orthodox should express their beliefs. A world without symbols—a meaningful nod, a painted sign—is impossible.

Yet the word for it is still "intolerance." For in a world dominated by symbols, there is a tendency for one icon to beget another. A cross is a symbol. Genuflection in front of the cross is another symbol. The order of procession into a church determining the order of genuflection is yet another. As the layers of symbol pile on thicker and thicker, the foundation becomes more rigid, its unquestioned correctness more extreme.[31] At Christmastime in America today, people decorate trees. They decorate whole houses. They put presents under the trees. They shop for presents. The stores play Christmas tunes for shoppers. One symbol begets another, begetting tradition and intolerance for the outsider. There's even a name for him: Scrooge.

It is not only that symbols multiply, but that they take on lives of their own, demand reverence, and prompt conflict. At one time the American flag flew at official buildings, post offices, or fire departments and at parades, especially on the Fourth of July. The wealthy or prominent family of a small town might have their own flag. In times of war and victory it was proudly trotted out. But doesn't a pledge to the flag hint that someone else might betray it? Suspicion and intolerance are accomplices. More recently, particularly during the war in Vietnam, the flag has come to mean what the accompanying bumper sticker says: AMERICA, LOVE IT OR LEAVE IT. Then even more flags spring up, the more flags the stronger the message: We don't like criticism.

· · ·

And so the very beauty of Constantinople and its strong religious beliefs imply uniformity and intolerance. This is Yeats' ageless, unaging empire—beautiful, conservative, closed. So we see that the three great strongholds of cultural Constantinople—Hellenic culture, imperial order, and Christian orthodoxy—had little place for tolerance, variety, or nonconformity. Not only were they founded on purity and orthodoxy, but they were all used against outsiders or barbarians. All the city's symbols of truth, beauty, and goodness, all of the signs of dignity, purpose, and meaning, spoke against outsiders.

But though there is no reason to believe that citizens of Constantinople in any way valued tolerance for its own sake, the city did have diversity. Constantinople was a center of sophisticated debate. There were translations of Western thinkers such as Augustine. But more important than mere exposure or tolerance, there was fashion. Bogomilism, one of the city's heresies, was "in vogue" among aristocrats in the capital for a time. This second Constantinople, the city of daily life, fashionable heresy, and de facto tolerance, is the city of political scientists rather than poets. It is the city of historical necessity.

THE SOCIAL CITY

Constantinople is a story of center and periphery. The imperial center of church, emperor, and school was the ideal, and the ideal was Greek. Yet all around the center, Constantinople, was a broad hinterland of peoples and customs. Broad boundaries mean broad differences. At its greatest expanse, during the eleventh century, the empire included blond, blue-eyed Slavs wearing furs in what is now Yugoslavia, and dark-skinned people called Mauroi, or Black, wearing linen in what is now Saudi Arabia.

Between the foundation of Constantinople and the end of the eighth century, Byzantium did much to assimilate the newer groups entering Asia Minor, including the Goths, Vandals, and Christians who were all fleeing from the Arabs in Syria and Palestine. Justinian II resettled peoples from Lebanon into Anatolia, a region near the capital that was almost completely Hellenized, and resettled over three hundred thousand Slavs in Bithynia. Very early these groups began speaking Greek.[32] Forced migration was a political tool and the goal was political and economic self-preservation. Constantinople needed newcomers. After the battles of the seventh and eighth centuries, the empire was diminished and so was the population of the capital. As much as possible, the emperor took in Greek-speaking populations, from territories in Thrace and the Aegean Islands, to repopulate the capital.[33] Although the preference was to disdain the outsider, the demands of war and trade strained the cultural ideal. Sometimes the empire gained warrior-allies, sometimes laborers, sometimes taxpayers. Eastern expansion in the ninth and tenth centuries incorporated many non-Greek-speaking peoples, and eastern Byzantine Anatolia contained a majority of non-Greeks: Kurds, Georgians, Lazes, Syrians, Armenians.[34]

While the center reached out to the provinces with its law, its tax collectors, its appointed bishops, even its imperial bride hunts, the periphery entered the center. Slaves and soldiers, students, fortune hunters, holy men, and, of course, traders flooded the city. Of the possibly 15 million inhabitants of the empire, possibly five hundred thousand, maybe more, lived in Constantinople.[35] (Perhaps thirty thousand of those were destitute, living in piles of straw or even dung for warmth, and perhaps another thirty thousand were thieves or criminals.[36]) As for minorities, numbers are difficult to estimate. The Armenian population of the empire was so high that each migration involved thousands, perhaps even twenty thousand to fifty thousand people. In some military campaigns over one-fourth of the Byzantine army was Armenian.[37] Although there were only about fifteen thousand Jews living in the empire as a whole, about two thousand Jews who followed the rabbinate and five hundred Karaite, or non-temple, Jews lived in Constantinople. That was only approximately one-half of 1 percent of the city's population, but Jews were five times more concentrated in the city.

Indeed, the city was shaped by its immigrants. It was physically shaped into neighborhoods, quarters, regions, usually around a church or other place of worship. The city's Moslems had their own section with a mosque, close to the city center and the emperor's protection. The

78

city's Jews were permitted to do business in the city but lived in Pera, across the Golden Horn. The Armenians, at least the ones who kept the old ways, also had a separate residential neighborhood.[38]

Some of these neighborhoods are known, their existence well established by decree or chronicle. Some, however, are inferred, based on the likelihood that newcomers to a city would look for aid and familiarity first. Villagers from Thrace or Cappadocia, the Mediterranean islands, or the deserts of Asia Minor arrived for work or to join relatives and probably went to what have been called "transplanted village-neighborhoods."[39]

There was also the large population of people living in the streets, a shifting population; few beggars could spend a winter on the streets of Constantinople and even fewer could spend more than one. Cold climate and ill health claimed many of them. Most of the people in the streets were newcomers to the city. In fact, life expectancy was short for all city residents. The city struggled to maintain its population. There were slaves in the city, even though the church opposed slavery in principle. But even the numbers of slaves fell unless actively augmented. When conquest slowed, after the twelfth century, slavery diminished for lack of defeated foreigners to sell as slaves.[40]

If the scholar Charanis is correct, that "it is a well-known fact that in its long history the Byzantine empire was never a true national state with an ethnically homogeneous population," how much more true that was of Constantinople.[41] The citizen of the city, as insulated from some quarters as he might have been, lived in a city whose form was a brocade of different peoples. He was bound to experience the diversity even if he did not meet every group. Wealthy families sent servants to shop, but even they passed the public monuments where beggars slept or saw the emperor's foreign bodyguard at a ceremony. In fact, after 988, when Basil II began recruiting Varangian, or Scandinavian-Slavic, soldiers, the imperial bodyguard, powerful and feared, was almost totally composed of foreign mercenaries. Were they respected, or viewed as scarcely trained wild animals, still barbarian? Either way, the citizenry experienced the city's breadth. Were there resentments or even riots? Yes, but not many. During the golden age of the Comneni, during the eleventh and twelfth centuries, Constantinople was cosmopolitan.

For the most part, the city not only was diverse, but it seemed to enjoy its diversity. Despite the very ideals of uniformity and orthodoxy that were the heart of Byzantine culture, daily life was relatively peaceful, relatively free from prejudice, and relatively open. The army, especially, was open to newcomers. In fact, the empire settled new populations to add new strength to its armies. Saracens, Bulgars, Turks, Slavs, Georgians, and others rose to prominence in the military, administrative, and ecclesiastical life of the empire. As one historian has said, "Byzantium knew no racial distinctions. Careers, one might say, were open to talent."[42] If a warrior was strong, an administrator wise, or an aristocrat well connected, he could, no matter what his origin, end up on the throne.

The Jews and the Armenians have been studied in detail, and both groups lived successfully and were assimilated surprisingly easily in Constantinople. Over the course of five and one-half centuries, there were three waves of serious persecution of the Jews, totaling about fifty years,[43] but the two and one-half centuries directly before the Latin Crusade of 1202–1204 saw what Joshua Starr, the leading expert on the subject, has called "undisturbed toleration."[44] An observer of around 1025 noted the protection afforded Jews, the fact that church officials allowed Jews to enter any church, and the ability of Jews to build their own temples.

> . . . the Jew in their lands may say, "I am a Jew." He may adhere
> to his religion and recite his prayers. No one brings it up to him,
> restrains him, or puts any difficulties in his way. . . .[45]

In fact, though, Jews did face some obstacles. They were bought and sold as slaves, subject to burdensome taxes, kidnapped and ransomed, and controlled in their livelihoods (often trading and textiles). These same trials weighed on almost all Byzantines, and Jews seemed to fare well in general. There exist for instance several bills of sale dictating that a community of Jews belonged to a monastery; they were not allowed to move and were considered part of church property, the way we think of medieval serfs in Europe. In other cases Jews were more like personal slaves, often tending as doctors. Yet there are also documents which illustrate the Jewish sale of Christian slaves, particularly, it seems, Bulgarians.[46] Starr's evidence shows that Jews were allowed to own their own homes and even farms. While they paid heavy taxes, there seems to be no mention of a specific tax demanded of Jews and not others, nor of spontaneous or arbitrary demands. The cost of war, and of empire, is high and the Byzantine system of taxation was thorough and burdensome. None of this speaks of a humane or even peaceful society. It simply shows that systematic oppression of a single group or even several groups was not part of Byzantine Constantinople. Not kind. Not gentle. But not tribal in outlook, either. The Jew was as likely to be slave as slaver, as likely dispossessed as proprietor. Neither singled out nor penalized, Jews were seen as a people, not an economic class.

Since the emperor was the empire's banker and most moneylending was a government affair, economic woes were not blamed on "outsiders," while "insiders" were unable to distinguish themselves in finance. This may be one reason Jews were neither forced into nor forbidden from particular trades. They played a part in the silk industry, a mainstay of Constantinople, and one in which most groups were involved. Jewish specialties were decorative embroidery and constructing garments. And trade. Here, too, Jews did not have a monopoly on trade, but through their contacts throughout the Near East and their language skills, they became involved in the high-risk/high-gain long-distance trade. A pier in the Constantinople harbor was set aside for Jewish ships. Jews appear often in the reports of travelers and chroniclers, probably because so many were involved in long-distance trade.

In short, Jews were segregated in their own quarter of the city, as were Moslems, Russians, Bulgarians, Armenians, rug dealers, perfume dealers, copper dealers, almost everyone. They were the object of the emperor's harangues about conversion and often faced proclamations of conversion and forced ceremonies. They were second-class citizens, generally unable to hold office and looked down upon. There were periods of persecution. Yet none of this was exceptional, conversions were forgotten the next day, and it all interfered little with their worship or daily lives. It interfered so little that visiting Talmudists and scholars were shocked at the laxity of Jewish religious practice in Constantinople. Instead of attending special ritual baths, Jewish women just went to the public baths with everyone else.[47] Some believe that the laxity was a result of Karaite influence—that is, the influence of non-Talmudic Jews, who formed a distinct sect. And cross influences explain a lot in Constantinople: the Jews appear to have been in contact or at least in close proximity with other ethnic groups. Jewish scholarship in Constantinople was closely allied with secular scholarship. When a visiting Jew asked a scholar which Jews he should study from, the local wise man said, "We study astronomy, geometry, and medicine here," and he named the most renowned gentile experts in the city.[48]

Joshua Starr's painstaking accumulation of documents and sources is enlightening but disturbing. It was written in 1939. How was his work colored by what he believed to be a "normal" level of intolerance, or by thinking of Jews as a race? A partial answer lies in a close look at another group about whom there is evidence, the Armenians.

Armenia, the same region that is now governed by the Soviet Union, was totally controlled by the Byzantines during the eleventh century. Some land had been won by conquest. More often Armenian leaders agreed to trades of land, then moved their people to other parts of the empire. In a way, then, Armenians were among the indigenous groups upon whom the empire was built. But not all of the Armenians in the empire came from lands held or acquired. Some came as adventurers or refugees when Armenia was under foreign control.[49] Judging from the fact that significant numbers entered the empire and its capital as refugees, it seems fair to assume that the Armenians did not encounter exceptional generosity in Byzantium. How, then, were they able to excel in scholarship and warfare, even to become emperors and found dynasties, in short, succeed in the most complete and extreme sense?

Assume, for argument's sake, the answer that is anathema to this book: there was something special, or nice, or commanding, or imperial about Armenians. Leave aside the fact that such an argument is circular: they succeeded because they were successful. Even if this assumption were true, what is the likelihood that Greek Constantinople would bow before such a truth? Remember the culture built around orthodoxy and conformity—Paideia, Basilia, Ecclesia. The ideals, the values, of the society would inevitably fail to bind and constrain the lives of non-Hellenic Byzantines.

Here are two very different stories of two Armenians who became emperor during the tenth century. Peter Charanis, who has written a monograph on Armenians in the Byzantine Empire, describes the first, Romanus Lecapenus, as poor, rural, and simple in origins. His father's great deed as a soldier, saving the emperor's life, brought the family neither wealth nor fame. Romanus Lecapenus was promoted from sailor to admiral thanks to his skill. Finally, he was able to exploit his power to become regent for and then co-emperor with the child emperor Constantine Porphyrogenitus. Meanwhile, his daughter Helen had married Constantine. In this way a humble Armenian became emperor and his daughter became the wife of an emperor.[50]

Of all the facts of this story, the most amazing is that Lecapenus rose in the navy on what seems personal merit. And on what grounds did his daughter marry an emperor? But then, personal merit in war and marriage had a place; it was called courage and beauty. In short, institutions existed to suck in the best of the outsiders. Constantinople did not value tolerance, and yet daily life included the give and take, the compromise, of diversity.

Our second Armenian emperor of the tenth century, John Tzimisces, was a privileged descendant of a wealthy and distinguished Armenian family, related through marriage to some of the wealthiest Hellenic Byzantine families. Murder figured in his ultimate accession to the throne, but his wife, Theodora, was the daughter of a Porphyrogenitii (Constantine Porphyrogenitus) and lent his reign some legitimacy. His Armenian descent seems almost irrelevant to the story.

The point is not that one or two Armenians succeeded in Constantinople, but that an Armenian could become an emperor; it was possible. While religious persecution of the largely Armenian Paulicians was violent and even cruel, most Armenians in the city still lived ordinary, even successful lives. It is not surprising that such a large minority group could overthrow an emperor or kill to obtain the throne. What is surprising is that members of the group could do so peacefully, with the support of the population. The very society which disdained barbarians allowed outsiders into positions of power, even in positions as educators, keepers of the culture. One historian notes, "These people appear, of course, thoroughly hellenized. . . . Yet it may be asked whether their hellenization was not unaffected by their original background, whether in being absorbed they did not modify the culture which absorbed them."[51] The resettlement of Armenians during the tenth and eleventh centuries, related to the eastern expansion and westward movement of the Seljuks, was one of the most important movements of people in Anatolia. Armenian princes and nobles acquired land and brought large retinues of followers and military aid.[52] Nicephorus Phocas, during the tenth century, asked the Syrian patriarch to repeople an entire city; huge numbers of wealthy merchants, physicians, translators cooperated at the behest of their patriarch, who in turn received the right to fill bishoprics.[53]

Like the Jews, the Armenians were not particularly wonderful, brilliant, or lucky. They simply lived in the same world and received the same treatment as other groups. We have seen that it was not an ideal of tolerance which invited this and other groups to share in the fortunes of the golden city on the Bosphorus. It was necessity.

NECESSITIES OF WAR AND TRADE

Of all the necessities of empire, the greatest were food and manpower. Constantinople had to be fed by the hinterland, and in an increasing spiral the demands for more wheat-growing land, hence more armies to obtain it, hence more men, hence more wheat, pressed on the Byzantines, just as they had pressed on the ancient Romans. Egypt was at first the main source of wheat for Constantinople as it had been for Rome. But when the Byzantines lost Egypt to the Persians at the beginning of the seventh century, they turned to Anatolia. The broad grain-growing plains there provided food, wood for shipbuilding, even manpower for a fleet. Yet the Anatolian plain was difficult to defend.

The increasing power of Islam encouraged expansion among the various Islamic tribes and dynasties, but it also led to fragmentation. As long as Byzantium could benefit from Arab disunity, as it could in the eighth century when it lost Egypt, it could hold on to Anatolia. But in the eleventh century Anatolia was at risk and part of the frontier was lost. The Byzantine administration was weak and the empire was further diminished by the defeat at Mantzikert at the hands of the Seljuk Turks, a growing force in Asia Minor. Loss of face, loss of resources, and loss of food led to chaos in the capital. The empire of gold had been debased.

From the West the Normans were steadily approaching and in 1071 they took the city of Bari in southern Italy away from the empire. They attempted to take Constantinople in 1081. But by the end of the eleventh century, the Comnenus dynasty, stronger and more militaristic than the earlier Macedonian dynasty, had begun to reverse the empire's fortunes. Anna Comnena was right to sing the praises of her father Alexius' military campaigns. The Comneni presided over a stable and continuous government, as well as a solid social order and a strong military power.

The Comnenus emperors resettled the conquered Slavs of the north in Anatolia in order to increase the labor force, extend cultivated land, and increased production. Even more than were the fields, however, the Comnenus armies were peopled with strangers. The constant need for armies spoke loudly against cultural fastidiousness. Officers complained about the discipline, but never about the ability of their foreign recruits.[54]

At court, too, war and its demands for resources made more room for outsiders. It is no coincidence that the stronger Comnenus dynasty was the one in which the number of titles multiplied and were frequently bought and sold. Outsiders could buy into the upper class. This gave the Comneni what they needed for their revenue.

The Comneni had inherited an empire weakened in land due to war and in population due to plagues; the university had declined and scholarship faded. But war demands that military skill be valued and rewarded. Soldiers who distinguished themselves in battle were rewarded with estates or the emperor's favor. And all status derived from the emperor's favor. Some scholars argue that there was no aristocracy in the Comnenus era at all, but a shifting upper class filled with those who could claim proximity to the emperor—through marriage, through money, through military prowess.[55] The aristocracy, then, was whomever the emperor needed—not liked, but needed.

The energy and passion demanded by war were a heavy burden for the Hellenic Byzantines, and perhaps for this reason alone they found it necessary to recruit and advance outsiders. Within Constantinople, a war-weariness and world-weariness made constant political passion impossible, even for the Comneni. Newcomers always had new enemies against whom to fight. The Armenians, in particular, dispossessed by the Seljuk Turks, had reason to fight. The court in Constantinople could not possibly feel the same passion.

The Byzantines needed outsiders to add energy even to the simplest daily events. World-weariness found concrete form in Constantinople. The wealthy and powerful retreated from the world once they were able. When the difficulties and tragedies of rendering to Caesar became overwhelming, many Orthodox Byzantines devoted themselves to the purer holy life and entered monasteries. They might endow a monastery, give all their landholdings to the church, and lead a life of peace and contemplation. For the holy to exist, it was a necessity to have unholy, in order to persist in the struggle. The keepers of the civilized world, shaken in their confidence, tended to look inward and back. They preferred compromise to despair.

Trade was a diplomatic tool in Constantinople, a form of compromise, and, like war, it strained the cultural ideal of orthodoxy. International trade was in fact not essential to the economy of Constantinople for most of its history; in fact, the emperor generally released as few goods, as little silk, as possible. Exports were carefully controlled through the *mitata,* or special quarters in the city for foreign traders. In these quarters foreign traders could be watched by government employees and their dealings restricted. Liudprand was infuriated and insulted when he, an ambassador, was searched on suspicion that he was taking silk and purple dye out of the country. Why then, during the eleventh and twelfth centuries, was there a huge Italian trading community in Constantinople, with its own docks, its own neighborhoods, banks? Necessity.

As the Byzantines lost their easternmost borders to Islamic forces, they turned more and more to their ambivalent Western allies for help. The Byzantines needed money for their two strategies, preventing war through paying "ransoms" and fighting wars. A ransom was sometimes paid to an antagonistic group to keep them from attacking; in other words, they bought a peaceful settlement through compromise. The Byzantines often used this strategy when dealing with the newly powerful Russians, a small tribe gaining in wealth. War often required far more money, as well as more technology and more hinterland to feed troops and provide men. And while troubles in the East often led to paying off invaders with pieces of the empire, troubles with the West forced the Byzantines to give away pieces of the capital city itself. Constantinople was forced to give away its trading privileges.

The troubles in the West had deep roots. The first half of the European Middle Ages, from about 500 to 1000, was a violent period of war and invasion. Northern Europe was divided into principalities and small kingdoms, and small armies were rewarded with land. Alfred in England, Charlemagne in France, and Otto in central Europe/Germany, all in about 800, made attempts to unify larger kingdoms, but for the most part invasions continued and could not be pushed back. After 1000, though, a more peaceful Europe, with more time for trade and agriculture, had less need for soldiers, less land with which to reward them, and consequently an expanded nobility of second and illegitimate sons without future or fortune.[56] Eventually, chivalry gave purpose to many young knights. So, shortly after 1066, when William of Normandy expanded his lands by going westward, Robert Guiscard of Normandy went east with the same general intention.

In the East, that is, east and south of Constantinople, the Arab peoples had become unified and had conquered large territories. The word of Mohammed the prophet had inspired the Seljuk Turks and later the Ottoman Turks, who adopted the new religion Islam and began a holy war to spread the word of the prophet. By the time of the Comneni they had crossed North Africa into Spain, controlled much of the Mediterranean, and were a constant threat to the Byzantines, who in the eleventh century asked their fellow Christians in the West to come to their aid.

When Pope Urban II declared the First Crusade in 1095, Robert of Normandy was already on his way, and he soon established a kingdom in Sicily and controlled many Italian port cities. As Byzantium's Eastern troubles multiplied, the empire sought help, but asking help from Robert would have been like asking charity of a wolf. Instead, the Byzantines approached the powerful maritime city, Venice. The Venetians had better, faster ships than the Byzantines. In return, the Byzantines released Venetian traders from paying customs duties and guaranteed Venice all the markets she needed on imperial territory. Then traders from Pisa got special consideration, then traders from Genoa. By 1171, Latin colonies in Constantinople totaled about eighty thousand inhabitants. Economically, these colonies added to rather than detracted from the empire; while they changed the balance of trade, the empire had never actually depended on foreign trade to stay solvent.[57] Socially, however, they flew in the face of orthodoxy: religious, linguistic, Hellenic, every possible dream of orthodoxy.

At this point policy and the public mood diverged. The late Byzantine emperors tried to conciliate Venice and its traders with promises and increasingly good terms. But with each new advantage, public opinion turned further against the foreign merchants, whom they saw as greedy and arrogant. In 1171 there was an uprising against the Venetians; in 1182 a massacre of Latins. By then the Latin colonies had become so big and powerful that their internal rivalries and disputes began to interfere with city administration. The cosmopolitan age ended as the Greek citizens of the capital fought with outsiders over real economic power. The Venetians, protecting their own interests in what they saw as a hostile environment, began to see themselves as sharing interests with the West and welcomed the Fourth Crusade to Constantinople, which finally took the capital out of Byzantine hands. Robert of Normandy took full advantage of Constantinople's weakness by raiding the city, in the first of several Western Christian attacks on the Eastern Empire. When Crusaders sacked Constantinople, they took many art treasures, like the horses that are now at St. Mark's Cathedral in Venice, but they also took books. And so the Greek works that had trained generations of Byzantines, preserved for so long, were stolen or "rediscovered." Thus is our Western culture Hellenic culture, and Italy the first site of the new humanism.

Until around 1100, Latin colonies were tolerated in Constantinople. There were even Latin churches, though the Eastern Church regarded Rome's religion as heretical. Outsiders ultimately destroyed the city, not because they wanted escape or dissolution, not because they did not want to be loyal, but because they felt the empire was rightfully theirs. Everyone wanted the golden prize. Only cosmopolitanism, the pride in taking the best of everything from everywhere and incorporating it, had opened Constantinople to outsiders. Then, when it was no longer able to take the best of everything from everywhere and incorporate it, Constantinople decayed. It did not have the resources to take everything. It did not have access to everywhere. It did not have the political continuity and unity needed for incorporation. Instead, the dream of a magnificent city gave way to competition over resources.

PAST, OR PASSING, OR TO COME

An aged man is but a paltry thing. But where in Yeats' Byzantium is the incongruity of an aged emperor and his aging wife gulping aphrodisiacs, denying their age? Romanus III so much wanted his empress, Zoë, to conceive that although she was already forty-eight years old when his reign began in 1028, he urged her to consult specialists one after the other. He tried potions and massages; she tried pebbles, charms, and ointments. He gave up in despair, although it might have been fatigue. The emperor was at least twenty years older than his wife.[58]

Byzantium was full of artifice, yes, but where was the dignity? The political necessity of an heir turned a seventy-year-old emperor into an odd symbol of the empire itself: aged, unrealistic, and denying nature. By 1453 Constantinople was weak and growing less important as advances in maritime trade made the Mediterranean the center of power. The old overland trade routes had all gone through Constantinople. But by 1453 the Arabs controlled North Africa and European kingdoms were gaining in power and importance. The hinterland was gone. A paltry thing.

Constantinople had had what all cosmopolitan cities have. In addition to a sense of meaning and mission, it had diversity forced upon it by historical necessity. War gave it refugees (as well as slaves), industry gave it laborers, power gave it the ambitious. And even though the city did not begin with the mission of tolerance, it is diversity itself which creates tolerance.

Constantinople had a sense of mission or purpose just as Babylon did. Its purpose was its religion, its tradition as the Second Rome, and its pride as the center of an empire. Constantinople also shared with other cosmopolitan cities the avenues of opportunity that we will examine more closely in Vienna and New York. The story of the Byzantine Michael Psellus, historian and snob, would sound familiar in any of these cities. A peasant in the provinces, he excelled in school. Determined to give him a better life, his mother brought him to the capital, where he distinguished himself in study and became a pillar of the establishment, first among many in defending Hellenic culture and scorning the barbarians.[59] Neither democracy, nor capitalism, nor freedom, nor kindness, nor brotherhood opened the world for him. It was cosmopolitanism.

It was no accident that Byzantium, the land of artifice, was also a land of opportunity. Artifice welcomes outsiders and gives them a chance. The man-made world is tolerant, in other words, much more tolerant than the mere biological world. Instinct demands hunters, runners, fighters. How many of us could exist in such a setting? How many of us owe our very lives and livelihoods to medicine and to knowledge, all artifice? Eyeglasses are artifice just as perfume and make-up are. In a world of such artifice there is more room for imperfection, and imperfection is characteristic of most of us. More importantly, the artificial world values clothes and riches, not skin color or height. Music and art in such a world are more important than physical prowess. So the old as well as the young, the weak as well as the strong, the Slav as well as the Armenian, could enjoy Byzantine prominence. The extreme of an aged emperor believing his aging wife could bear children may seem absurd. But the same world of artifice allowed Michael Psellus, a poor, insignificant boy, to become a great scholar. The man-made world is often absurd, but seldom as cruel as the natural one. The very word "nature" is often a weapon, while in the world of artifice, looking different is not a threat and being an outsider is not a sentence of death.

Byzantium did not decay like a carcass, eaten away from within by parasites and predators, no more than Babylon had too many peoples or fell under its own weight. Treason and betrayal are common explanations of the decline of these multiethnic empires. Certainly, there were internal problems, and the death of opportunity is one explanation which we will examine more closely later on. But what is most important here is that Byzantium, like Babylon before it and the Habsburg Empire after, was an actor in a complex international scene of kingdoms, empires, tribes, and peoples. Constantinople fell in war, as did Babylon and the Habsburg Empire. Centuries of internal weakness may have led to its capitulation, but Constantinople could never have wished away its external enemies, nor could it have halted developments in other parts of the globe. In other words, the whole scene of international alliances, trade, and power struggles was changing and, weak or strong, the Byzantines could not stop it. If we begin with a belief in the Babel story, that peoples cannot and should not live together, we will surely find traitors. Traitors, however, are not the weak link in these heterogeneous empires. It is their own sense of mission, their own goals which fail these empires. Competition takes the place of cooperation. Outsiders ask for equality, not just inclusion. But all of this we will come back to later.

Byzantium rose and fell in the estimation of historians. Until the fourteenth century the inhabitants didn't even use the word "Byzantine," but called themselves Hellenes. Each history says more about the age in which it was written than it does about the empire: during the twentieth century we see the empire as a dynamic superpower; at the end of the nineteenth century Constantinople was called a soft city of decay. William Butler Yeats wrote in the early part of this century, an Irish patriot among the English, a moderate among Irish patriots, intellectual among philistines, old among the young.

When Yeats felt himself an outsider, he dreamed of Byzantium.

III

The Jew and the City:
A Look at the
Urban Diaspora

More than earth or fire or water, concrete or lights or harbors, the city is made of air. Air is the city's lifeblood. It makes men free. Skyscrapers, like cathedrals, are buildings of air— it's not the earth which holds them up, but the sky which holds them down. It is the air that carries rumor and excitement and fashion. The city air takes your breath away, inspires and exhilarates. It is only natural that men of the city exist on air. Jewish culture has contributed a powerful image of city life, even though Jewish culture has not been uniformly cosmopolitan or even urban.

The *luftmensch* is exactly what the Yiddish word describes: a *mensch*, or man, of *luft*, or air. He lives by his wits, trading in nothing, inventing expertise, investing in speed and the fleeting nature of time. He is the opposite of those solid, reasonable citizens whom "the world always needs." The world always needs food, right? The world always needs clothes, right? Lawyers, doctors, bakers, teachers—none is a luftmensch. But consultants, brokers, critics, analysts, designers, editors, arrangers, criminals, and their therapists, everyone with a scheme, everyone who knows the next big deal, everyone with his finger on the pulse of something or other, sniffing his income in the breeze, these are all luftmenschen. The luftmensch is a city character; he's light on his feet. Groucho Marx introduces himself, "I'm Professor Wagstaff from Huxley College," and gets the chilling reply, "That means nothing to me." So he tries again: "I'm Professor Huxley from Wagstaff College." And the answer this time for this man who would be anyone: "You weren't at the other college very long."

It began by necessity, this living on nothing. There was nothing. Why are luftmenschen so dependent on and so associated with the city? There is a paradox here. The Jew has become identified as an urban figure, yet for centuries Jews were not even allowed within city limits. Is the urban

Jew a fiction? A reality? Does history make city dwellers not only free, but visible, while country souls are lost? Or is the urban Jew a recent development, a product of upheavals and immigration? Is Judaism an urban culture?

The Jewish diaspora is an unavoidable subject in the context of Western cities, not only because religion has given meaning to much of urban history. The Jewish experience provides background and context and detail; it is the long-distant consequence of Babylon, the sequel to Constantinople, and the background to Freud's Vienna. More importantly, it is proof of a premise of this whole work: cities are the refuge of the displaced and estranged and, indeed, diaspora Jews are city dwellers.

As important as the great cities are, there is something more important—cosmopolitan culture. It isn't a place, but an attitude, a way of life. Since Jews have been ridiculed and attacked as rootless and cosmopolitan, they must be present at cosmopolitanism's defense. Yes, there is an attitude which favors peace and the arts. And, yes, Jews have sometimes taken part. The urban diaspora holds within its story many of the elements of cosmopolitan culture. There is diversity and variety in the problem of exile and assimilation. There is public life in the liberated cities of the West after the French Revolution. There is a peculiar division of labor in the predicament of the luftmensch. The result is a group of people who carry within them the tensions and strains of city life. The diaspora, like the mistral, is a wind, but it blows cityward.

AFTER BABYLON:
A HISTORY AMONG OTHER PEOPLES

When the Babylonian king Nebuchadnezzar destroyed the First Temple, the Jews became a people in exile. Over the centuries traders, travelers, and students lived throughout the East and throughout the Roman Empire. When the Romans destroyed the Second Temple in A.D. 70, however, the Jewish people became for the first time a people without a land. According to one interpretation, the Romans who had fought in Judea took Jewish wives and slaves away with them when they were transferred north to the region of Vienna. Other accounts describe similar events in other cities settled or fortified by the Romans. There were Jewish tombstones in Bath. Jewish traders went with the Romans to Strasbourg. Scholars trace Jewish roots in European cities this way, as if there were purpose or precedent in the early migrations. Perhaps there was. Under Charlemagne and his heirs, between around 800 and 900, there was a Jewish princedom in what is now France; analysts point to this self-governing province as evidence of early French toleration. Yet most Jews simply lived as did all other survivors of the Romans, wherever they found themselves.

Often they found themselves in cities. Or, at least, historical sources and records often locate Jews in cities. Benjamin of Tudela, a twelfth-century Jewish traveler, wrote extensively on the circumstances of Jews.[1] For the most part, he wrote about cities. Barcelona, Marseilles, Genoa, Constantinople, Antioch, Damascus—his broad itinerary provides a glimpse of how widespread the Jewish community was. For the Jews and many others, cities were the point of departure, the seat of study, the center of piety.

As Arabic armies and culture spread across the Mediterranean, the Jews naturally accompanied them as citizens and traders across North Africa into Spain and Portugal. In the growing struggles between Christians and Moslems, Jews were victims. Only under Christian pressure did the Moslems begin to demand of the Jews signs of faith and obedience.[2] The West's intense, systematic persecution of the Jews began with the Crusades. In this protracted holy war zealots attacked Jews as the enemy. At the same time, as travel increased, plagues spread across Europe, and the Christians blamed the Jews. The church organization also coveted Jewish resources.

Up until the time of the Crusades, cities had Jewish quarters and sometimes special Christian quarters. Constantinople had separate sections for different peoples, professions, and purposes. Yet after the Crusades what was once habit turned into an excuse for quarantine and punishment. One theologian declared in 1480 that Christians were debased living beside Jews. In 1555 Pope Paul IV declared the need for segregation, arguing that it was absurd for Jews to live among

Christians.[3] He ordered the establishment of ghettos. The word "ghetto" was coined in Italy in 1516 to describe the Jewish quarter of Venice. The origin of the word is obscure—it could come from *ghetta*, the cannon or casting factory which bordered the first ghetto. Or the word may be a variant of *borghetto*, the word for a neighborhood or district. It also resembles *guetto* or *guitto*, filthy creature. The pope's pronouncement was a decree of impoverishment for the Jews, since isolation meant economic disaster in a world of market stalls and market squares.

Catholicism fought hard for its dominance during these years, not only against local customs, but against increasing attempts at reform. In the turmoil of the Middle Ages there were expulsions of Jews who would not convert or who were charged with spreading plagues, bewitching Christians, and drinking blood. The most notable of these expulsions was in Spain in 1492 at the time of the Inquisition. From Spain many Jews sought refuge in Italy, from Italy some went north. Many had answered the invitation of Boleslav the Pious in Poland, who invited the Jews to settle there in what was then a flowering kingdom. Since the 1200s Poland's universities had been renowned, home to the arts and sciences, and throughout the 1500s Poland enjoyed a golden age. The king invited the Jews for their experience in trade. The Jews stayed, but Poland disappeared.

Conquest eroded the Polish Empire. By the 1700s the west was part of the the Austro-Hungarian Empire and the east was annexed to the czar's Russia. Over the centuries conditions in the east and the west varied immensely and political events decreed a decisive difference between German Jews and eastern European or Russian Jews. Both became communities of city dwellers and both were severely restricted in where they could settle. Gluckel of Hameln, a widow whose memoirs vividly depict Jewish life in Germany in 1690, recounts how the Jews were expelled from Hamburg, then allowed to return, only to be hunted again.[4] Charles VI's Familiants Laws for Bohemia, Moravia, and Silesia in the early 1700s resemble nothing so much as the South African Passbook Laws of this century. Each Jew was assigned a number which could be passed down to only one son, permitting him to marry and settle. The many who were not allowed to marry or to live anywhere permanently wandered as beggars before migrating further east.

PUBLIC LIFE IN THE CITIES OF THE WEST

The great difference between East and West was that national revolutions and the Enlightenment turned the West into a haven of liberty and freedom. Napoleon's armies liberated the ghettos of western Europe and declared equality. Even earlier the Jews, who had been expelled from London in 1290, were invited back by Oliver Cromwell after the English Revolution of the 1640s to help bring about economic recovery. Jews were often invited to fill new jobs that others were not willing or able to do, jobs demanded by urban life. Urbanization, Enlightenment, and industry went together. In 1780 Emperor Joseph II of Austria extended full rights to Jews. By 1860 Jews had full civil equality in almost every country in Europe. In 1858 Jews began to enter the British Parliament and in 1870 they were permitted to attend English universities.[5] Newly opened schools in many countries drew the sons and grandsons of peddlers into the professions. Opportunity called and Jews answered. In Germany twenty-six out of one hundred Jewish boys attended the gymnasia, schools preparatory for the universities, while only three out of one hundred Christian boys attended.[6] By the end of the First World War, over 25 percent of the lawyers in Vienna and Berlin were Jewish, as were over 15 percent of the doctors. The presence of Jews in London, Paris, and Vienna reflected increased opportunities for education and work in the professions.

Western urbanization and prosperity combined with opportunity to create among Jews a strong middle class, closely tied to urban life. Around 1900 Jews made up about 1 percent of the population of Germany, but 5 percent of the population of Berlin. In absolute numbers urban Jewish communities blossomed. During the last half of the nineteenth century the Jewish population of Berlin almost tripled and the Jewish population of Vienna increased fifteen times over, although the total Jewish percentage of the population declined—prosperity brought a declining birth rate and urban life threatened tradition. Just before World War I a third of all Jews married non-Jews in Berlin and Hamburg. In Copenhagen mixed marriages represented over half of all marriages involving Jews, and in Amsterdam by the 1930s over 70 percent of Jewish marriages were mixed.[7]

Urban life became associated with assimilation for Western Jews: increased social acceptance, decreased orthodoxy, material success, increasingly close contact with non-Jews. Many became "pillars of their community," even entering "non-Jewish" fields like the shipping or electrical industries. And like most pillars, there they were, concrete, solid, necessary. Not men of air at all.

Cosmopolitans love their city for its openness. These Western Jews, touched by the Enlightenment and taught by the French Revolution, were patriots; they loved their country for its distinctiveness. Thousands of Jews left Strasbourg so they could stay in France after 1870 when France lost Alsace to Germany in the Franco-Prussian War. Likewise, Jewish Germans heeded their government's call and moved into the newly annexed region at the same time. It is by now a sad and tired story that many Western Jews were sincerely shocked and baffled by Europe's growing anti-Semitism after 1880, culminating, of course, in the Third Reich.

THE ECONOMIC POSITION IN THE EAST: THE LUFTMENSCH

As for the Eastern or Russian Jews, their survival under crushing poverty and cruel restrictions was a mystery. "Caravans come and go . . . but the Luftmenschen of Kislon and Kabtziel go on forever,"[8] a Russian Zionist of the early 1800s wrote. Where in the West polity and economy cooperated to further the situation of the Jews, in the East polity and economy buffeted them with misfortune. Years before when Polish noblemen had invited Jews to settle and form towns on their property, they had found the working and living conditions free of traditional restrictions. Some of these towns, like Lodz and Bialystok, grew in importance with the growth of industry and large Jewish populations concentrated in these cities. Yet this concentration was not by choice, at least not after Poland was divided and the Russian czar started ruling the territory. Jews were forced to live in the strip of territory that had been Poland or the newly annexed Turkish territories. They were denied permission to settle anywhere else, denied entrance to cities, and denied the right to work in crafts or as innkeepers, in short, denied the livelihoods and lives most familiar. The Russian Pale of Settlement exemplified the narrow boundaries allowed Jews. The term was coined in the early 1800s under Czar Nicholas I, who included restrictions on Kiev, one of the few big cities within the Pale. Under Alexander II, in the middle of the nineteenth century, there were some exceptions: some Jews were allowed into Moscow, some students allowed into the unversity there. After the infamous May Laws of 1881, however, and the expulsions of all Jews from Moscow, the death of Jews from starvation was second to death from violent assault. The May Laws not only prohibited Jews from going beyond the Pale, but granted local peasants the right to demand the expulsion of Jews among them, effectively permitting violent riots or pogroms. The May Laws and expulsions in 1891 and 1892 especially made Russian Jews seek refuge in the West, particularly in the United States.

The Pale of Settlement held 94 percent of all of the Jews in Russia, and many small towns there were entirely Jewish, but even in this heavily Jewish region Jews made up only 11.6 percent of the population. (Today Jews account for roughly 10 percent of the population of the state of New York, for comparison.) Jews there, though, made up 36 or 37 percent of the urban population. Even with restrictions—numbers limited, occupations restricted, areas of settlement limited—the eastern European Jewish population was a people of cities. The city of Minsk was 58.8 percent Jewish; Grodno was 57.7 percent Jewish. Compared to this, even the great cities slightly further west, known for their Jewish populations, cities like Budapest and Warsaw, seem barely touched by Jewish culture. (After World War I Jews constituted 23.2 percent of the total population of Budapest.) Experiments in agriculture, often prompted by a Russian government eager to be rid of the Jews, ended in dismal failure. When the Russian government tried to send Jews to farm, they sent them to impossible land with no tools and no skills in an attempt to starve them. Urban life did not represent assimilation for Eastern Jews—only survival.

While the sixteenth century saw the foundation of private Jewish towns by Polish nobility and the nineteenth century saw impoverished industrial life, in between was the *shtetl*. Shtetls were little Jewish towns that varied in size from one thousand people to twenty thousand or more. They were cities in an empire where Jews were barred from the major cities, communities in an empire where Jews were scattered, religious centers in an empire where Judaism was a religion despised. Centuries passed and these villages still had no police forces—so strong was the hold of religion and social opinion, so insistently preserved were the values. As in any village, the outsider was suspect. Yet unlike other villages, these were dependent upon outsiders—they were middle villages between country and city, buying produce from peasants and selling it in cities, buying finished goods there and bringing them to the countryside to sell. What else could they do? Denied country land and city life, Jews made homes in between. Study, relative social position, and religious celebrations were the boundaries of a life lived in these marginal villages.

If the shtetl was a collective answer to insecurity, the individual answer was to take to the air. Here is the problem: The population, increasing in Malthusian proportions, was squeezed into a smaller and smaller area. At the same time, there were no jobs. Jews were forbidden to go to the cities to find work. At the same time, the demands of a burning religious devotion required attention—time for prayer, time for family. The answer to this forced, constrictive competition was to find something else. Luftmenschen had to develop a high tolerance for insecurity and take whatever work came along, never knowing in the morning what endeavor would bring lunch. They sold what there was to be sold and sold more. The answer to inhuman competition is the smaller and smaller division of labor, locating a task so specialized that no one else had thought of it. Peddle influence, if you have nothing else, peddle knowledge. When the luftmensch left the life of eastern Europe, he became a stock character everywhere the division of labor was exact and exacting. An urban figure.

. . .

Jewish writers wrote often about luftmenschen in the Old World's cities. Characters in their stories frequently represent the shady underside of a bitter and difficult life. Isaac Babel, for instance, wrote in the early part of this century about Odessa. His character Benya Krik is a criminal because crime is the natural province of the man who is light on his feet. Benya Krik, the burly, aggressive king of crime, makes his living through extortion and other intangibles. And some tangibles. Krik traded the goods he stole from Odessa's ports.

> . . . fat-bellied jars of Jamaica rum, oily Madeira, cigars from the plantations of Pierpont Morgan and oranges from the environs of Jerusalem. This is what the foaming surge of the Odessa sea bears to the shore; this is what sometimes comes the way of Odessa beggars at Jewish weddings.[9]

Odessa was a city where a Robin Hood could turn a profit. But criminals were not the only luftmenschen of Odessa. There were also writers. The city was a great literary center, where Russian, Yiddish, and Hebrew literature blossomed, as the critic Robert Alter has explained.[10] Odessa was not only a new city, opened to Jews after 1791 when Russia wanted to settle the regions newly won from Turkey, it was also relatively open to international influence. It was far from the center of power in Moscow and closer to the ships that arrived in its ports. The poor drifted in and lived off the salt sea air.

The more rarefied air of Lublin, home of a center of Talmudic study, sustained scholars and others, as Isaac Bashevis Singer describes in *The Magician of Lublin*. The whole story is a sad comment on the Jew's ambivalence toward the material world. Like a scholar determined to care only for ideas, not food, Yasha, a magician, is determined to fly. He has always been a confidence man, a cad, a man who will earn his bread by showing people what they want to see. Now in the ultimate immaterial act, he wants to fly away, to escape, and sure enough, the air saves him; the true luftmensch, he is transformed into a bird.[11]

Hutchins Hapgood's *The Spirit of the Ghetto* is a poignant look at the inner life of New York's Lower East Side in 1902. Here, too, there are luftmenschen: writers and actors, café intellectuals and laborers who will work at any job. But more interesting than any figure in the book is Hapgood's friend Abraham Cahan, who gave him the idea for the portrait of the Lower East Side. As soon as Cahan arrived in the United States, he offered to the American papers an eyewitness account of the czar's recent coronation, a scene he had just left. At the same time, he sent articles to Russia as a New York correspondent. By parceling out pieces of himself—his knowledge of English, his knowledge of Russian, his immigrant status—he developed a career as a writer and editor. Only after success in English-speaking America did he return to the Lower East Side, where he edited the *Jewish Daily Forward,* the most influential Yiddish newspaper in America. American success stories, more astounding than fiction, are often the stories of luftmenschen or, put in American terms, entrepreneurs in the world of ideas. Their careers take shape only in retrospect.

Emigrés from eastern Europe, like Cahan, brought the luftmensch to New York and to the United States, where such a figure was made widely popular in the comedy of the Marx Brothers. Who are their characters except struggling unfortunates, eager and willing to do anything to squeeze out a living? Chico and Harpo will do anything anywhere as long as it is not heavy lifting: in *Horse Feathers* they kidnap football players; in *Duck Soup* Chico gives up peddling to become a spy; in *A Day at the Races* they sell racing tips; in *A Night at the Opera* they are managers of someone or something—it's doubtful; in *The Coconuts* they are shady characters who sell information. In each case Harpo's sly innocence and Chico's accent convinced the audiences of the twenties and thirties that they spoke for all immigrants and newcomers. The Jewish eastern European luftmensch had entered the American city.

It is Groucho, though, whose characters have particular significance. He is a fast-talking confidence man swept by circumstance into positions of prominence: a college president, a nation's president, a doctor, an impresario, a hotel owner. Yet in each case he is an outsider, his tenure is precarious, he happened in by chance. In his low, just-between-us crawl, he creeps around to the other side of the desk and laughs with the audience. True, I'm a hotel owner, he seems to say in *The Coconuts,* but I could just as well be one of these hobos. True, I'm a professor, he implies as he tweaks the beards of the professors in *Horse Feathers* who resemble members of the German academy, but not for long. Groucho Marx was not only the air salesman par excellence, but he made an important revelation to the modern urban world: all of your fancy folks are air salesman.

The Jewish image of the man with two feet in the air was an apt image for the modern world. As a result of this one image, used often in novels in this century, the Jew has become not a stereotype so much as a shorthand, a metaphor for all existence.[12] Saul Bellow's characters, and especially Mr. Sammler, seem to be wandering, eking out existence in an urban world. Philip Roth's men are all unhappy writers except for Portnoy, who is very important in something involving administration and reports, but we are not sure what. Joseph Heller's men are light on their feet when they succeed, but the true luftmensch is Gold—selling ideas, juggling book contracts, always looking for another way. City folk in America are air folk. Londoners have country seats, Parisians have lived in their apartments for centuries, but Americans look at urbanites with the same wary eye they reserve for skydivers.

AN URBAN CULTURE

Jewish culture has been by choice, by necessity, as well as by description, urban. With each upheaval the Jewish population was forced another step into the future, and the future was always urban, more and more urban. Industrialization brought everyone into cities and the Jews more than most. By the twentieth century most Jews lived in town, usually in large towns. In 1925 23 percent of all Jews lived in centers which held more than one million people. Only about 10 percent of the world's Jews lived in small towns in western Europe and about 20 percent in small towns in eastern Europe. The small towns were obliterated and the big cities changed—there is no visible Jewish presence in Prague, Budapest, Warsaw, or Vienna today.

By 1937, after substantial waves of immigration, 3.7 percent of the U.S. population was Jewish; 30 percent of the New York metropolitan area. Twenty years later the United States was one of the three countries that were home to the majority of the world's Jews, along with the USSR and Israel. In the U.S. 96 percent of the Jewish population lived in urban areas while 64 percent of the general population did so. In the USSR 95 percent of the Jewish population lived in cities while only 48 percent of the general population did so. Even in Israel, with no history of restrictions, 89 percent of the population lived in urban areas. As of 1967 the New York metropolitan area held almost half of the Jewish population of the United States. Today 2.4 percent of the American population is Jewish. In the highly urban industrialized Mid-Atlantic states Jews constitute 7.3 percent of the population. In the state of New York alone they are 10.6 percent. New York City, Los Angeles, Philadelphia, Chicago, Odessa, and Tel Aviv are home to most of the world's Jews.

It is true that most Jews live in cities, though not all do. They have not founded them, for the most part, nor built them, nor ruled nor run them, for the most part, nor named them. Often they did not choose whether to live in one city or another. They have simply lived in them.

Some cities, cosmopolitan cites, have welcomed Jews, just as they welcome all outsiders and newcomers. Those cities have had beliefs and ideals broad enough so that even Jews could take part; mixes of population so great that Jews could contribute to and benefit from the experience of other groups; a public life so inclusive that all peoples felt welcome; and avenues to escape from poverty.

Of all the cosmopolitan cities, New York was an exception among exceptions. Cosmopolitan cities are rare and New York the rarest. Although the largest group to emigrate to the United States in the first twenty years of this century was the Italians, Jews tended to stay in New York more often after their arrival. At the height of Jewish immigration in the early years of this century, 73 percent of the Jews who arrived stayed in New York City.

New York held jobs, family, schools. Jews settled into New York as a large minority and had a widespread effect on it. From 1915 on, 85 percent of city college students were Jews. Small business, the professions, the civil service, real estate, academic life, the garment industry, and the union movement would have been entirely different without Jewish participation; it made New York the center of all of these professions and trades. Jewish cultural life, theater, and newspapers flourished thanks to the large numbers of Jews in New York, the variety of their backgrounds, and their joy in their newfound freedom. Jewish speech, food, humor, gestures, and attitudes gradually expanded beyond the Jewish community. In return for their contributions Jews received an education in worldliness, a polish and sophistication unavailable to any previous Jewish community. Jewish culture in New York took on a cosmopolitan flavor.[13]

Jews were not the only group New York embraced. But New York represents a particular moment in Jewish history. Today American Jews are retreating into the suburbs and the spirit of the shtetl. The suburbs are urban without being cosmopolitan; they are large concentrations of people with little public interaction. There is none of the meaning or mixing or mobility of the great city centers. Suburbs are static; no one gets ahead there. In that way they resemble the shtetl, the day-to-day workaday world of sameness. Anyone who is really successful leaves, even if it is only to go to another suburb. Not only Jews but much of America is retreating to village life, as if in an attempt to return to the villages their grandfathers and great-grandfathers left. Shtetls and suburbs are small cities, small in area and outlook. They are compromises between belonging and estrangement.

Jews are largely assimilated in American life. Yet there is a paradox in assimilation, a paradox reflected in the fact that Jews still live in large concentrated numbers. Here is the problem: The harder you try to forget, the more you must remember. The harder you try to fit in, the more your attempts bring you back to your own identity. At each step toward being like someone else, you will be expected to be more yourself. If you are successful in job and status, you will carry the burden of seeking recognition. American life favors civic-mindedness and community leaders. So you must have a community. When, in an attempt to leave the city, as many Jewish Americans did, you seek a mixed community, you may end up among Jews. "Mixed," to most respondents to a survey cited by Nathan Glazer, meant about 50 percent Jewish. But this idea of mixed neighborhoods often makes Jews end up alone, as Glazer points out.

. . . 50 per cent, which is twice the proportion of Jews in the city, and three times their proportion in the metropolitan area, would strike most non-Jews as too much. It is probably not a stable proportion in home-owning developments. . . . In some good suburban areas non-Jews have fled from incoming Jews. . . .[14]

Historically, too, attempts at assimilation have backfired. During the eighteenth and nineteenth centuries German Jews trying to reform outmoded religious observance in order to fit into the context of the German Enlightenment created a group of people far more enlightened and reformist than most Christians of the age. The Hasidim, the most Orthodox Jews of eastern Europe, however, cared nothing for assimilation. They were by contrast in tune with the fervent spiritualism and superstition of most villagers of eastern Europe. It is hard to forget and costly to change.

Or, put another way, nothing is totally forgotten, but its signs reappear in another form. The more effort it takes to forget, the more visible the strain. That is how Sigmund Freud explained memory and its repression. You can forget the past and all that it meant, but when the strain of forgetting becomes too much, the distant memory may drive you to other endeavors. To create music and art, form unions, write novels, conduct scientific research. The Jewish tension of memory and forgetfulness, of uniqueness and assimilation, has animated cities for centuries. One resolution of this tension is shtetl life; in the shtetl or suburb one can live in the shadow of the assimilated city, but live daily life in a small community of memories. One resolution is life among the luftmenschen. The luftmenschen make an art of necessity and live a life of forgetfulness because it is the only way to make ends meet. And one way to resolve the tension, a way described and lived by Freud, is to enjoy the life of cosmopolitan ideals and hopes, to sing music, to write books, to contribute to a civilized forgetfulness always fired by a burning, relentless memory.

IV

Vienna:
The Creation of a
Public Life

Sigmund Freud, like the biblical Daniel, was an outsider drawn by chance to a cosmopolitan center. Freud was a Jew born in Freiburg in predominantly Czech Moravia, part of the Austro-Hungarian Empire, 150 miles northeast of Vienna; his family moved to Vienna when he was eight years old. Like Daniel, he was an interpreter of dreams. And like Daniel, he knew about and aspired to the ways, the purpose, the dreams of his adopted city. Freud recalled:

> One evening at a restaurant in the Prater, where my parents were accustomed to take me when I was eleven or twelve years of age, we noticed a man who was going from table to table and, for a small sum, improvizing verses upon any subject given to him. I was sent to bring the poet to our table and he showed his gratitude. Before asking for a subject he threw off a few rhymes about myself, and told us that if he could trust his inspiration I should probably one day become a "Minister." I can still distinctly remember the impression produced by this . . . prophecy. It was in the days of the "bourgeois Ministry"; my father had recently brought home the portraits of the bourgeois university graduates, Herbst, Giskra, Unger, Berger, and others, and we illuminated the house in their honor. There were even Jews among them; so that every diligent Jewish schoolboy carried a ministerial portfolio in his satchel. The impression of that time must be responsible for the fact that, until shortly before I went to the University, I wanted to study jurisprudence, and changed my mind only at the last moment.[1]

What sort of place encourages a minority immigrant to believe that he, and others like him, not he alone, could be a cabinet minister in an aristocratic empire governed by a family of autocrats? Certainly not the

Vienna of Freud's adulthood, when Karl Lueger became the city's mayor on a platform of anti-Semitism. Vienna of the 1880s could only tolerate as a pathetic joke a fortuneteller who taunted little Jewish boys with dreams of a place in government. Earlier, though, earlier, something made Freud's childhood a world of possibilities. It began much earlier. Vienna was a cosmopolitan city before Freud was born.

FREUD AND THE IDEA OF PUBLIC LIFE

Between the years 1750 and 1850 a lot happened in Vienna. Haydn composed and played. So did Mozart and Schubert. Johann Strauss' waltz was unleashed. Napoleon besieged the city after the French Revolution. The Congress of Vienna celebrated the rise of a conservative Europe; the defeat of the revolutionaries of 1848 etched it in stone. A world-famous medical school opened its doors. Three emperors ascended and left the throne. Several wars divided German Prussia from German Austria. Within those years Beethoven lived, wrote, and died. Those who attribute great works to genius find a lot to explain in Vienna. Or rather they find nothing to explain. In the words of one historian:

> The whole point about genius in any shape or form is that it stands outside society. It represents not a development, but a mutation, and such mutations may come singly, or in constellations. There appears to be no rhyme or reason in it; the mutations simply occur.[2]

But the Vienna of the late eighteenth and early nineteenth centuries seems consistently full of "mutations." All of a sudden child prodigies blossomed like wildflowers, composing and playing some of the most beautiful music which had ever been heard. Foreign musicians, medical students, and merchants flocked to the city only to be unmasked as "geniuses," "mutations." Is this idea of mutations really possible? Could it be rather that the culture itself fostered and encouraged genius, that that culture later touched the childhood of a genius who would bloom later, the genius Freud? Could it be that it is Vienna itself which merits attention?

Often an individual genius and his principles can direct a study of more general issues. The scholar Carl Schorske has studied Vienna through Freud's work and has seen a struggle between fathers and sons, an eruption of nonrational impulses in the late nineteenth and early twentieth centuries.[3] Freud's ideas parallel events of his time. Just as Freud posited an eternal Oedipal struggle, so the younger generation of radical artists and students was at that time trying to overthrow the simple rationalism and homebody boredom of their nineteenth-century fathers. Just as Freud insisted that the irrational id must be acknowledged (or it will be revealed suddenly or unexpectedly), so Viennese politics became more violent after years of suppression. This is Vienna through Freud's eyes.

Now Freud through the filter of Vienna. Medical reality of the time contributed to the theories Dr. Freud developed. A limited understanding of biochemistry, a limited arsenal of drugs—these date Freud's work.[4] At his time, for example, sex and sexuality were truly dangerous and real sources of anxiety. Venereal disease was of such epidemic proportions in the Vienna of 1830 that most known members of the avant-garde and most musicians, including both Schubert and Beethoven, had it. Added to this medical fact was the social fact that a marriage could be prevented if the future husband could not prove evidence of a lucrative trade; virtually every class, then, lived in fear and ambivalence, afraid of sex and afraid of never having sex. Or as one author put it, virtually no one in early-nineteenth-century Vienna had a normal sex life.[5] As Freud would be the first to admit, the sexual experience of parents affects the children's ideas about sex. So Freud's emphasis on sex may well have been tied to Vienna's social reality.

Attempts to explain Freud by explaining Vienna, however, are controversial and suspect. Critics tend to gravitate toward a discussion of Freud's patients and his own family. Whether kindly, noting that anti-Semitism forced upon him Jewish patients unwanted by other doctors, or unkindly, the finger points to Judaism. So either Freud is seen as a unique genius without society or else psychoanalysis is seen as a "Jewish science," even more as a "German-Jewish, Viennese, upper-middle-class science."

Here is a typical social interpretation of Freud's life and thought:

Embarrassed by his minority status, Sigmund Freud, like many other Jewish intellectuals, felt forced to explain the glaring difference between eastern European Jewish incivility and western refined culture.[6] Out of embarrassment, Freud accused the West. It is not rudeness which harms the psyche, Freud is forced to argue, but your pretense of manners that represses feeling and causes neurosis.

Rudeness? If this interpretation rings true, the self-hatred certainly runs deep. The point of this interpretation, like so many interpretations, is that Freud's ideas, born of his marginal status, are Jewish ideas, and the Vienna that molded him was Jewish Vienna. The way to understand a minority member, these theories claim, is through his different background. But that is not true. The way to understand a minority member is through his dream.

According to his biographer, Ernest Jones, Sigmund Freud kept a childhood ideal of public service all his life. Jones points out that Freud literally dreamt of being a cabinet minister years after he was a child, and by then the idea of actually becoming a minister must not have been something he thought of much, if at all.[7] Freud never wanted to retreat into a private, familiar world where manners were unnecessary. Just the contrary. His ambition was to bring the deep recesses of private fear into the public world, where the light of rationality could shine upon them. Freud's theories are a tribute to the public world. In other words, Freud's ideas do represent something of Vienna, an ideal learned in childhood: the ideal or dream of cosmopolitanism. Freud does not advocate irrationality, withdrawal into privacy, the abandonment of manners; his theories are an expression of the cosmopolitan dream, especially in its emphasis on public life.

For Vienna had a sense of mission, and a mix of peoples, but what made it a truly great cosmopolitan center was its public life.

Public institutions, including education, the military, and the arts, public parks, public streets and museums, and public bureaucracies, all serve as channels for opportunity and advance. They take the newcomer and suck him into the whirl of activity, toward the mainstream. This is a social idea, not a political one. Political liberalism might add to it, but wasn't present in many great cities such as Babylon. It is not democracy that is needed, but opportunity. The case of Vienna will demonstrate how the ordinary could become extraordinary and the extraordinary could become genius.

Before traveling on to examine Vienna as a whole, however, let us do justice to Sigmund Freud. If he represents the public world, it should be obvious enough. If his theory is an affirmation of a childhood dream and not an accusation to a world of strangers, it should be clear enough. And it is.

First, the norm or standard for emotional health was public behavior, according to Freud. So what if a woman coughed every time she saw a glass or refused to drink water from a glass? Not only did Freud not excuse lapses from civility, they were the very yardstick by which he measured the psyche. When asked what the "normal" person should be able to do, he answered, work and love. Both are social activities. His answer was not "express himself" or "enjoy life" or "get by" or "function." The very measure of an individual's health to Freud was his ability to act in a public world.

The public world, moreover, included the doctor's consulting room. Even if Freud's clinical behavior was more lax than is now the norm and the doctor showed more emotion and personal concern or judgment, and even if he wanted the patient to rid himself of inhibitions, the patient was still judged on how well he or she could contain himself and remain mindful of an outside world. Analysis was a "talking cure." Primal screams, masturbation, or other nonpublic display was not part of the therapy.

Most importantly, though, Freud's broader theories of society were expressions of belief in public life. *Civilization and Its Discontents* is an affirmation of civilization, difficult as that may be to achieve. In order to live together in society, Freud asserted, men and women have to repress many of their feelings and inner drives. Students may think about sex during a slow lecture, but no lecture could take place if couples actually paired off and lay down in the seats. Antagonisms and desires must be squelched in favor of more long-term goals. And so bridges are built, and cities founded, upon men and women's displaced feelings and postponed desires. Civilization is possible only where men and women do not withdraw into perpetual, private love-making. And as a result of suppressing and displacing their inner drives, men and women feel the steady ache of unnameable discontents; neuroses are the symptoms of that strain. Not only is Freud's whole idea an argument about public life; he concludes that public life is worth the strain.

In order to understand how far Freud carried his childhood dream of an open, public world, look again at his theories. Why does a doctor believe that individual distress is at all related to the social world? Moreover, why is a doctor writing about his cases for a broad audience? Why did he believe he would be famous? What made him think people would read his ideas? Simply, he believed in a public.

There is a name for people who believe that ideas have a public and that they have a duty to speak to that public: they are intellectuals.[8] Intellectuals are created only where people feel a commitment to public life and a duty to speak to that public. Dedicated newspapermen may chase stories and dog down a hot lead; that does not make them intellectuals. Witty aristocrats may pen their memoirs and find themselves coaxed into showing friends; that does not make them intellectuals. Professors, theologians, jurists may follow the exacting standards of their profession, may be honored and revered. But if they feel no moral duty to speak about public concerns, broad questions which touch a broad public, they are not intellectuals. Only a place with a great public life can create great intellectuals. That kind of place makes the ordinary into the extraordinary, the extraordinary into genius.

The pace picks up and faster and faster the whirl of city life speeds past. Clockwise and around in a grueling exhilaration, the speed draws you into the larger motion, sweeps you in, leaves you panting. It is so expensive. It is so intense. The waltz makes Emma Bovarys of all who dare to try; anything less becomes less than life. Throw your head back; inhale the air rushing past. Industry sings the tune and pounds the beat. The crash of waterfalls sets your pulse. City life, at once intimate and daring, draws you into a public whirl.

EMPIRE OF MANY PEOPLES

Vienna, a frontier fort founded by the Romans, became the ruling center of the Habsburg family and the center of the Habsburg Empire. What gave the empire its sense of mission and drive toward greatness: was it the family history, its shrewd policies, or simply its geographical position? The Habsburgs ruled Austria for seven centuries, from 1282 until 1918, when the Austro-Hungarian Empire was dissolved following the First World War. The question "Why Austria?" must include the Habsburgs in its answer.

The family was at once everything and nothing. The Habsburgs were the keepers of the Holy Roman Empire—but the obsolescent Roman Empire gained more prestige from the family than they did from its name. During the Middle Ages the dynasty claimed to be descended from Julius Caesar—this seemed safe politics rather than imperial glory. During the Reformation Roman ancestry, the Habsburgs knew well, kept the family in good stead with the papacy and a safe distance from the German Hohenstaufens, who financed Protestant disobedience. The family was everything, the empire itself was simply the product of the dynasty's drive for expansion and glory. And yet its beginnings were not exceptionally glorious and were without much sense of mission.

Guntram the Rich is probably the earliest known Habsburg ancestor. A count in the Nordgau region of Alsace, he was deprived of his substantial properties in A.D. 952 because Otto, then head of the Holy Roman Empire, found him guilty of treason. If Guntram really is the right ancestor, the Habsburgs can be traced to eighth-century Alsatian dukes. Why was the family rich? Because of their land in Alsace, the fertile, well-traveled plain southwest of the Rhine, as well as holdings in Switzerland. Bishop Werner of Strasbourg, brother or brother-in-law of Guntram's grandson Radbot, built the Habsburg, or Habichtsburg ("Hawk's Castle"), in what is now Switzerland in around 1020. Radbot's grandson was the first to use the name Habsburg. Its ever-increasing lands let the family engulf more and more of central Europe. Rudolf of Habsburg became king of Germany in 1273 and, after expanding his lands, gave his sons control of Austria in 1282, the beginning of legal Habsburg rule in Austria. The whole Habsburg story is one of large expansions and small retreats, adding lands for service and through alliances.

Is a long history itself a glorious one? The Habsburg story is hardly unique and even less eventful than most—no messages from God or visions, not a glamorous crusade. Just feudalism in working order, land for military might, land through alliances. The surprise is not how the family came to power, but how they stayed in power. Long after feudalism had given way to modernizing monarchs in the rest of Europe, Austria-Hungary managed to dominate them all with its old rules and landed aristocracy and, above all, its role as a personal Habsburg domain. The personal influence of the Habsburgs cannot be overestimated: Leopold I's love of music is credited with bringing into the empire throngs of musicians in the late 1600s. Maria Theresa's hausfrau tastes were the cause of mid-eighteenth-century censorship and public morals police throughout the empire. But there was something else that gave unity and purpose to the empire so that its capital city was more than a plaything or pleasure palace. It was Austria's special mission that made it glorious.

The alliances the House of Habsburg made in Europe were often the result of successful, strategic marriages. These marriages were so successful and so strategic that despite frequent war making, the later empire had around it the shawl of a peaceful, cozy matchmaker, more interested in security than adventure.[9] Maria Theresa's daughter Marie Antoinette was offered in what then seemed to be a secure match with powerful Louis XVI of France. And when the tide had turned and Napoleon, on the heels of the French Revolution, demanded international recognition, the Habsburgs obliged with another daughter. Marie Louise did not meet Napoleon until after they had married, "and when she finally met him," as one historian puts it, "she hated the 'Antichrist,' and she cried a bit, but she did as she was told."[10] One ditty of the era sang, "Louise's skirts and Napoleon's pants now unite Austria and France." When the tide turned again and the Congress of Vienna celebrated Napoleon's defeat, his Viennese wife simply returned home to watch.

Marriage made the empire stable and gave it the legitimacy of love, in all its forms. Family life—cozy, comfortable, and stable—was the ideal around which the Biedermeier style was built. The passion and idealism of Romanticism, the coquetry of dance, platonic bliss, love, and sex were values intrinsic to Vienna. When Maria Theresa, the powerful empress, imposed her sensibilities on her subjects, love became more than policy and more than sacred duty—it was a national ideal. At one point Maria Theresa was dismayed to learn that her daughter Marie Antoinette slept apart from her husband Louis. Even after learning that it was the custom at Versailles, Maria Theresa said, "I must accept that what you tell me is right. But I should have liked it better if you could have lived in the German way and enjoyed that certain intimacy which comes of being together."[11] What is more, the success of the Habsburg family came in large part from luck in love and marriage. While the life expectancy in the Middle Ages was abysmally low and the European population declined, the Habsburgs were fruitful beyond hope. Having lots of children assured succession as well as expansion. Maria Theresa herself had sixteen children, making possible many alliances.

When alliance was not possible, there was always war. Like other cosmopolitan centers, however, Vienna did not describe its mission as conquest for its own sake, but as preserving the balance, the precarious balance between East and West and old and new. Even war was joining, blending—a kind of marriage. The Habsburg Empire saw its mission as the "eternal counterpoise."[12] When it went to war, it was to keep peace or prevent further war. When the Turkish threat was broken in 1683, Vienna was between Russia and France, Prussia and Poland, not only geographically, but politically. Vienna was the feudal counterpoise to the Enlightenment, the Catholic counterpoise to Reform, the conservative counterpoise to revolution. Without outside causes, peoples, alliances, and persuasions, Vienna, the eternal counterpoise, would have been without justification. Its very mission was the rest of Europe. The symbol of the empire, its two-headed eagle, represented a state which looked both east and west, which was, according to the historian Oscar Jászi, a fatal flaw. As strongly as the dynasty may have sought unity, Catholicism, or German culture, they could not be had. These goals were not consistent with the broad expansion and underlying sense of purpose of the empire, to engulf all of Europe through alliances and expansion.

The posture of political balance only thinly disguised the Austrians' moral purpose: conservatism in the face of Enlightenment ideals and the French Revolution. The French Revolution, along with the Industrial Revolution, changed history irrevocably and gravely threatened the monarchies of Europe. The idea that ordinary peasants could make decisions or that all men were brothers, this was dangerous enough. But that the people killed their king, carried out a program of retribution against aristocrats, and hoped that other countries would follow them, this was intolerable to European kings. France was waging war on all the rest of Europe. But also, more personally for many heads of state, many aristocrats fled France and went to foreign courts where they had friends or relations. Although many of them returned safely to France after the war, European nobility was shaken.

Austrian conservatives reacted to the Revolution by forcing unity on their empire, unity of thought and action through censorship, for example. And yet the very unity they were trying to defend was a unity of many nationalities. As the emperor Francis said:

> My peoples are strange to each other and that is all right. They do not get the same sickness at the same time. In France if the fever comes you are caught by it at the same time. I send the Hungarians into Italy, the Italians into Hungary. Every people watches its neighbor. . . . The one does not understand the other and one hates the other . . . . From their antipathy will be born order and from the mutual hatred, general peace. . . .[13]

Divide and conquer, perhaps. Yet the unintended result was an empire of peoples who retained their languages and an empire whose very justification was diversity.

Metternich, the powerful prime minister, was opposed to nationalism. For nationalism was a product of the Enlightenment ideal of a self-directed life, a government for and by the people. The idea of a unique cultural destiny for each nation, and of real differences in identity between them, came straight from the Enlightenment emphasis on rationality. The philosopher Immanuel Kant (1724–1804) posited "categories of mind," or different predispositions toward different parts of reality. Different peoples, then, view the world differently. Let each people direct its own future! The young poet Lord Byron lent freedom-fighting glamor by joining the Macedonians in their struggle. The early 1800s, the Romantic, youthful age of passion and freedom, saw the first stirrings of nationalism. Metternich, meanwhile, and the empire he represented, were undeniably opposed.

German nationalism was a strong force in the Austro-Hungarian Empire, but it was not a pillar of the empire. Germans were a skilled group of migrants who often held government positions where they helped to modernize regions in Hungary and the East. Maria Theresa insisted on use of the German language, not to replace Hungarian and other languages of the realm, but to replace Latin, an outmoded and useless language for administration. Maria Theresa supported the idea that people keep speaking their native languages, while she encouraged German language and culture. When it came to the possibility of a German state, however, an Austria joined with Prussia or Saxony, Austria was not interested. First, Metternich argued, what need of a German empire? Austria already was an empire, the Holy Roman Empire. Secondly, there was strength in diversity. Separate, balanced powers would ensure a more stable world than would attempts at German union. A federation would be fine. "If Austria were above any other state, he thought, there would be anarchy, internal feuds and foreign cabals."[14] Metternich's slogan was "unity in multiplicity." He was a reactionary theorist for the Habsburg throne, and although his ambition was total control, he actually contributed to Austrian diversity.

Most paradoxically, though, Metternich and the Habsburgs believed that peoples like the Prussians, Bavarians, Saxons, etc., had too little in common to become a German state. Metternich saw no reason why a political state had to coincide with a cultural group. Why should people be brought into one group and not another?

In this way Austria believed in differences among peoples at the same moment that the empire was seeking orthodoxy. Foreign tongues were spoken at the same time that political stirrings were being repressed. The empire preserved peoples' identities at the same time it valued them least. The paradox became most apparent years later, years after Metternich and Francis I, when the empire found that its own attitudes had squashed its own goal, that unity in dogma was not possible.

With a policy of expansion and a mission based on multiplicity, it goes without saying that the Austro-Hungarian Empire had within it a wide variety of peoples. Here is the full title of the reigning emperor:

We . . . by God's grace, Emperor of Austria; King of Hungary,
of Bohemia, of Dalmatia, Croatia, Slavonia, Galicia, Lodomeria,
and Illyria; King of Jerusalem, etc.; Archduke of Austria; Grand

Duke of Tuscany and Cracow; Duke of Lothringia, of Salzburg, Styria, Carinthia, Carniola and Bukovina; Grand Duke of Transylvania, Margrave of Moldavia; Duke of Upper and Lower Silesia, of Modena, Parma, Piacenza and Guasletta, of Ausschwitz and Sator, of Teschen, Friaul, Ragusa and Zara; Princely Count of Habsburg and Tyrol, of Kyburg, Gorz and Graduska; Duke of Trient and Brixen; Margrave of Upper and Lower Lausitz and in Istria; Count of Hohenembs, Feldkirch, Bregenz, Sonnenberg, etc; Lord of Trieste, of Cattaro and above the Windisch Mark; Great Voyvat of the Voyvadina, Servia, etc., etc.[15]

While Germans and German culture set the standard for the empire, one that was often imposed by the throne, Germans made up only about 36 percent of the Austrian part of the monarchy and 10 percent of the Hungarian part during the nineteenth century. Otherwise, the empire consisted of Magyars (.04 percent of Austria, 55 percent of Hungary), Czechs (23 percent of Austria and 11 percent of Hungary), Poles (17 percent of Austria), Serbs, Ruthenians, Croats, Italians, Rumanians, Jews, and other, smaller groups.[16] Each of these had a language and a history. The Magyars and the Germans were the two most powerful groups, most represented in government and finance.

As for Vienna, it began the nineteenth century as the third largest city in the West, after London and Paris. Increasing after 1820 at the rate of about 5,500 people a year, the population was up to about 320,000 by 1830. Its size, and its population increase, were largely due to immigrants.

> . . . in 1830 only 8.25 % of all Viennese were foreigners . . . the percentage doubled by 1825 and by 1840 nearly 43 % of Viennese residents were foreign born. Many of these people came from the East, including Hungarians, Poles, Bohemians, Czechs, Slovenes, Moravians, Silesians, Serbs, Croats, Armenians, Turks and Greeks.[17]

One scholar's interpretation sounds hauntingly familiar; he doesn't say "melting pot," but crucible, and describes a harmonious blend where people retain their original identities but also take on a new, Viennese identity.[18] One memoirist whose grandfather took him for walks in the old Vienna commented on the many different peoples he saw:

> Tailors were Czechs, cobblers Poles, waiters Hungarians, brick-layers Italians, each nation in accordance with its natural gifts and talents. There was a large reservoir of talent on which the imperial residence could draw.[19]

So many of the immigrants had wealth, he said, that palaces were named in every language. The language, too, changed. Johns from all countries were called "Schani," even those not originally called Giovanni, and all Josephs were "Pepi."

Madame de Staël, the shrewd and opinionated observer of differences between the French and the Germans, while unimpressed with Vienna's variety, was certainly witness to it. She visited Vienna in 1808 for, of all things, a royal wedding. She was taken with the city's public life, its parks, its picnics, its music. "In the midst of the crowd you often meet with Oriental, Hungarian, and Polish costumes, which enliven the imagination; and harmonious bands of music at intervals give to all this asemblage the air of a peaceable fete. . . ."[20] But the baroness set as her task the analysis of national character, that is, what made the Austrians Austrian. Her very goal in writing is to distinguish one people from another. Of course she notices that Vienna is multilingual and many-peopled. She finds it tiresome.

Were Vienna merely German, at least it would have integrity, despite the Viennese lack of wit, Madame de Staël believes. But the Viennese insist on attempting foreign manners. Who are these Germans who refuse to speak German? They turn out to be Poles or Russians.

> The Poles and Russians, who constituted the charm of society at Vienna, spoke nothing but French, and contributed to the disuse of the German language. The Polish women have very seductive manners; they unite an Oriental imagination with the suppleness, and the vivacity of France. Yet, even among the Slavonic, the most

flexible of all nations, the imitation of the French style is most often fatiguing. . . ."[21]

And then her prophetic statement reveals her true feelings: "A foreign language is always . . . a dead language."[22]

This statement summarizes much of modern history and expresses the nationalist ideal of self-determination, all in a few words. For it says that real beliefs and feelings can be expressed only in one's native language, and any other language is so much baggage. Madame de Staël would know personally the truth in this idea. When a discussion is held with a foreign friend, often everything is said twice; first in one's native language so the speaker may speak his own sincerity, then in the foreign language so the listener may hear sincerity. The lover who never has the opportunity to say words of love in his first language (regardless of whether or not he is understood) has never unburdened his heart and remains locked away and distant. All this Madame de Staël would know from her own romances.

It is the privilege only of those who know foreign languages to agree with her. She takes for granted that people know several tongues and can always communicate at least the minimal requirements of court ritual. Her world was just emerging from the power of Latin. So she insists on national uniqueness, and is somewhat confounded in Vienna.

Madame de Staël as well as other observers looked for causes for the seeming harmony of the peoples living in Vienna. Nature seemed an obvious answer. The city on the Danube was lush and graceful; its atmosphere or its landscape "acclimated" visitors.[23] Nature, simplicity, peace, harmony—these were the explanations. Madame de Staël's description of the Prater, the public park, sounds like a mix between Jean-Jacques Rousseau and Isaiah:

> There is no great city without its public building, its promenade, or some other wonder of art or of nature, to which the recollections of infancy attach themselves; and I think that the Prater must possess a charm of this description for the inhabitants of Vienna; nowhere do we find, so near the capital, a public walk so rich in the beauties, at once of rude and ornamented nature. A majestic forest

extends to the banks of the Danube; herds of deer are seen from afar passing through the meadow; they return every morning, and fly away every evening when the influx of company disturbs their solitude.[24]

What better place for the lion to lie with the lamb or the Magyar with the Ruthenian? Yet if greenery were so conducive to peaceful mixing, why is there less commerce and society in the countryside by definition? Perhaps a little green goes a long way. There is real truth to the *Natur* explanation of Vienna's cosmopolitan character, beyond the Romantic notion of the noble savage which seems to move Madame de Staël. Just as in Constantinople a vital public life accompanied an inner world of secrets, so Vienna balances broad public life with private contemplation. *Natur* is at once public and private.

Kultur in winter, *Natur* in summer; the social season was winter—the opera, the waltz—and in summer one's mind could wander. One could stare at a tree, gaze at clouds, could momentarily absent oneself and still be within bounds. *Natur* belonged to everyone. But before you relax in comfort and relief (at last a natural-landscape-architectural explanation, at last an inescapable, determined, nonsocial explanation), think again. Why parks? Why public parks? Why a crowded social season of balls and concerts? Public life is a social creation and it in turn creates a cosmopolitan culture.

So we are back in the Prater, the public park of private restaurants, where public amusements exist for the enjoyment of private tables. Sigmund Freud's parents do not know when they call over the public fortuneteller that their son, too, will become a public poet who will pronounce on the fate of private persons. And he does leave the private sphere of his parents to become a great public figure.

ADMINISTRATIVE REFORMS: THE CREATION OF A PUBLIC WORLD

Aristocrats fumed when Joseph II, then coregent with his mother, Maria Theresa, first opened the Prater to the public in the winter of 1765–1766. His ruling not only allowed the common masses in the park, it commanded them not to pay attention to members of the royal family nor the emperor himself while in the park. In order to understand the effect of a public park, imagine extremes of wealth and poverty the likes of which few of us have even seen. All land, every parcel and every twig on every parcel, was owned by the nobility. Remember that in England at this time a man could be hanged for shooting a rabbit for dinner and in France equally punished for picking up more than his rightful bundle of twigs from the forest floor. Weighed out in minute quantities, the rights and ordinances of the feudal world were designed to set men apart, not bring them together.

The nobility hunted for sport on lands right next to the capital city. They had lands cleared for formal gardens or forested and filled with beasts. The hunt rode fast and roughshod; excitement trampled vineyards and woodlands and whatever was in the way. Or aristocrats promenaded past carefully tended trees and lawns, in silk, in jewels, in huge hoop skirts. Remember that an aristocrat not only commanded respect by privilege and tradition, leaving curtsies in his or her wake like a wind through a flower bed. An aristocrat was also an inescapable expression of beauty, glamour, perfection. Would you turn away or, better yet, simply not notice, if you saw a vision, a deity clothed in a rainbow? And yet Joseph told the common people to do just that.

Imagine a public park. Air for all city dwellers. A place to go, first, to admire and see the nobility, but then to be like the nobility. No curtsies, no embarrassment. Everyone could promenade and pretend to be the emperor. No wonder the Viennese were so attached to their daily promenade. Madame de Staël thought it might be boredom, all of society traipsing over morning and night to walk in the same place every day, the same route. Parisian society had so many other amusements, she said, such long walks wouldn't be enjoyable. She did not see that in the public parks imperial decree had freed the people of an emperor.

It is not surprising that the aristocracy objected to mixing willy-nilly in this way. Joseph was undermining their aristocracy and differentness, destroying their hunting grounds, and inviting in the very people they were trying to escape. Didn't the lower orders bring disease? (The answer to this question, by the way, is not a simple yes. The aristocracy, in their desire to distinguish themselves, refused all vegetables as food for peasants. Consequently, their unhealthy diets caused malnutrition and numerous digestive complaints which drove them to spas like Karlsbad for relief. There they sipped hot mineral waters which might actually have helped them.) Was there no escape? The city was full of petty shopkeepers, struggling musicians, clerks, and general riffraff, and the aristocracy saw them all too much in the streets.

The parks were the nobility's last refuge; the city of Vienna was for the most part mixed and crowded. Housing was in short supply as industry and commerce demanded more space and drew workers into the city. A strange public life developed in the streets and houses themselves. The aristocracy chose the central city for its nearness to the court and the emperor, to fashionable society. Still, cities were centers of disease and the smart aristocrat maintained his country house. Madame de Staël remarks that in Vienna the nobility did not choose the suburbs, but stayed clustered in their town houses, maintaining a lively social scene. More than an affectation drew the nobility to the hunt and the promenade. They were also pushed by a need for fresh air. But the poor lived in the city along with the rich, crammed in between and among them, often sharing a staircase. There were no ghettos or specialized neighborhoods in the early nineteenth century: for the most part, there was not enough available housing for people to be able to choose neighborhoods or cluster in groups. Nobility and wealthy bourgeois owned huge town houses, but lived on two floors and rented out the others. Franz Schubert met a supporter this way. An aristocrat who lived in his building heard Schubert's music, became an acquaintance, and helped his career. Vienna was a teeming hodgepodge, all very public—the hallways, the staircases, the streets.

This, too, was in part Joseph's doing. Why did the nobility give up floors of their buildings? There was an official decree that all first floors of all buildings must go to housing his civil servants. It was not choice on the part of the aristocrats. Nor was it even love of money. So we turn to Joseph. What motivated him? Love of his people? Hatred of privilege? Joseph's personality has often been used to explain his reforms. True, he hated hunting, and doing away with the hunting grounds hardly disturbed him. He disliked display and ostentation, including religious ritual. Until the outcry became overwhelming, he ruled that there should be no caskets or funeral rites, only simple burials in mass pits lined with lime. This reform, rather than disrespect, influenced the funeral of Mozart, so coldly portrayed in the recent film *Amadeus*. The son of Maria Theresa's progressive doctor arranged for Mozart's funeral in 1791 with what he believed everyone's best interests at heart.[25]

Joseph's mother loved the Jesuits; he detested them. No sooner did his mother die than he seized all monastery property and declared an act of toleration for Protestants and a limited (but extensive for the time) toleration for the Jews. Joseph was a harsh, demanding autocrat, but he was not simply cruel or heartless. He had always felt disliked and never much felt like one of the club. His first marriage ended in tragedy, his second in farce, and thereafter he was a lonely, isolated workaholic. Many of his reforms could be seen as acts of love, although others look more like acts of hate, others sheer perversity. Throughout his life he sought affection and never received it. Unhappy with his identity, he often traveled incognito. He was suspicious. He employed spies. He admired Frederick of Prussia and wanted German culture enhanced in Austria.

But can a personality create a trend of reform? Even Maria Theresa, Joseph's mother, made a reforming mark, although she was a pious, uncultured woman who began her reign as a gay, flighty, love-struck girl and ended a simple dowager. She disliked and feared change, especially Enlightenment ideas. She liked most being surrounded by her enormous family, feeling warm and complete in happy domesticity. In her youth she loved the grand spectacles of royalty, in her age the grand spectacles of religion. Her personality was so different from Joseph's, yet both actually contributed reforms.

While personality may count as something, especially among the Habsburgs, whose empire was seen as a personal domain, there is more to history than kindness or grief or even logic. Past events and future hopes make an emperor act. Maria Theresa, and her son even more so, wanted to consolidate their lands and ensure a future for their empire. These goals, shared by two very different rulers, had nothing to do with personality. Their future relied on more universal concerns, such as increased revenue for war and diplomacy. It relied on a new way of managing the empire, a more efficient way. Administrative reform was behind all of Maria Theresa's and Joseph's decrees which resulted in a public sphere. Thanks to them, Vienna, the capital of administration, could absorb massive numbers of foreigners. The empress demanded that her subjects be educated, and foreign students flocked to the city. The emperor demanded that his bureaucrats be housed. Vienna's higher purpose, the Habsburg Empire, swept thousands and thousands into public service.

The paradox in Vienna's creation of a public life was that while all around Europe Enlightenment ideas were taking hold, ideas which argued for the very reforms Maria Theresa wanted, Maria Theresa disliked Enlightenment philosophers and did all she could to keep their works out of her empire. Their notion that all human beings, endowed with reason, could act upon the world, could learn new ways, could become educated, frightened her.

The outlook of scholars and artists was fast changing. The wonder of the human body, a legacy of European humanism, was only a short step from the wonder of the human mind, of human life in communities. "What a piece of work is man, how infinite in faculties"—the words a great poet gives to his hero, Hamlet. The Protestant Reformation, which saw each man facing his God alone, made God more distant, less all-consuming. And if one tried on the perspective of that distant God, turned the telescope around, so to speak, then how small those humans looked—so small and so similar, ants upon an orange.[26]

Enlightenment thought seemed to iron out differences among human beings, but ideas were not the only fast-changing influence. The marketplace was an unforgiving forum: what value the trappings of privilege when wealthy merchants could buy as good or better, when any man was as good as another to work a loom or turn a wheel? This insistence on equality may have been the work of wealthy burghers frustrated at their growing importance and lack of power. But even the looms and wheels themselves changed people's thinking: technology provided the metaphors—the lenses, telescopes, microscopes, clockwork.

Maria Theresa's Austria had no love of classical learning or of Protestant reformed ideas, but it did have a marketplace. It needed money.

When a threat to the crops and therefore the solvency of the empire arose, Maria Theresa was eager to aid the serfs. In 1769 the peasants of Silesia struck and the issue of servitude became part of an economic inquiry. How had she judged the peasants? First, economically.[27] She did have an impulse to free the serfs, but her advisors warned against it. Only her son, Joseph, would take that extreme step. Her reforms, then, begun in 1767, limited the obligations on serfs, with the goal of solvency. Each peasant, according to one law, should be able "to support himself and his family, and also to pay his share of the national expenditure in time of peace or war."[28] Even the individual reforms, which now read as a book of the horrors of forced servitude, were instituted in part to make her economy more efficient: men were forbidden to beat pregnant women, free assistance was to be given by midwives and treatment given to persons bitten by mad dogs, and orphanages were established.[29]

The same marketplace which made men sing of freedom made Maria Theresa worry about finance. As one historian says:

> Maria Theresa's intention was clear, and her peasant reforms
> offer a good illustration of the workings of her . . . utilitarianism.
> The peasants must be raised up because it was wrong that the weak
> should suffer; it was also expedient to treat them well because they
> were needed in the interests of the economy.[30]

Careful management and reorganization balanced the imperial budget in 1775. Maria Theresa was still no child of the Enlightenment. She simply could not avoid its influence.

An increasing spiral of trade, technology, and exploration took Europe's ships farther and farther a-sea in the years before Maria Theresa's reign. Navigation improved, travel created new markets, trade demanded more secure ships. These travels provided another, more exotic proof of Enlightenment ideas. One of the most profound of the new ideas was Europe's invention of the savage.

Could this dark-skinned warrior, wearing feathers and paints instead of a powdered wig and make-up, could this be a human being? What manner of human being would live without palaces or salon witticisms? Explorers bringing back to their kings' courts examples of these beings were surprised to find they could be taught to live as Europeans, especially the children. They could learn a language or a manner. They were like children, the Europeans thought, like the childhood of man. They were noble and innocent, unbent by centuries of feudal servitude.

The shock of seeing these very different beings forced Europeans to think about their own habits and customs. Here are people without clothes. Why do we wear clothes? Why do we make some men worse than others—why are some of our people in chains? The invention of the savage and the beginnings of social inquiry were two sides of the same newly minted coin, the growing self-criticism and self-interest of Europe. Its monumental consequences cannot be ignored—the very words "Third World" echo with its effects. Both the drive for domination and the drive for equality grew out of this European awareness. Both great philosophers and grotesque slave-mongers lived in its shadow.

MARIA THERESA AND THE LEGACY OF THE ENLIGHTENMENT: UNIVERSAL EDUCATION

Maria Theresa was not surrounded by Indians and Africans. Her empire colonized the Old World, not the New, and even had she received one of these people as a gift, she might not have thought much of it. She was not of a philosophic bent. Yet Maria Theresa experienced the same shock of discovery upon seeing her own people. She did not sympathize with Voltaire or Rousseau, but she could not block out her own experiences, which were themselves symptoms of her times.

Every account of Maria Theresa's "natural" sympathy for her serfs includes the word "shock." She was shocked at the condition of the peasants. How could an empress be shocked by the condition of her peasants? Peasants were, of course, a different species of human being to her. They were like Indians or Africans explorers described: they ate differently, spoke a different language, lived in primitive conditions. Emperors had believed this for centuries and certainly emperors had seen peasants. Yet Maria Theresa was not trained to be an empress. Her father, Charles VI, had wanted a son. Long past the time when it was obvious he would leave behind only daughters, he ignored Maria Theresa's education. Like any court lady, she learned music and marksmanship and poetry, but as one scholar writes, that type of education was an absurd way to prepare her to rule.[31] Her Jesuit tutors schooled her from the *Ratio Studiorum,* a book at least 150 years old by the time Maria Theresa got to it. It was more concerned with biblical trivia than Austrian history. While other heirs apparent might have been taken on tours of their lands, the young Maria was not allowed to ride.

So instead of a toughened ruler who had been trained at her father's knee, the empire had a queen ready to be shocked by the condition of the peasants. Her Jesuit training, designed for ladies of the court, stressed charity. It was this lesson of charity that she retained. She opened her eyes as an empress and had a true Enlightenment experience. Although she detested the "new philosophers," she shared in experience, if not intellect, their meaning. She looked carefully at her fellow human beings. Not because she was a woman, but because she was trained as women were; not because she was kind, but because she was trained to be kind, did she begin reform. In an age of reform, even the most determined reactionary cannot hide from the changes being wrought. Perhaps out of personal regret, or feeling for her peasant-savages, or amazement at the variety of humankind, Maria Theresa's greatest reforms were in education.

Education was immediately tied to reform of the administration, since the state needed well-educated personnel.[32] In order to understand the need for new schools, imagine scholarship as it was in Europe for hundreds of years. Elementary education, where it existed, was in the hands of the clergy. The Society of Jesus, or the Jesuits, a teaching order of the Catholic Church, conducted many if not most lower schools, where religion was the main subject of study. The Jesuits were alternately loved and hated, rejected and relied upon. Their most sparkling successes were students destined to be priests. It was widely believed that ordinary people required very little education. In any case, few could afford to release a child from moneymaking chores long enough to attend. For most Europeans, school was a form of piety in which states or governments had no role.

A little higher up the social scale, more aristocratic, or older, one could receive in Europe the same education that Anna Comnena received in Constantinople. The wealthiest merchants could give children more advanced instruction, which included the trivium and quadrivium, the classical curricula which included math, music, Latin, and rhetoric. The state was not involved here either and most often a private tutor gave instruction. The daring character in John Barth's *The Sot-Weed Factor*, a novel which takes place in the 1600s, is leaving for the New World to become a tutor. "What if they ask me to teach something I don't know?" the nervous novice asks. The response is funny ("In that case charge double; it's harder to teach something you don't know"), but his fears are unfounded. There were few innovations in this middle-level education. Trades were learned by apprenticeship. Lucky the bookworm who was apprenticed to a printer. Often he could learn languages and many new ideas, as did the young Benjamin Franklin or many of the most active citizens in the French Revolution.[33]

Finally, there were universities, usually for aristocrats, where some of the newest philosophies were expounded. Oxford, Cambridge, the Sorbonne, and the great German universities were filled for centuries with the small group of scholars who traveled great distances at great expense to read, teach, and think. The government, any government, had no claim on these schools. They had direct charters from independent free cities or popes and they existed beyond states. The Danish prince Hamlet attended a German university, remember, where his friends Gildenstern and Rosenkrantz were also students. Had Hamlet lived or, rather, had Hamlet been resigned to seeing his uncle Claudius reign, he might have returned to Denmark to exert some influence as a minister and perhaps gone on some diplomatic missions. As a prince, he certainly could have done this without university training. The tragedy of Hamlet might even be read to say that his university training was a hindrance.

Now, it will be clearer what kind of revolution the antirevolutionary Austrian empire began. The government had nothing to do with education at all, and in becoming involved, Austria created a revolution. Maria Theresa took counsel in this matter from her doctor, Van Swieten, who had come from Holland and was anti-Jesuit. She saw him as a trusted personal friend and an expert on children and education. Van Swieten first obtained permission to extend the crown's influence into the University of Vienna. In 1749 the sovereign took the right to appoint professors to the faculty. Van Swieten's reforms raised intellectual life in the empire, culturally as well as politically. Strong universities increased Austria's prestige, especially compared with Prussia.[34]

Maria Theresa also approved the creation of new colleges of higher education. She founded an academy of Oriental languages for the training of consuls who traded with Turkey and the East. She founded in 1746 an academy for poor young nobles, and this school, the Theresianum, taught political economy and mathematics, subjects needed by able administrators. She appointed prestigious scholars to chairs in the faculty of law at Vienna who helped the subjects of natural law and political economy gain in status.

The Jesuits were out of the business of controlling education; first, they were not given appointments as deans of faculty, then in 1773 Joseph suppressed them. They were replaced by more practical-minded religious orders and instruction was in German, not Latin.

The state also entered the business of elementary education, mandating instruction for children in village schools. Senior schools taught Latin, history, geography, natural history, and drawing. Three colleges to train teachers were opened in Prague, Brünn (Brno), and Vienna. While the training colleges taught in German, all other schools were taught in the local language, either Czech or German or, in Hungary, Magyar, German, Slovak, Croation, Ruthenian, Illyrian, or Wallachian. In Hungary, similar reforms did not succeed in the countryside, but in the towns both Catholic and Protestant secondary schools flourished and a mining college opened in 1763.

In other words, by 1780, the year of Maria Theresa's death and nine years before the French Revolution, all Christians in the empire had access to schooling. (Joseph extended this to people of all religions in 1781.) Not only did they have schools to attend; there was a hierarchy of schools so that the empire could encourage and promote the best students. There was at least one *Trivialschule* in every small town or parish, at least one *Hauptschule* in every district, and at least one *Normalschule* in every *Land*. There were also special refresher schools which taught a class for two hours each Sunday after mass for students between thirteen and twenty years old. All boys and girls had to attend school until they were twelve years old. Any speaker of any language could become an educated person. While the system had flaws in practice (including a shortage of teachers), it meant that the Austro-Hungarian Empire was becoming full of potential civil servants, spies, engineers, and thousands of other professionals who spoke all the languages of the empire. The most successful and prestigious spoke German. But the body of talented, useful people from whom Vienna could draw was very great.

It is not opportunity that is at issue here, but inclusion. Opportunity through education is an old theme and a complex one. Many people, even today in America, find their only path to success through a maze of phonics workbooks, science experiments, and homework assignments. The language of the majority, once learned, leads to the culture of the majority and through that culture lies the way to power. But don't be mistaken. Social scientists have consistently found that careers and opportunities are best predicted not by how much school you've had, but by how much money your parents have had.[35] As for Vienna of the late eighteenth and early nineteenth centuries, how many benefited from these schools? How many who learned to read remembered how? What wonderful careers awaited the educated poor but jobs in the growing factories? Schools may have trained them to arrive on time, sit in rows, fulfill assignments, but the working conditions in the textile mills of Silesia or the glass factories of Bohemia were hardly rewards for scholarship. Education helped the economy more than the individual. But the individual, every individual, was included.

The results of this inclusion are revealed by two examples. Under Maria Theresa women were drawn into public life, where they had more dealings with men than before. The empress herself set an example of the capability of women. Although she was described as mother of her country and she even resorted to tears and feigned weakness when trying to persuade Hungarian nobility, she was the ruler nevertheless. Early in her reign, she seemed to prefer late-night dancing to the serious questions of government. But by the time Marie Antoinette was queen of France, Maria Theresa saw the gravity of monarchy and had definite views on the role of women. Louis XVI, it seems, was at first unable to consummate the marriage. A flurry of letters from her mother urged

Marie Antoinette to help her husband. (It turned out to be a physical problem cured by a painfully late circumcision.) When the marriage was better established and Marie Antoinette was reputed (largely by her mother's spies in Paris) to have many lovers, the letters changed. Sex and orgies were not the province of a queen. If Marie didn't realize the seriousness of her responsibilities, she would be ruined. Maria Theresa did not think of women as ornaments or unthinking dolls. That Marie Antoinette did was her downfall.

Maria Theresa was convinced that morals were too lax in Vienna, and two highborn, conservative observers of the age seemed to agree. Madame de Staël said Viennese salon life had no substance, particularly since censorship stifled conversation, while Caroline Pichler complained that food was so cheap and the poor so haughty that attempts at charity failed, leaving the highborn with no one to care for but themselves. Many people believed that the balls and dances, especially the waltz, brought men and women into dangerous proximity. Music made society indiscriminate. Music also provided careers for women.

The city was an important center for women. Unlike England, where the aristocracy had a social life on their country estates, Austrians had only Vienna. It was the social center, the marriage market, the source of income, the potential for stability. Whether or not morals were lax is hard to say. Close proximity or the new freedom of the city might have influenced newcomers. Then again, close proximity may just have made everything more obvious.

Ironically, after Maria Theresa instituted her morality rules, the situation probably worsened. Casanova gives in his *Mémoires* the account of a renegade and well-traveled Italian adventurer who described the mixed effects of Maria Theresa's new laws.

A legion of vile spies, . . . adorned with the attractive name of Commissioners of Chastity, were the pitiless tormentors of all girls. The sovereign did not have the sublime virtue of tolerance where it concerned what was called illegitimate love, and, pious to the point of bigotry, she believed herself to acquire great merit in the eyes of God by her minute persecution of the natural propensities of both sexes . . . [This] gave rise to all kinds of infamies which her tyrannical Commissioners of Chastity committed with impunity in her name. They carried off to prison, at all hours of the day and from all the streets of Vienna, poor girls whom they found alone, who in most cases went out only in order to earn an honest living . . . when a girl entered a house, the spy who had followed her waited outside the door and then arrested her for interrogation. If the poor victim showed any embarrassment and hesitated to answer in a manner satisfactory to the spy, the tormentor took her to prison, first, however, despoiling her of her money and jewels, which were never returned. The only means girls had of not being molested was to walk through the streets demurely with lowered heads and chaplets in their hands.[36]

Another of Maria Theresa's attempts to protect women, a law ensuring that a prospective bridegroom had to have a steady income, also actually harmed them. By delaying marriage, the rules left women either alone or dependent on their fathers, who were undoubtedly none too pleased, and eager to marry the burdens off. The education Maria Theresa made possible, at least, helped women toward self-sufficiency, as insecure as that might be. Women were in a precarious, though very public, position. From the very highest nobility, through the bourgeoisie, down to the lowest peasant or prostitute, women in Austria were not secluded. We have already seen that they faced mandatory schooling, although they had to sit on separate benches and not wear corsets, which, presumably, would have made them too distracting to boys. Women were also essential to dances or celebrations. They hosted the social circles which later gained in intellectual importance. They were factory labor. They were rulers. Inclusion did not mean opportunity; women were not equals and in fact were quite mistreated. But women did develop a sense of belonging and the same civic awareness as men. Women graduates of certain teaching schools, for example, were required to teach at least six years in the service of the state. Years later this civic consciousness blossomed into strong initiatives by women for social reform.

Just as Maria Theresa included women more fully in the life of Vienna, Joseph included people from different backgrounds and classes in his secret police force. Joseph said anyone could be employed. "Messengers, drivers, nay, under certain circumstances, even Jews who do good service. Nobody should be considered too low."[37] Those in the government's employ gained in numbers. Joseph reorganized the espionage system by unifying all the police so that they were responsible to the emperor rather than to provincial governments. Joseph appointed and trained the police chiefs which he sent to the provinces; the chiefs reported to the minister of the interior in Vienna.

The secret police created by Joseph are doubly interesting, not only for who did the spying, but also for who was spied upon. Everyone was a potential spy; switched loyalties were fine as long as they were loyalties to the empire. Unlike his predecessors, Joseph even encouraged a policy of immigration, in order to have more potential employees. He was fond of repeating a popular joke: A bureaucrat asks a priest why the clergy had become too proud to employ the humble mount of the Savior. The clergyman answers coldly, "Because the emperor has taken so many jackasses into his employ that there are few left for us to use."[38]

Those spied upon meanwhile were the administrators and officials themselves. Joseph's goal was to keep a check on his own government, or, rather, the new organization he was expanding. His instructions to the spies were that no one should know they existed—the official police were a cover for the secret police. The police control was extreme. All "suspicious persons" on their way to Vienna were reported. Everyone, especially strangers, was registered. So Joseph's motive was not love of foreigners. As Joseph attempted to create a new, efficient administration, though, the results were broader inclusion and a bigger public life.

JOSEPH'S REFORMS:
THE SPIRIT OF BUREAUCRACY

Joseph expanded radically on Maria Theresa's reforms. The spirit of enlightened despotism filled his Edict of Toleration in 1781, in which he not only allowed all religions access to education but also allowed all his subjects to worship publicly. The vehement opposition of his counselors, the clergy, and the nobility were justified; once Protestantism was recognized, the number of Protestants more than doubled in five years. He also liberated the Jews, a reform Maria Theresa would have never even considered. He abolished the yellow patch Jews had been forced to wear and repealed the special tax they had to pay. When Joseph's first outline for toleration of the Jews met with protest, he proceeded more slowly, first granting rights to the Jews in Lower Austria, then Bohemia, Moravia, and Silesia, and finally Galicia. Each province received special treatment, as each had with almost every reform. Yet the goal was to bring them all toward a rough, easily governed parity. Similarly, toleration for the Jews was aimed to make the empire more governable. "With a view of rendering useful to society the large class of Israelites who inhabit our hereditary lands," Joseph began his first statement.[39]

What was it that would take a group and make them useful to the empire? First, Joseph demanded that the Jews conduct their affairs in the language of the land they inhabited, and they could attend public schools provided for the purpose. They were also permitted into higher schools, although the number of Jews in Vienna was still controlled. The numbers of Jews in the Austro-Hungarian Empire were not inconsequential, and Joseph found another use for this resource: he made all Austrian Jews eligible for military service.

Military service was universally hated, not only for the dangers, loneliness, miserable conditions, and disruption in men's lives, but for the very effect Joseph knew he would achieve: the army is a great leveler. It pulls men away from their pasts, away from family life, religious observance, local traditions. It makes all men equal in the service of a higher necessity, the state. In doing so it introduces peasant boys and cloistered scholars to new places, new ideas, and to each other. The army mobilizes a population and creates a nation. One scholar has argued that France was not a truly unified nation until as late as the First World War, when compulsory service created a population that could speak the same language and share the same values.[40] The United States, too, experienced the equalizing effects of the military in the Second World War. The military, for many black soldiers, was an opportunity for prestige based on merit, opportunity that was too often missing stateside. When these black soldiers came home, they demanded more as equal partners in America.

The army levels in another way as well. All minorities can be incorporated into the nation, not only the least dignified, but also the most exalted. Forced to serve with those less privileged, the upper crust must develop a more forgiving veneer. Just as the idea of public parks shook the power of the nobility, so did public armies. Public life is a step toward accepting strangers as contributors. Joseph had no love of strangers, but he wanted all the contributions his people could make. He explained that his goal was

> education, enlightenment, and better training for this nation. The opening up of new sources of income, the repeal of the hateful constraints, the abolition of the insulting badges on clothes—all this, as well as rational education and the extinction of their language, will serve to weaken their own prejudices, and either lead them to Christianity or improve their moral character and make them useful citizens.[41]

With Joseph, as with his mother, it is not kindness nor goodness nor an ideology of openness which increases tolerance, but an arrogant desire to make use of a resource already there. Joseph's grating personality and impolitic impatience made many of his reforms hated; many were repealed, as were his attempts to limit censorship. Yet the clock can never be turned back. The public life begun when Joseph II's own reign began in 1780 helped create the Vienna of arts and science, the Vienna we think of at century's end, the Vienna of Sigmund Freud.

An example of such long-term effects was Joseph's Central Book Censorship Commission, developed to take censorship out of the hands of the provincial governors. There were still many prohibited works, but they included among them works of the church which Joseph considered superstition. His goal was not to encourage sedition, but to put all power into the hands of the emperor and take it away from the provinces and the church. Joseph believed that prohibitions caused more harm than did benign neglect. So, for instance, while a book might have been banned in German, it was allowed in the original French on the assumption that few people read French. Prohibit it completely, the theory went, and the people would learn French.

Works which contained "immoral utterances and unclean obscenities" were still prohibited, but Maria Theresa would not have recognized her moral empire. Titles which flooded Vienna at that time included *Concerning Viennese Girls,* and *Magister Jocusus Hilarius' Wonderful History of an Old Virgin who Remained Unviolated for 30 Years, Told in Clean Rhymes.* [42] All books listed in the Papal Index, the pope's list of banned books, were made free. Anyone could print and distribute foreign books. Above all, however, learned books were encouraged.

Scientific works were considered entirely beyond control, as long as some authoritative person vouched for their authenticity. This step toward what we now recognize as peer review was revolutionary. No matter how short-lived Joseph's ruling, it created an audience of authorities. Because any authoritative person could vouch for a work, not just government-approved censors, writers began to have a responsibility toward a public; they answered to their readers or potential readers, not the academy.

In 1787 Joseph granted the city of Vienna complete liberty of printing and publishing. Just as the pitch of libel and insult was steadily raised, the revolution in France frightened monarchs and made printers suspect. Censorship was reimposed in 1789. Literary freedom had lasted no more than nine years. Printing presses, though, seldom disappear. In its heyday of literary freedom, Vienna had become a city of intellectuals, printers, and publishers. By the end of the eighteenth century, the school reforms started by Maria Theresa had produced readers eager to buy books, and in Vienna alone there were over four hundred professional writers. Even when the books disappeared, the writers and their public were still there.

Literate subjects are productive subjects and obedient subjects. Joseph's censorship reforms had as their impetus the desire for a better-run empire; this is also why Joseph reformed the administration of the empire, again broadening public life and including more groups. Family or connections no longer suited an official; he had to show knowledge of his region. Joseph wanted educated officials, but especially officials loyal only to the state. The emperor decreed that bureaucrats would receive pensions and that their widows and children would be supported because he knew that their allegiance would reduce jealousies and prejudices. [43]

The new bureaucrats had plenty of business. At the end of Joseph's ten-year reign, six thousand decrees and over eleven thousand new laws were on the books.[44] The emperor's district commissioners were instructed to inspect their lands and observe not only whether the laws were carried out, but whether the houses were numbered, whether there was any superstition, and whether there were sufficient precautions in the sale of poisons. All of these instructions, and many more, were legislated. All of this legislation created a loyal bureaucracy which, in turn, drew more and more people into a more public world. But why? Why not fill the posts with aristocrats, keep laws to your liking, and simply rule? In order to understand this, we must retreat a little into the world of bureaucracy.

Bureaucracy as we know it has a bad name. Whenever there's a line at the post office or another form to fill out to file an insurance claim, bureaucracy is blamed. Americans are taught to hate bureaucracy and bureaucrats, those lily-livered city slickers who hide behind their desks and pretend not to see you. Bureaucrats wear wrinkled suits and smell of their lunch. What's more, they are parasites, taking home exorbitant pay and too many vacations. The government would be better off with fewer of them, Americans cry. We don't like bureaucrats.

The social theorist Max Weber, the great social scientist who first studied bureaucracy, called it an iron cage, the extreme of rule by law and system.[45] We pound against the cage's bars. Bureaucracy is rule by offices, not persons; the bureaucrat merely fills an office. He is impersonal, cold, sees each client as a number. We hate the bureaucrat for his impersonalness; he doesn't care about us. The bureaucrat's interest, like anyone else's, is to keep his job; but unlike other workers' jobs, his is to proliferate rules, forms, or documents. We hate the bureaucrat's insistence on petty rules. Weber says the bureaucrat is chosen by merit. We hate his self-righteous exam mentality. Weber says he takes no personal gain from his office, but simply draws a salary for his position. We hate his complacent lack of initiative. Weber says the cage grows around him, locking away his feelings, hardening his heart, keeping him apart from the warmth of others. And isn't it true? We hate the bureaucrat.

But wait. Civil service, open to qualified people of all backgrounds, subject to government regulation, has consistently been an avenue for minority advancement. Do we say bureaucrats wear wrinkled suits because they really do or because we hold their lack of privilege against them? Do we say they are lazy because we think they are lazy or because we think "people like that"—Jews, Italians, blacks—are lazy? What do we really mean when we say we don't like bureaucrats?

Imagine a world of unreined emotion, where local noblemen can have you flogged, or beat you themselves. Each interaction with an official is a terrorizing experience—you are at the whim of anyone's emotion. Such a world is not only terrifying, it is unpredictable. When bureaucracy enters this world, it is a form of deliverance. Bureaucracy is predictable and exact—the same tax at the same time every year. It is rule by law and document—anyone can read the rules and need fear no single person's retribution. You need not bribe anyone, do favors for him, give him your wife. What is more, you will be treated the same as the next person. The world of emotion is cruel, fickle, and unfair. If your neighbor curries favor, his burdens are lighter. If his brother is in office, his burdens are lighter still. How much better the impersonal, beautifully dependable bureaucracy.

What is more, every person has the opportunity to serve. It could be you behind that desk and you would be enforcing the same rules and ruling on the same cases. Bureaucrats are like all of us—no better, no worse.

By exalting the bureaucrat and therefore making the world more predictable, Joseph contributed to the increasing rationality of the world, as Max Weber would describe it. According to Weber, the world has developed steadily over time toward systematization. Over thousands of years, Weber says, the world has been demystified as people chose means that could efficiently achieve their ends, just as Emperor Joseph chose bureaucracy to carry out his desire for absolute control and his Enlightenment ideals, or as a farmer relied on new plows rather than new prayers. As the world steadily becomes more and more subject to human control, the original positive effects are lost. What was meant to be a light cloak has become an iron cage.

Now, Weber says, we are trapped in a world where people care only about means and ends. What must I do today to have this tomorrow? Fine. Get out of my way. Bureaucracy has become burdensome and so has all of human interaction. The warmest handshake says nothing when it is only a means of currying favor and the object is a step up on a career ladder. Luckily, all of this is the extreme, the "ideal" case. None of us is so perfectly rational, and we are better off for it.

THE LEGACY OF THE FRENCH REVOLUTION

In the years after Joseph's reign his reforms, or at least the reasons behind them, were increased and expanded. As Austria moved between revolutions—from the French Revolution of 1789 to the world-wide liberal revolutions of 1848—it continued to expand its public realm, drawing in peoples and expanding contacts until it could do so no longer.

But while Maria Theresa and Joseph II were reformers, Joseph's successor, Francis II (changed to Francis I when he assumed the throne), was not. The memory of the French Revolution frightened him; he tightened censorship, he resisted change. Yet change went on without him.

The memory of the French Revolution did find sympathy among intellectuals in Austria, just as it did all over Europe. Liberty, equality, and fraternity had resounding echoes in every part of intellectual life. Even as censorship was increasing, writers wrote more and more vehement articles, flouting censorship strictures in favor of liberty. Even the Congress of Vienna voted a condemnation of slavery despite the conservatism of Francis and his prime minister, Metternich. Their ruling outlawed the Negro slave trade almost fifty years before the United States, the supposed seat of freedom, did the same. As for equality and fraternity, from these grew the ideas of nations and nationalism. The American colonies had rebelled in the name of colonies; the French people revolted in the name of a people. They claimed fraternity, a bond similar to family ties, but broader and stronger. Not only did the Freemasons and many other societies blossom in Europe in the late eighteenth century, but friendship itself became a new institution founded on choice and the individual.

As the cold, dry reason of Enlightenment thought gave way to passion and feeling, fraternity grew more and more important. Could men not express who they were, express the genius of their country? Nations were carved out of larger units. Under the influence of equality and fraternity, every people wanted to express its unique identity. Many poets, painters, and scholars reflected early-nineteenth-century Romanticism with an interest in the world of the faraway—costumes, languages, the past. In Vienna a librarian of Slovene descent studied Slav dialects and had wide influence among Slavs. A Serbian almanac, *Danica*, was published in Vienna between 1826 and 1829.

Nationalism had a surge in the Austro-Hungarian Empire as well. In part, German nationalism was strengthened by Napoleon's invasions, which stimulated other peoples to seek out their heritages. Yet the years between 1789 and 1848 were not years of growing Germanization in Austria, due in large part to the government. Nationalism, according to Metternich, was one of democracy's ugly faces, a mask for anarchy. But, the argument went, "on the other hand, there was no reason why a state should not permit its diverse subjects to retain their national customs and traditions,"[46] as long as the "moral pentarchy," or the old order of Austria, Prussia, Russia, England, and France, remained intact and upheld peace and order. Vienna's concern was not loyalty to one culture, but loyalty to an order.

> In Vienna, marriages between different national groups, without extinguishing the pride of national lineage, diminished it some-what, transforming the representatives of the old noble orders into a new society united in its deepest interests, its way of life and its common loyalty to the emperor and the Empire of Austria.[47]

Liberty and equality might have been hard to see in the conservative empire, but fraternity was there, poised delicately in a balance with empire loyalty and the status quo. For the moment, all men seemed to be brothers.

The mechanism of this balance was law; this was an age of constitutions. What better way to express the genius of a people than in its laws and written principles. The new Legal Code of 1812 subjected the whole empire to a unified set of laws which both helped and increased the growing bureaucracy. This was also an age of contracts: laws for the whole society, marriages for the nobility, alliances for the international powers. Francis himself may have feared law, liberalism, and change, but he could no more resist his age than could Maria Theresa or Joseph. When the Congress of Vienna convened in 1815 after the ravages of Napoleon's attempts at conquest, the goal was a set of alliances and laws. The congress' final act put 121 articles into writing.

All of this was very serious; but while the idea of law and contracts was modern, the content of the alliances was reactionary. No matter the substance, in Vienna nothing changed and no one paid attention. The congress at which these laws were made was an excuse to throw Vienna into a flurry of parties, dances, music, festivities, and booming business. A famous bon mot of the age was born when a diplomat was politely asked, "How is the congress going?" "The congress isn't going," he answered, "it is dancing." The Viennese press, along with the Viennese people, remarked endlessly on the love affairs and exploits of Europe's royalty, all gathered together and feted by Francis himself. Czar Alexander, above all, the powerful thirty-seven-year-old victor over Napoleon and a dashing figure, was a constant source of wonder, consternation, and disgust. His love affairs took him not only into the boudoirs of the legendary beauties of Vienna, but into the lowest brothels. He was more than a moral problem to his hosts; he was a security problem, wandering in the lowest, most dangerous districts of the city. Even a political event as serious as the congress involved Vienna in a social, not political, excitement. Austria's tradition of political repression and reform from the top down left little room for popular participation in politics or political awareness, even on the part of the aristocracy. Yet public life can be other than political. Like Babylon and Constantinople, Vienna was not a democratic city. Unlike Babylon and Constantinople, Vienna was on the edge of a modern, democratic, industrial world.

Even after the congress ended, Vienna continued to benefit from the bursting demand for goods, services, and favors. There was a lively trade in uneaten food from the tables of monarchs. Ceremonial courses, untouched by those too stuffed to speak, became the perquisites of officials who had it conveyed "right out of the walled town . . . and in at the back door of a restaurant." One scholar credited the congress with a general rise in the Viennese diet.

For the poor, or in fact for anyone who cared to help themselves, there were tidbits to be had for nothing. On the evening of a ball at Court, whole tubs of half-squeezed lemons, prepared and uneaten strawberries, oranges and ground almonds were put out in the courtyard. The really needy could in any case always present themselves at the Hofburg kitchens. . . .[48]

Almost everyone felt the rising standard of living. The Congress of Vienna increased the population of the city by a third.

As afraid of change as Francis I may have been, economic progress was advancing on Vienna. The national bank he created in 1816 made credit possible for industrialists. The technical institutes he founded increased invention and industry. Industrialization, twin revolution to the French, brought in its wake both liberation and misery. The poor and displaced swelled the ranks of beggars. A tax on consumption instituted in 1829, a rising cost of living, and heightened expectations made the new industrial population both poorer and more impatient. The state monopoly on alcohol took potatoes and wheat out of market use. By the 1840s Vienna was industrial and struggling. It was a great commercial center—there were more than 430 silk mills in Vienna in 1845. It was a center of the new railroads—by 1841 ten thousand people regularly traveled between Vienna and Wiener Neustadt, a nearby city. A newer, faster, impatient city was ready to take up western Europe's cry for change in 1848.

The new ideas engendered in the French Revolution culminated in the wave of revolutions that rolled over Europe in 1848. People in every country demanded freedoms, economic reforms for relief from the emerging industrial hardships, and proclaimed the rights of peoples or nations. It was youth, enthusiasm, Romanticism, hope, with a strong dash of nationalism. Mostly these revolts failed, although a new order, the industrial order, the order of the bourgeoisie, gained on the aristocracy. The goals liberty, equality, and fraternity were gradually revealed to be contradictory. If all are free, as the bourgeoisie hoped, how can all be equal? If all are equal, what, then, is fraternity? And are all men brothers when liberty allows some to oppress others? After 1848 the contradictions grew deeper.

Vienna from 1750 to 1850, then, was a growing world of different peoples, different languages, different classes, brought together in a whirl of public life, before the competition and consequences grew bitter. It was a changing world where new figures appeared: the journalist, the intellectual, the industrialist, the engineer, the teacher, the bourgeois. A new prosperity made life more enjoyable and refined. It was the century when peoples or nations were invented, became self-conscious, sought out their history, and then joined in the general life of the empire, its schools and streets and festivities. The Vienna Freud entered was invented. The Austrian Empire itself was invented, renamed from the conglomerate of inherited lands and dominions that it had been and forged as something new—although it was hard to say what.

Austria's unique genius was its many peoples—these peoples needed to join together to ensure opportunity and autonomy for each one of them. Reforms in the empire's administration drew members of national minorities, like Serbs, and Macedonians, and Rumanians, into Vienna. Events throughout Europe, rather than tearing at Vienna's cosmopolitan character, reinforced it by turning the city into the social capital of Europe. Even the new ideas of Romanticism and nationalism only reinforced the empire's insistence on its purpose. Austria's very mission was to protect these smaller peoples and at the same time remain powerful. If Austria had not existed, František Palacký, the Czech historian and archivist, said, it would have been necessary to invent it.[49]

MUSIC: INCLUSION AND OPPORTUNITY

Music was a form of public inclusion in Vienna. Music in the street, in the concert halls, especially in the theater, was believed to be something everyone could enjoy, in which everyone could take part. One way or another. Whether as business office, fashion showroom, or romantic rendezvous, the theaters served as public meeting places.[50] The theater was a central gathering place; it was, aside from official ceremonies, the only place where large groups were allowed to gather. It may have been this special role of music which prompted an observer to comment in 1810:

> . . . all the great public diversions and amusements are enjoyed
> by all classes without any abrupt divisions or offending distinc-
> tions—in these respects, Vienna is . . . quite alone among the great
> cities of Europe.[51]

Public concerts were still a novelty in the early 1800s; music was just
emerging from the chambers and gardens of the nobility. Yet much of
Vienna's social life revolved around these concerts and theatricals. In
1824 alone 75 major concerts took place in Vienna. Between 1826 and
1827 there were at least 111 concerts in Vienna. (The same year there
were 125 concerts in London and 78 in Paris.) Other cities had concerts,
but Vienna was alone among the great cities of Europe in the make-up
of its audience. There were usually crowds, even when government plans
or censors made the hour inconvenient. On Sundays, holidays, and
during the dinner hour (1 to 3 P.M.), almost everyone found it possible
to attend, even city officials and bureaucrats. There were occasional
outdoor concerts on a summer evening or late at night. Most concerts,
though, were indoors, midday, during the season (from late autumn to
late spring), and often on religious or state holidays *(Normatagen),* when
dramatic theaters were prohibited from opening. On these occasions all
classes of people crowded the halls.[52]

Each concert was negotiated *ex nihilo* by the composer or star
musician, who rented a hall and a supporting orchestra, arranged for
light and heat, notified the authorities, of course, and arranged ticket
prices. There were no concert halls until 1830; musicians had to rent
theaters or churches. Concerts were arranged for as many reasons and
events as people who organized them. Musicians arranged concerts for
the income they provided. Concerts were arranged to benefit the blind
or aged, for the victims of disasters. Or to commemorate birthdays,
weddings, royal occasions, the emperor's recovery from illness, anniver-
saries of important events. On May Day, for example, the Viennese
always went to the park and attended the traditional 9 A.M. concert in
the Augarten.

Religion, traditional customs, or language may have varied, but concerts were so plentiful and varied in purpose and price that everyone
could attend. In fact, the purpose of music and musical concerts was

itself open to interpretation. While many great works rose from the fertile musical environment, the preferred works were sheer entertainment. Amazing, gee-whiz virtuosity thrilled the Viennese, as far back as Maria Theresa, who loved a good time. Scholars have often commented on the classlessness and universal character of music in Vienna, and for good reason, but not because Everyman was of refined sensibility. As early as the 1770s, Maria Theresa saw the prodigy Mozart, and all Vienna marveled at his skill. Yet many lost interest, preferring instead easy melodies or what one critic has called the "pleasing embroidery on an accepted theme performed in an accepted manner."[53] Maria Theresa, like all of Vienna, wanted to be entertained.

Beethoven was loved. But Paganini was worshiped. Viennese audiences liked tricks, child performers, skill at an instrument, quick improvisation. Although the Society for the Friends of Music, founded in 1814, did provide a place where the greats could be heard, these concerts, whose choral portions were sung in Latin and German, had a middle-class didacticism. The upper and lower classes wanted novelty. The growing middle class liked Beethoven, but his concerts did not bring in the biggest profits. His works were long and serious. When Paganini appeared playing violin solos, playing a whole piece entirely on the violin's G-string, his concerts were not only successful, they were a craze. His concerts of 1828 were the most popular and lucrative of any in Vienna. He was foreign, he was a virtuoso, and he was adored. Food, clothes, were named after him. People screamed and fainted. One music historian noted, "Even the city's five-florin notes . . . the admission cost of his concerts, were temporarily called "Paganinerls.""[54]

Viennese music was the center of social life in the city, whether as a brilliant show, a magnificent experience, or the background hum for an interesting conversation. The public was promised an uplifting event, cajoled by claims of amazing feats or dragged in by pity and woe. But everyone went.

The government not only encouraged musical interest, but demanded it. Every ceremony and event had its music. Treaties, buildings, victories were all commemorated with public concerts. Johann Strauss, Sr., wrote the *Kettenbrücken* Waltzes on the occasion of the opening of a suspension bridge. Of the five theaters in Vienna, two, the Burgtheater and the

Kärntnertor, were run by the state. Theater tickets were given as perquisites or rewards to bureaucrats. Above all, the emperor was the city's primary patron of the arts. While periodically a burst of German cultural feeling would break through, the imperial interest in music included support for Italian opera, visiting virtuosi, and music students from all over.

The Royal Music Society was by the nineteenth century an Austrian institution. Founded by Maximilian I in 1498, its history was one of distinction and glory. It appears in Dürer's wood engravings. In 1548 the poet Wolfgang Schmelzel praised the Hofmusikkapelle:

> I praise Vienna . . . above all cities of this country, because of the profusion of singers and instrumentalists who may be heard there, come from all parts of the kingdom and often indeed from abroad.[55]

The same was still being said in the early 1800s: Vienna, the city of court administration, was the city of glorious music. One reason, certainly, was musical education. The Hofmusikkappelle, in addition to playing for feasts and operas, masses and parties, also housed the most prestigious music school in the empire. Only advanced students were admitted. The Stadtkonvikt, another music school, was established for gifted but poor students. Music was a public good in Vienna, paid for to a large extent by the emperor.

Music was also controlled by the emperor. Just as the theater was censored, so were musical concerts: around the time of the French Revolution works with "freedom" in the title were suspect; polonaises or any other Polish dances were also regarded with suspicion, as that country was associated with progressive ideas. The names "Jesus" and "Mary" could not be sung in certain contexts. The time and place of concerts were strictly regulated for maximum security—and they never competed with state-run events.

It has been argued that censorship in all other areas left music the only free field for Austrian creativity—this would explain the flourishing music world of Vienna. Madame de Staël certainly blamed the censors for Vienna's lack of intellectual excitement. Yet music itself was censored. And, as one author points out, censorship did not prevent the work of a Voltaire in France or of a Dostoevsky in czarist Russia. In terms of international comparison, there is another important fact: music was flourishing everywhere. Mozart was more warmly received in Prague than in Vienna and Haydn was heralded in London.[56]

Vienna, however, had a broad, public place for music, room enough, both literal and figurative, for geniuses to find their way in and be recognized. Swept in on waves of public interest, musicians found their way to fame. Great geniuses did not bloom in isolation in the streets of Vienna. Hundreds, thousands were involved—probability itself demanded genius. So many musicians flocked to Vienna that some were bound to be good. Expert musicians could not avoid performing in the city with the greatest interest and most musicians. Mozart and his sister were only two of many, many child prodigies paraded before a fascinated public, as one historian of music recounts:

> In Vienna during the year 1822 alone, Franz Liszt made his debut at 9 years of age; the brothers Carl and Anton Ebner (aged 9 and 10) from Pest gave violin concerts; and Fanny Salomon (aged 12) . . . gave a private piano recital. Several children from the same family often appeared together, as did three members of the Hobmann family (aged 7, 8 and 13). . . .[57]

Vienna, with its many musicians, then, had a creative atmosphere which not only attracted musicians, but created them. Genius is a result of broad-based interest and encouragement. The same mechanism which assimilates outsiders into the cosmopolitan dream gives the cosmopolitan city its glow of talent and perfection.

The church, like the state, provided a setting in which music flourished. The baroque Catholic tradition of the late eighteenth century was a fertile setting for musical creation. The mass had long been revered as an aesthetic experience, and increasing attempts to glorify God's name provided some of the most beautiful compositions of the Western world. Some must have thought the musicians were divinely inspired. In fact, they provided what the church could well afford to buy—masses to commemorate the dead or consecrate great events. Music expressed the awe of birth, marriage, death—all of the moments celebrated and regulated by the church. Music ennobled the ritual and filled the senses. Just as one felt closer to God seeing sunlight filter through inspired stone arches, the churchgoer felt closer to God hearing inspired counterpoints through the ethereal acoustics of the great cathedrals.

Wealthy patrons eager to emulate the emperor's taste for music and a religious liturgy heavy in emotional symbolism contributed to the flourishing concert world in Vienna. More importantly, but less directly, the budding industrial age made its contributions. The democratization of concerts represented yet another element of life brought into the marketplace; this time music was for sale. No longer the privilege of those born to talent or to aristocratic entertainments, music was emerging as a source of profit, a commercial venture. At the end of the 1780s Joseph II's imperial beneficence provided the public entertainments; by the 1840s the public could choose its own entertainments.

The most fundamental contribution of the industrial age to the music world was the public itself. Business owners and even laborers had leisure time thanks to industry. Even unskilled workers now had time for things other than work, thanks to mechanization, which meant workers received more pay for fewer hours. Able to support themselves with eleven or twelve hours of work, laborers could spend the thirteenth or fourteenth hours at a dance or concert. Vienna's abundant resources made leisure possible and leisure made audiences possible. Just as factories created large gatherings of workers, they created large gatherings for other purposes, including music.

Music was a form of public inclusion, then, because it was so much a part of life—social, political, religious. It was almost impossible to escape it. Its boundaries were unclear, its purposes widely interpreted. And while the concert world was just starting to take shape, so was the idea of musical performance. Music was a form of public inclusion, then, also because anyone could play. There were few amateur/professional distinctions.

The distinction between professional and amateur had always been blurred at the top of the social hierarchy, and especially within the royal family. Not only was Maria Theresa an accomplished musician, her father, Charles VI, was more gifted as a musician than as an emperor.

Joseph I, whose reign began in 1705, was such a gifted composer and performer that he was compared favorably to all professionals except in one respect: they had more time to practice.[58] Austrian emperors spent hours each day working at their music and they, along with many aristocrats, loved to perform. One of the most unusual charity concerts played at that time included Rossini's Overture to *Semiramide*, arranged by Carl Czerny for sixteen pianists at eight pianos, performed entirely by Austrian aristocrats and royalty. The concert was an overwhelming success.[59]

Even in wider circles distinctions between levels of commitment were blurred. A composer who wanted to present his work would have to hire musicians. Caught short, many of the musicians might not be what he had in mind. A local student might have to suffice. Or for a flat fee he could have the theater's usual group, but some of those might be beginners. In a certain sense all were beginners. Musicians did not rehearse— the hall cost extra for rehearsal and might not be available in any case. The most extensive rehearsal, at the vehement insistence of the composer, might be three or four sessions. Beethoven demanded even more rehearsals for a concert which included his Mass in D and the Ninth Symphony. Some orchestras were more proficient than others. Regional differences were so marked that a composer could hear his works totally transformed if they were played in a city where the musicians freely embellished them in their own style. Musicians not only were expensive and unreliable, they might not obey conductors and most were unused to rigor or discipline. A virtuoso performer could avoid the whole mess, and reduce costs, by recruiting accompanists from his family or friends. In this way professionals were buoyed by amateurs, or vice versa.

Franz Schubert, a dedicated, prolific composer, freely played his lieder for friends who gave him ideas and encouragement in return. His Schubertiades, evenings when his songs were performed in salons, were arranged by these same talented dilettantes—his friends. Beethoven, too, was encouraged and supported by friends. His friend Ignatz Schuppanzigh was concertmaster directing the string section for the debut of the Ninth Symphony. Surrounding each "lone genius" was a world of amateurs. The musical world had room for everyone who cared to participate.

This broad inclusion of different kinds of participants increased

Vienna's musical vitality. Local working-class composers with talent found work in taverns and dance halls. They brought with them folk tunes or regional melodies which they wove into their dance music. There is even one interpretation of the waltz itself as a common-denominator dance which, in the words of one observer, combined elements of "Tyrolean landler, Hungarian czardas, the mazurkas and polkas which originated in Poland, even the kolo from the Balkan highlands . . . superimposed on the dances generally practised in the eighteenth century: the gavotte, the minuet, and so many other national and provincial dances which vanished almost entirely when the waltz appeared."[60] All of this was blended with one other element: speed.

The dizzying, dangerous pace of the waltz (popularized in the 1780s, but omnipresent by the 1820s) demanded huge ballrooms. The bigger the ballrooms, the huger the crowds. A journalist observed in 1809 that every evening fifty thousand people packed these dance halls, and that therefore one in four Viennese must have spent any given evening waltzing. The night in 1808 that the Apollo, the extravagant restaurant/ ballroom, was opened, police had to keep order. Opening-night festivities cost five times the ordinary price, yet not only were the four thousand places filled, an extra thousand people were admitted. Still, there were crowds outside, and when no more were allowed in, they tried to break into the hall.[61]

The ballrooms were decorated to rival the palaces of aristocrats and often succeeded. One had a ceiling which opened to shower rose petals on the dancers; some were in open air; several held special masked balls or featured scenes of fantasy, such as grottoes or arbors. The atmosphere was exhilarating, even for a contemporary journalist hesitant to take part.

> . . . It is a very mixed company, but its ingredients are not to be despised. . . . Under illuminated trees and in open arcades people are seated at innumerable tables eating and drinking, chattering, laughing and listening. In their midst is the orchestra, from which come the new waltzes, the bugbear of our learned musicians, the new waltzes that stir the blood like the bite of a tarantula. . . . The motley crowds jostle each other; the girls, warm and laughing, push

their way among the lively youths, their hot breath tickles my nostrils like the perfume of tropical flowers, their arms drag me into the midst of the tumult. No one apologizes. . . .[62]

If the crowd was mixed, it was not always motley. During the Congress of Vienna, Europe's crowned heads entertained themselves at the Apollo dance hall, along with its usually middle-class clientele. Music—and dance—in Vienna included all classes.

The Viennese also listened to music in salons, where the distinction between professional and amateur was further narrowed. If classes and peoples did not exactly mix in the salons, they did all value music as training for society. A piano was a mark of good taste in a home. Women could enhance their marriage prospects and men their careers with their musical proficiency.

The salons, for several reasons, seem to contradict the premise of a public life. After all, the aristocracy, by the 1820s or 1830s, losing money to war and extravagance, were becoming defensively exclusive and were losing much of their purpose, if not their glitter. Their patronage of music flagged. They never spoke of politics. No industrialists or leading lights of the age were invited to their homes. Even their own physical beauty had diminished after generations of restrictive marriages. Weren't their salons, then, dull evening get-togethers where unimpressive women stooped under the weight of the family heirlooms hung around their necks?

And what about the bourgeoisie? Don't their salons represent the very essence of retreat into private life? Small informal gatherings where amateur musicians provided a background for games of riddles or casual flirtation seem hardly a cosmopolitan stronghold. Musicians met supporters only seldom at such gatherings. Where then, the simple modern asks, is the significance of the salon?

It has, first, significance for our age. It is a significance in retrospect, perhaps, or a place in myth and memory. The beauty of the salon, the pleasure of being with friends in fancy dress, is seldom recaptured. It cannot be. The witticisms or bon mots now seem petty, irrelevant, and out-of-context. The flirtation is now unnecessary. The stiff and stylized mannerisms of men living up to a distant, abstract standard or simply aping the aristocracy look silly through the glass of time. The salons were a silliness, but if we strain, we can see their charm. We can see that the participants, despite their love of gossip and pretense, devoted time and talk to a world beyond themselves—music, theater, even games. And more importantly, the constancy of social ties surrounded each player with known attachments and predictable obligations. The hostesses of salons were more powerful than we can imagine today. By deftly manipulating guest lists or arranging entertainments, the grand hostesses could determine the career of a musician, influence a bureaucrat's policy making, or simply arrange an advantageous match for one of their daughters. No one, not the most glamorous, the wealthiest, the most brilliant socialite, could now command a constant party, bringing back devoted guests two or three or five nights in a week for years. Not even the most loyal friends spend every evening together. Today some people, many from European backgrounds, meet regularly to hear music, or talk on the phone daily, but that is on a far more intimate scale. What we can appreciate, even identify with, in the salon is the dream that beauty or truth—or what we might call career goals or personal aspirations—need not exclude social warmth. And social power.

The exceptions to standard salons are especially revealing. Not all were meaningless private parties designed to display the household's wealth. Jewish families involved in finance fostered salons that rivaled those of the aristocrats, from whose salons Jews were excluded. Every single day from midday to midnight Fanny Itzig Arnstein, one of the most famous, if not the single most famous hostess of the late eighteenth and early nineteenth centuries, was at home receiving guests. Friends and admirers thought it an exceptional sacrifice; most hostesses were "at home" only one or two nights a week. In part due to his wife's influence, Nathan Adam Freiherr von Arnstein was ennobled. Indeed, the great Jewish families became a shadow aristocracy and were enthusiastic supporters of music. The Arnsteins took in Mozart for eight months, arranged for concerts in their home, and made loans to Beethoven, as well as sponsoring music in their salon and playing music themselves. The Arnsteins, though, were not alone. Other financiers wielded similar cultural influence.

The financiers were not the only brilliant exceptions who made the salon a significant institution. There were other middle-class patrons of the arts and hosts of notable salons. The concerts at the home of Josef Hochenadel, an official in the Imperial Ministry of War, presented some of the most serious music in Vienna. In fact, serious music was largely kept alive by bourgeois amateurs in private homes. The level of difficulty of salon music increased over time. Publishers pleaded to keep salon music simple enough for a wide audience, yet simplicity became less necessary as more people became proficient. As more and more people played and practiced, a distinctive genre of salon music emerged. Through the exceptional salons this music was preserved, treasured, encouraged, and augmented. Not everyone was just playing cards.

Among those who held musically exceptional salons were three friends of Franz Schubert. All three men were from outside Vienna and first moved there to attend the university and work in the bureaucracy. They invited to their musical evenings family, friends, business associates, and relatives. The music Schubert wrote for these evenings was fine, yet relatively simple and short; his longer, more serious works were for other audiences. Certainly, their association with Schubert is what makes these salons at all noteworthy. Yet they also encouraged Schubert, not only giving him social companionship, but, more important, helping his work itself.

This leads us to examine the salons that followed more traditional patterns. The common denominator of these salons was their role as a school for social life. The salon taught the rudiments of shared values. First and foremost, the shared value was music, of course. Schubertiades helped Schubert—they taught him the significance of his own gift. Musical salons kept music teachers employed, demanded that household servants be proficient on various instruments—in other words, rein-forced the importance of music. Salons and their child prodigies social-ized men and women into a world of music performance and appreciation. Music helped music. The products of the salon system could recognize good music even if they didn't play it, even if they didn't like it. A world of educated listeners is a world in which musical genius will flourish, and in Vienna it did. Knowing one's own abilities is the surest way to recognize merit in others. This is not to say that merit was always rewarded. Merit, however, in musical talent as in Joseph's bureaucracy, was entering more and more minds as a criterion for judgment. Also, as more and more people shared ability, a common bond developed, a democratic-type approach to others. So while the salons retained class distinctions and fought for prestige, they inculcated the more universal idea of merit.

More than merit, though, the emphasis was on social cooperation. These closed foyers where amateurs competed for praise taught two great lessons about modern social life: the value of realizing one's talents or individual fulfillment, and the importance of shared activity or, if you will, public life. Another paradox. The closed doors led to the salon that taught openness. Think back to an age of agriculture and tradition. A singer might bring pleasure on a feast day, but constant practice and attempts on his part to improve could only be a disturbing anomaly. Look at him—he'd rather sing than work. The sin of pride tinged his efforts. Between the French Revolution and the Revolutions of 1848, though, the individual was celebrated, as were his unique talents. The broad encouragement of individual talent made possible the idea—and the reality—of the genius, or gifted, marvelously unique talent. The salon was the birthing room to the genius.

At the same time, it was a primer for public life. Think ahead to an age, our age, when leisure time is often spent alone. There may be others on your baseball team or running beside you, watching television next to you or reading in the same room, but the lesson is not to go outside yourself. One keeps one's eye on the ball, concentrating on the task at hand, discussing little. The salon stimulated conversation, curiosity about the world at large, by teaching the young a world writ small. So although the private house and private delights shaped the salon, the salon shaped the public world.

Besides, musicians needed work.

THE LIVES OF THE MUSICIANS

Vienna's preeminence in music is directly tied to the opportunity music provided for outsiders—many of its luminaries were not Viennese. But they came to Vienna and stayed. Just as many of Vienna's lower-class musicians added folk elements and rhythms to the city's music, foreign musicians also added new melodic themes, new performance practices, and sometimes special expertise in building musical instruments. Of sixty-four foreign-born musicians living in Vienna between 1815 and 1830, the fourteen from Germany included Beethoven; the three from Italy included Antonio Salieri. The depth of Viennese public life contributed to the welcome these foreign-born musicians felt. Some salons were open to them, some concerts; the emperor and all of royalty demanded their services; in the streets and parks they could learn local styles and play for money, and, above all, the popularity of all music helped launch their careers. Despite the popular image of a musician out of step with the demands of his time, the lives of the great musicians show a remarkable pattern of benefit from public life and the position of music in Vienna. They were simply more refined in their musical tastes and skills than were the majority of Viennese. They were, of course, also victims of their age, succumbing to the many diseases which kept the Viennese mortality rate high. Life expectancy for a Viennese man was thirty-six to forty years: Mozart lived to be thirty-five, Schubert thirty-one; Beethoven died an old man at fifty-six. The infant mortality rate was high and anyone who lived survived a devastated home. Mozart and his sister were the only two of seven children to survive infancy. Schubert's father married twice and had nineteen children, only nine of whom survived. In Beethoven's family only three of seven children grew up. The mother of Johann Strauss, Sr., died when he was seven, and not much later his father, after remarrying, drowned in the Danube, a suspected suicide. Genius did not cause musicians to die young or suffer exceptionally. Musicians were not exempt from their age.

Musicians were neither rich nor poor, but depending upon the specific job and their degree of fame and success, as well as their seniority, they could be struggling or comfortable. In short, not all musicians starved in garrets, broken in humiliation and penury. Compared to the 100,000 to 150,000 florins a year that the highest nobility might count as income, the 2,000 florins of the court Kappellmeister, or music director, might seem small. Yet the 40 florins a year a woman factory worker might earn, and the 400 earned by a junior lecturer at the university, provide another point of reference. Senior civil servants and ministers were more highly paid than most musicians, but musicians tended to rank far above ordinary laborers.[63] Poverty, abuse, and despair were not the natural lot of musicians because art is misunderstood or prophets go unacknowledged. Rather, they were the result of a music world changing in small, halting steps, rendering old ways obsolete.

The age was not constant. The hundred years from 1750 to 1850 saw drastic changes in the lives of musicians in Vienna. In 1750 Maria Theresa's school reforms were barely in effect; one hundred years later any peasant could be a schoolchild and every schoolchild learned music. During that time aristocratic patronage was on the wane and the power of rich burghers was increasing. Just as valets and ladies-in-waiting were turned into laborers, musicians left off being servants and took up being employees. The lives of great composer-musicians so clearly show these changes that we can follow them one by one as opportunity and the greatness of Vienna ushered them into fame. Franz Joseph Haydn, born in 1732, faced a different world than did Wolfgang Amadeus Mozart, born roughly twenty years later. Ludwig van Beethoven, born roughly twenty years later still, was removed from the aristocratic world of his predecessors, but not entirely. Franz Schubert, born a generation later, in 1797, had yet a different type of career, which was quite unlike that of Johann Strauss, Sr., who was born in 1804. How lucky we are even to reflect on these great figures. How awe-inspiring that they all lived within such a short time span. But leave off the elementary-school music appreciation and early piano lessons that teach about Haydn the courtier and a Beethoven angry and tormented. Shed the dust of history that obscures their origins and filters their careers. Now look. They were all part of a cosmopolitan Vienna.

Franz Joseph Haydn, the son of a wheelwright, had no musical ancestry, although a cousin first introduced him to music. At eight years old he became a choirboy at St. Stephen's Cathedral in Vienna. Had it not been for the fact that the emperor's music director was there, always looking for young voices, Haydn would not have had any entrance into music as a career. Vienna, the center of opportunity, was also the center of training. Even though Haydn was dismissed from the choir as soon as his voice changed and thereby thrown into poverty, he had the training and contacts to find a distinguished teacher. Were there music books or teachers in Rohrau, in Lower Austria, where he was born? Certainly not comparable to Vienna's.

Haydn's career is a remarkable one for the son of a wheel maker. And yet he remained a servant his whole life, albeit a dignified one, only a short step from his craft origins. He was a music director for various nobles, then musical director for Prince Nicholas Esterházy, the aristocrat for whose court Haydn wrote his most memorable symphonies and string quartets. The original agreement stipulated that Haydn must not sell or give away his compositions. He received a generous salary, a free hand, and good working conditions. Haydn saw himself as a master craftsman who was allowed to experiment freely, and not as a genius or a marketable commodity. Even after making an extraordinarily successful concert tour in England, he returned to his patron and to Vienna.

The age of patronage has its prime example in Haydn. Not because of the wit and refinement of his music, nor because of his aristocratic manner. Simply, he was poor when he was outside imperial music-making and rich within it. The *Surprise* Symphony, reputedly composed to keep a drowsy emperor awake, or the *Farewell* Symphony, a signal that the musicians wanted to return home, were not acts of power but of weakness, an artistic last resort. At his death Haydn was honored, recognized, and acclaimed. Music had brought him opportunity and taken him into the public sphere.

Mozart's background prepared him more fully for the world of patrons, yet he rejected that world, partly because Vienna itself was changing. Mozart's father was a musician and he already knew that music was a route to success. The path to fortune still led to the doors of the nobility, and in tour after tour his father introduced the young Mozart to reigning monarchs and aristocrats. And indeed, the nobility remained powerful arbiters of taste throughout Mozart's lifetime.

Yet as he matured, Mozart worked less and less within the established world of patrons. Not that Mozart broke away completely. His appointment as court composer to the emperor crowned his brilliant achievements. Yet more and more he tried to break from the role of servant and exist as something else. Increasingly, he relied upon teaching and public concerts—that is, works for the subscribed public concerts or operas of

Vienna. Unlike Haydn, he cared about his appeal to wide audiences and for much of his life lived in poverty.

Amadeus, Peter Shaffer's masterful play and screenplay about the life of Mozart, is an attempt to uncover the meaning of genius and divine inspiration. The title and pith of the play is *Amadeus,* the love of God. Mozart, like most men, is part animal and part angel and both his natures do glory to his Creator. Shaffer's Mozart is an unlikely genius, immature, often not even likable. But then there is Salieri. Antonio Salieri, the powerful Kappellmeister of the Habsburg court, was a distinguished, acclaimed musician. But few people today see him as anything but a rival to Mozart. Shaffer's Salieri is mediocre, a scheming, untrustworthy wretch. He represents for Shaffer all of those who try and try, but are not divinely touched. Perhaps they try to hard. Perhaps they misunderstand the very meaning of devotion, suppressing the human qualities that God intended, sadly aping some painter's idea of divinity. Perhaps they are hypocrites. The mediocre, like Salieri, recognize genius, adore it, feed off of it, destroy it. Salieri makes Mozart's life miserable, but it is Mozart's work that lives. The mediocre, like Salieri, are confused, frustrated, bitter. So Shaffer gives us the natural beauty of genius and the tragedy of mediocrity.

And now, in praise of mediocrity. Is it really sad that so few people have Mozart's gift for music or that so many are simply mediocre? Only if one believes in nature and not in education, in isolated actors and not in society. Some people believe that nature provides whatever pathetic endowments you've been dealt. Mozart was born to be magnificent. And Salieri, as Shaffer has him lament, was given his modicum of mediocre sense, no more, no less. But there is another way to understand talent, as the product of education. Where mediocre spirits can be encouraged to better themselves, there is a value on talent. The truly gifted person will be recognized. There will be audiences, classrooms full of aspiring students, in short, the setting that "creates" genius. Mozart encountered audiences who loved him, teachers willing to teach him, and, finally, influential men like Salieri willing to give him work. All of these extras in the life of Mozart were mediocre. Without a Salieri, a Mozart would be impossible. It is the broad public world of the second-rate which allows the first-rate to flourish.

How could a nation create a whole generation of brilliant physicists? By teaching science to as many as possible of its children, of course. The wider the net, the more chance that the truly talented person will fall into it. The same is true of music, dance, art. A society teaches what it values to its children. Vienna taught music. If we were to wonder whether or not a Mozart could live today, we would have to keep that in mind. Chances are he would not be a serious composer today, since serious composers have little contact with a broad public; they are esoteric, academic, highly specialized, and little known. John Lennon might be his modern equivalent or Sid Vicious, musicians who benefited from the very public notoriety they tried to reject, establishment successes who were antiestablishment. It is just as likely, though, that a modern Mozart, especially in America, would be a math graduate student or a computer hacker. A child may show a precocious gift, yet the gift is interpreted in different ways at different times. Numbers can spell either intricate rhythms or scientific equations. Some gifts, such as an extreme sensitivity to emotion, may not be recognized at all.

And so genius grows where mediocrity is tolerated. A genius for critical reasoning and discussion grows where amateur critics thrive. A genius for democracy, or willingness to debate, compromise, and innovate, Alexis de Tocqueville wrote of the United States, grows where all citizens are in the habit of participating, cooperating, and voicing opinions. Where this can happen, there is public life, rather than private bushels. If everyone hides his light under a bushel, there is no way of knowing if that light is bright or dim.

Ludwig van Beethoven is even more of a puzzle than Mozart and his career represents a different step toward the public music world. He struggled less than Mozart to remove himself from the whims of wealthy patrons and was actually quite successful in winning commissions. Son and grandson of musicians, he rose through established patterns and became revered and loved in his own lifetime. At the same time, however, he struggled more than any musician ever had to earn high fees from publishing and selling his music. He managed to convince himself that his livelihood depended on music sales, one musicologist wrote.[64] As more of life was bought and sold and industry took hold in Vienna, Beethoven played the part of a music salesman, demanding high prices with the threat of publishing elsewhere. His ties to business and his increased contact with the growing business class made Beethoven's otherwise traditional career unique: it marked a step toward democracy and away from aristocratic patrons.

The mythic Beethoven is an irascible, temperamental artist, tortured by deafness, embittered and alone. In truth, even this irascible Beethoven was surrounded by friends and admirers who helped him stage concerts, loving amateurs who appreciated his talents. His written conversations with friends fill shelves of notebooks; these notebooks were his main form of communication in his later years. Though deafness drove him to despair when he realized its severity and permanence, he returned after one or two years of depression to a social and productive life. Deafness had no direct tie to his death at the relatively old age of fifty-six; he probably died of syphilis complicated by numerous other ailments. He never married, that is true, but remember that the law forbade marriage for those who could not demonstrate a stable income. Many musicians did not marry. Beethoven's intense guardianship of his nephew Karl and his many love affairs served as his emotional supports. Irascible, perhaps, but not alone, and not impoverished. Perhaps his business acumen paid off: Beethoven owned a house in Vienna, something few musicians could afford.

Beethoven was a man of middle-class sensibilities. When first introduced to Goethe at a Habsburg extravaganza, Beethoven found him snobbish. Beethoven was deeply affected by the ideas of the French Revolution and Emperor Joseph's attempts at reform. He is quoted on the subjects of liberty and progress and he admired Napoleon for his humble origins. And if he could be judged by the company he kept, then his sympathies seemed to be with the forward-looking. While his music stands beyond time and place, accessible to anyone ready to listen, the man stands firmly in his age.

Although they did send him to elementary school, Beethoven's musical family was eager for him to be a virtuoso on the model of Mozart. He toured as a virtuoso, listened to music in the Prater and the Augarten, when he moved to Vienna from his birthplace, Bonn. His parents encouraged him and gave him lessons. In general, the opportunities he had were typical of Vienna at the time and the obstacles he faced were standard for the age. The illnesses he complained of plagued almost everyone in Vienna. Beethoven is exceptional only in his longevity.

His adult career also mirrored the events of his times—he composed for special occasions and royal personages, certainly. But he was also buoyed by the Congress of Vienna, which took place when he was at his peak of popularity. The continuous balls, concerts, and other musical occasions of the time provided time and place for a composer. But by the end of his life even Beethoven lagged behind the changing music market. His music still sold, but popularity and public relations gained prominence in the concert world. The myth of Beethoven the hero was more popular than the man himself.

Beethoven's career is a striking contrast to that of Franz Schubert, who was just over twenty years his junior. Schubert, too, had a career in music thanks to the institutions of Vienna. His father was a schoolmaster and introduced Franz to music, which was a mandatory part of each school's curriculum. Schubert became a choirboy, like Haydn. As a schoolboy, he sold his schoolbooks in order to attend Beethoven's *Fidelio.* He took lessons from Salieri, even after he finished school and was teaching in his father's school. In short, he was surrounded by the best opportunities of his age. His facility and seeming effortlessness at songwriting made one biographer write, "Music, it seemed, simply flowed from him, or through him."[65] Music also flowed around him.

The days of noble patronage were gone. Schubert's work appeared in music journals and was played in public performance, in benefit concerts or subscribed concerts. But he was very much a product of salons, where his music was heard by distinguished audiences. He also wrote for the theater. Yet he never knew the luxury, nor the servitude, of an aristocratic commission, and his music was always music among equals—much of it quickly jotted down to play among friend-amateurs that evening.

More than any of his predecessors, Schubert was popular. His lyrical, touching melodies were instant successes. Schubert was fast, prolific, and easy to play, three popular characteristics for a composer whose world consisted of amateurs eager to play new pieces. By the time of his death at thirty-one, he had written more than six hundred songs in addition to masses, operas, and symphonies. Moreover, he was the man of the hour: a true-to-life, in-the-flesh, Romantic genius. He had more friends than money, all of them young and impassioned. They shared cramped quarters and sacrificed the stability of home and marriage in favor of Art. He represented the free man, not free politically, but spiritually. Not only was he the first truly popular composer; he was also the first composer to rapidly lose his public to whim and fashion. Schubert was a plump little schoolteacher, not a wild musician. He was not a matinee idol, and as a man of the hour, when his hour ended, his music lost its audience. Upon his death his songs seemed to disappear. Suddenly, no one cared about anything but waltzes.

Johann Strauss, Sr., a Jewish child of the working class, had no more than a gift for the fiddle and the good luck to be in Vienna. His father was an innkeeper, not a musician, and he died when Johann was very young. Strauss was not in a boys' choir and did not have the benefit of private lessons. And yet he knew where there was music. He ran to the musicians playing at the inns and ballrooms of the Vienna Woods, the parks on the outskirts of the city, and received from them help, lessons, and jobs. Josef Lanner, a popular musician of the time, allowed him to join his group of musicians, which eventually became the biggest, most popular dance band in the city. When Lanner split the orchestra, Strauss became the leader of his own group. Suddenly, Strauss was no longer just popular, he was prestigious. In 1835 he became the director of the imperial court balls. Where else could such a meteoric rise even be thinkable?

The waltz was a sickness and Strauss was both contagion and cure. His wild, dark good looks added to his mystique. His friendly competition with Lanner worked as a natural public relations gimmick. Strauss had more than that, though. Here was a real hero. He was a virtuoso in a city which adored technical proficiency. He looked foreign at a time when the exotic was chic. The notes he drew out of his violin, impassioned, plaintive notes, were more than any other virtuoso could do. And he had something new and growing in importance, the waltz. Once he turned the popular dance form into a craze, only he could satisfy the public with his wild improvisations and new compositions.

His son, Johann Strauss, Jr., elevated the waltz into highbrow symphony in works like *The Blue Danube* and *Tales from the Vienna Woods.*

It was the elder Strauss, however, who took the waltz to the public in the first place. Public music was his whole career. He had no patrons but the public, no admirers but the public. He had no concerts but the balls, no private evenings in bourgeois salons. So he is a fitting figure in the age of public life and an example to show that the public world is the cosmopolitan world—the different is admired, the new extolled. The changing careers of musicians from Haydn to Strauss demonstrate the changing public participation in the music world. Democracy, industry, the marketplace—these figure in the telling. But when you ask where art flourishes, the answer is not in those elements. Each musician here, often thought to be a unique genius, benefited from Vienna's audiences, instrument makers, schools, or public parks. A long history of imperial support for music, including the church choirs and mandatory music training in public schools, created the foundation. Thousands of mediocre musicians and music students contributed to a city where truly great musicians would be recognized. Then a tradition was built, and students went to Vienna to study with the greats, to hear the powerful sounds of Beethoven and to be seduced by Strauss. Art flourishes where it is for everyone. Public life gives greatness to the cosmopolitan city.

THE PUBLIC WORLD

Finally, Vienna's public life can be heard in its music. Just as speech can whisper, chat, or proclaim, a musical sound can speak in many ways. The idea of public music is not so very strange. We have all heard marches and military airs in parades or before speeches. Public music accompanies ritual: at the beginning and end of weddings, worship, baseball games. Even the morning ritual of leaving for work often includes listening to the radio, as we are ushered from private worries to public work. At other times music is private solace. Late at night a familiar lyrical turn marks retreat and surrender, as you sink deeper into a chair, leave off the struggle, hear only something that your whole body knows to be true. Not all music is the same. There is public music and music made for small companies, music which excludes and music which is a form of inclusion. The music of Vienna was a form of inclusion, an invitation to participate in a shared city.

More and more, Viennese composers wrote for large audiences. Symphonies replaced chamber music. Although Beethoven still wrote string quartets, he preferred the symphony's larger scale. Even Schubert, whose talent was for melody, tried his hand at the symphonic form which was the mainstay of the age. The symphony, like the mass, was accessible and predictable. Also, the emotion of the works of this period was transparent and accessible. The more emotional the work, the broader the audience who could enjoy it. Haydn's musical jokes were obscure, Mozart's still a little abstract, but by the time of Strauss everyone felt the passion. And the themes of the period, the messages and motifs, tended to be immediate and folksy rather than obscure or private. Mozart's *Marriage of Figaro* and *The Magic Flute* were broad farce and fantasy. Schubert used the well-known folk story of William Tell. And Beethoven drew on themes almost everyone could understand, from war and heroism to a walk through the woods.

The music of the period evokes the large expanse of public Vienna, its openness and grandeur. Maria Theresa opened schools and set about creating great universities in Vienna. Joseph opened the parks and expanded the national bureaucracy into an enormous public service. Even Francis, with his parties, presided over a broad, inclusive city. Cosmopolitan Vienna was the world's musical center. Certainly, as a great musical center, it drew toward its heart foreigners, peasants from the hinterland, and any others who could play and had ambition. But it did this because music was a form of public life and an avenue of opportunity, not because geniuses came to light there. The crowds in the ballrooms, the crowds in the Prater, bureaucrats rewarded with concert tickets, schoolchildren learning by rote, all of them were part of music's public world.

No piece better exemplifies the period than Beethoven's Ninth Symphony. The power and magnitude of the work demand a big concert hall and a big audience. The use of a choir doubles the power and size of the performing group. The suspense of the second movement and the melodic theme of the fourth appeal to the trained and untrained ear alike. The text, Schiller's *Ode to Joy*, is an open plea for communal understanding.

The scene: The scratchy, tentative sounds of a first violin are followed by lower and lower voices. The orchestra begins like a boy whose voice is changing, growing deeper and surer. The crack mid-word is replaced by lyric emphasis as low replaces high, loud replaces soft, strength replaces weakness; the conductor pulls from his orchestra the power of speech and the human voice. The conductor is Beethoven and he pulls from the orchestra the first notes of his Ninth Symphony, the stylized description of an orchestra beginning to play.

The hall is full, although difficulties in negotiating the price of tickets delayed the concert. Friday, May 7, 1824, is too late for Vienna's high society, whose summer season has begun; they have retreated to summer homes or long vacations. The emperor is not there. Even so, there are enough followers, aficionados, and the musically curious to fill a hall. Beethoven is an unlovely figure, but old and admired. The audience hangs on each note. Each movement seems to be the most beautiful ever heard. And then the next movement surpasses it. There is authority in the tones and restrained seriousness. There is also passion. During the second movement the audience cries out, bursts into applause, yelling, "*Vivat!*" Five interruptions and the police commissioner intervenes; it is illegal to yell *Vivat!* in the theater.

Vivat! Long live the composer—illegal because only the emperor has the dignity and authority to be wished long life. *Vivat!* Long live the music, whose excitement thrills the crowd. Each interruption gives the performance more fire, the audience more tense power. *Vivat!* In the name of music, we utter an illegal oath, we join as a public and deny all authority but the authority of music.

And then the crashing of symbols and a fanfare of optimism. Joy, Joy. The deep voice of wisdom and understanding sings of joy, the lyric voice of romance, the round, luxurious alto and the airborne soprano sing of joy.

All men, All men, All men. All men will be brothers.

V

Paris and Tokyo: The Not-Quite Cosmopolitans

A whore in Paris bends over a filled washtub. She is dressed. She is coiffed. Her face is obscured. And yet there is immodesty in her pose. A strand of hair falls free and she is not in a functional squat, but a bend from the waist, a self-conscious pose of seduction and servitude. Around her are signs of the Orient: the wallpaper is patterned with a rough calligraphy; there is a fan on the wall. A vertical line or doorpost interrupts the scene, outlining her already outlined form. So Toulouse-Lautrec's Parisian resembles another seductress, a bare-breasted Japanese woman who also stoops above a filled washtub in allure, whose scene, drawn in Western perspective, is also interrupted vertically and who also is surrounded by calligraphy.

Both Paris and Tokyo of the late nineteenth and early twentieth centuries were cities of adventure, cities of seduction. Like these two paintings, the two cities were touched by foreign influence. *Japonisme* had a strong influence on progressive painting in Paris of the Third Republic; Western points of view revolutionized Meiji Japan. As touched by foreign influence as both cities were, though, they remained like the seductresses of these paintings—preoccupied and private, engaged in their own ritual, even disdainful of admirers. After all, it is the narcissicism of these beauties which attracts the viewer. Each beholds her image in a pool. The stranger may come, but neither woman awaits or welcomes him.

Other paintings reveal other things, both privilege and servitude. The Artist Kitao Masanobu Relaxing at a Party is surrounded by geishas anticipating his needs. Directly in front of him is a screen, a vertical panel. Yet he looks at neither the screen, nor his servants, nor his musicians and guests in the background. He is lost in his own thoughts, oblivious to the Western visual perspective around him, oblivious to all but his own significance. Then there is the Parisian bourgeoise At the

Milliner's. She is oblivious to the shopgirl cut in two by the vertical panel of the mirror. She cares only for her own image in the mirror—an image lost to us, as the Artist Kitao Masanobu's thoughts are lost to us. They are two more Narcissi at their pools. Like Tokyo and Paris, they benefit from foreign style, from privilege. They are fashionable, worldly, beautiful, advanced, wicked, all the words one can summon for taste, refinement, and innovation. Yet they do not represent cosmopolitan culture.

So far, the cities in this book have all been cosmopolitan cities. What is more, they have been imperial cities, uncomplicated, so to speak, by the age of nation-states and the demands of mass politics. Now, taking another step forward in time, we find ourselves in the age of national fervor and chauvinism at the end of the nineteenth century. At this point Paris and Tokyo have a lot to tell us. Why were these glamorous cities which seemed to have some cosmopolitan characteristics never truly cosmopolitan? The answer lies in the rural roots of nationalism. Paris and Tokyo were at heart garden nations held captive by their hinterlands. This chapter, in contrast to the others, tells of the power of the provinces in forming values.

When in Rome, do as the Romans do. If the Romans are now braiding their hair like Ethiopians, braid yours. But if they are not, then, by all means, don't. Fashion, in short, is not tolerance. Paris and Tokyo of the early part of this century were capitals like Rome, famous for fashion, not tolerance. Or more precisely, they were national capitals whose nationalism dampened their cosmopolitan culture. They had not escaped from their rural pasts.

These glittering new eras were ushered in, in both France and Japan, by conflict with outsiders and an intense ambivalence toward foreign influence. In both countries, foreign influence, as positive and even exciting as it could be, had the lingering taste of defeat. France felt defeat by Germany in the Franco-Prussian War. Internal dissent over the terms of the defeat hastened the collapse of the French government, and the chaos of war set the scene for the Paris Commune of 1871. The subject of this broad urban revolt was not only the peacetime treatment of workers, but also the lower class' closer relationship to the dangers of war. France was internally divided over the conduct of the war, whether or not to continue it, how and where to capitulate. Out of the ashes of the war and the Commune arose the great Bourgeois Republic, the Third Republic. The Compromise of 1875, which conservatives and liberals pieced together in order to form a stable government, included universal suffrage, a parliament of sovereign representatives (a parliament of independents, favoring local notables), and an independent president. The legacy of the war was more than administrative reform, though. The Franco-Prussian War had lasting effects on the relationship between France and outsiders.

The provinces of Alsace and Lorraine had been ceded to Germany after the war—those who once were insiders now became outsiders as refugees from these provinces fled to Paris. As loudly as Parisians may have cried for revenge or the return of the lost provinces, they were equally suspicious of these strangers, the German-speaking French in their midst. It was at this time that the French committee on colonizing Algeria devised a plan to settle Alsatians in Algeria, one of hundreds of displacements which would eventually haunt our own century. The Alsatians were only one small part of a grand ambivalence. Who was enemy and who was friend?

The French had admired Germany. German philosophers and historians were lionized. After the defeat, admiration redoubled. For it was put about that the war had been lost to the German schoolteachers, whose successful pedagogy—and propaganda—created good citizens and better fighters. Techniques of German education filled French discussion. France viewed England, too, and its other competitors, with renewed fear and desire. The nation had been forced awake and it became insomniac.

Japan's Meiji Restoration, like France's Third Republic, began with a fight over foreign intervention. Before 1853 Japanese law decreed death for any foreigner entering the country (although the law was not always enforced). In 1853 the American Commodore Matthew C. Perry arrived, backed by an armed fleet, and demanded trade relations with Japan. When he returned in 1854, the Tokugawa regime had no recourse but to submit to his demands, since the American forces were so obviously more powerful. Foreigners were officially permitted to settle in five port cities and the cities of Osaka and Edo after 1858. But internal conflict also accompanied this defeat. Just as in France, preexisting factions split on the new threat. The powerful shogunate, or aristocracy, fought against the emperor in favor of their own power, even as they cried, "Honor the emperor—expel the barbarians." Newer, less powerful lords took the opportunity to "restore" the throne in 1868, moved the capital to Edo (from Kyoto, home of the imperial palace), renamed the city Tokyo, or "Eastern Capital," and formed a new government. No faction really supported the foreigners. And yet it was impossible to expel them.

If German schoolteachers had defeated the French, American engineers had vanquished the Japanese. Japan began its intensive effort to absorb Western technology with grudging admiration. The constitution which Japan adopted in 1889 was the result of careful study and comparison of various European constitutions. Japan, like Europe, began building an educated citizenry and began mobilizing a broad-based army. Yet here, too, the effects of defeat went beyond administrative reform.

Meiji Japan, like France of the same age, was a land of grand ambivalence and fears of inferiority. It entered the competition for conquest and colonies. It took on a fashion for things foreign. Yet national self-consciousness overpowered even the international seductions of a Paris or a Tokyo.

THE SEDUCTIONS OF THE FOREIGNER

The first places to modernize in Japan were the places where the foreigners lived. So Tokyo was one of the first cities with public waterworks and public sewers. Foreign technicians oversaw the construction and foreign laborers laid the foundations. The face of the city changed as architecture took on a European look. Josiah Conder, the most famous of the foreign architects in Meiji Japan, not only designed buildings himself, but taught a generation of Japanese architects the elements of Western style. His most famous design was the Rokumeikan, a sort of palace of international style. Begun in 1881 and finished in 1883, it was a state-owned hotel/convention center/public monument and a deliberate attempt to cater to Westerners. It was two-storied, huge, with ballroom and billiard room, and most extraordinarily, water thundered from the faucets.[1]

Another Englishman, William Barton, advised on the Japanese construction of the Royunkaky, popularly known as the Twelve Storeys, built at the same time as the more elite Rokumeikan. The Twelve Storeys, the tallest building in the city, brought foreign style and technology to the broad buying public. It was a shopping mall, observation tower, and recreation center. Not the least of its attractions was the first elevator in Japan, imported from the United States. The goods which filled the shops were for the most part foreign. "There was a Chinese shop with goods from the China of the Empress Dowagers and sales girls in Chinese dress."[2]

It was fitting that foreign goods be housed in foreign architecture. The allure of the foreign seemed almost whole cloth; one could wrap oneself in it completely. New-style parties and dances required new clothes, new ballrooms, new music, new food. New clothes demanded new hairstyles, new jewels, even new posture, a new gait, new gestures. All with a desire to be modern or civilized or worldly. Of course, one did not have to be wealthy and one did not have to play the whole suit in order to enjoy the new Western game. By the early 1900s most schoolgirls wore European buttoned shoes no matter what clothing they wore. Almost all men gladly gave up the traditional hairstyle—a shaven head with one long queue or ponytail dressed on top of the head—for the simpler, cheaper Western haircut. Men grew mustaches, a style first dared by the Restoration government officials. And the custom for married women to blacken their teeth as a symbol of enduring love faded.

Thus there were substantial populations of foreigners, including English traders and Chinese and Korean laborers; renewed public-mindedness; and a new civil service in Meiji Japan. There was a mania for the exotic, a mania for fashion, and a mania for fitting in. Just as Viennese women had dressed their hair "à la giraffe" after seeing a giraffe for the first time, Japanese women styled their hair in the "penthouse style" or in the "203-metre hill knot," named in honor of the new architecture or new military prowess. The pompadour known as "eaves," from its sweeping projections, was called "high-collar" if it was too extreme.[3] Anything extremely or affectedly foreign came to be called high-collar, although the term expressed grudging admiration as well as derision. Derision changed to admiration as publicity, the public world, changed oddities into necessities. As one Japan scholar wrote:

> The big change, the domestication of the foreign, began in late Meiji, at about the time of the Russo-Japanese War, and the advertising men and the retail merchant may have been responsible for it. Perhaps it would have occurred without their aggressive urgings. Yet the old dry-goods store became the modern department store.[4]

Edo had not been a market city as much as an administrative center, yet it was its commodities that made Tokyo daring. In its pleasure quarters, all signs of intimacy could be bought and sold, from the pouring of a cup of tea to the draining of total desire. As the Meiji era and its drive for Civilization and Enlightenment wore on, prostitution became increasingly divorced from ritual and increasingly a more direct financial transaction. The pleasure quarters had been called the streets of flower and willow, from the poet Li Po's description of the geisha as the willow and the courtesan as the flower.[5] The geisha had specialized in ceremony—in music, dance, and the tea ceremony—and the courtesan in affairs carnal. Just as traditional ceremony brought observers to each flower festival and garden scene, seasonal ceremonies brought observers to the streets of flower and willow. The Yoshiwara, or pleasure streets, had been the place of grand courtesan processions, festivals, open houses. Licensing reinforced ritual—the quarters were licensed, the brothels were licensed. As foreign visitors brought with them a differing moral sense and the spirit of Civilization and Enlightenment pervaded Japan, a change came over the pleasure quarters. In 1872 the courtesans were "liberated," largely as a result of a national fear and sensitivity about accusations of slave trafficking. Many women, thus released and prohibited from private prostitution, lost their means of subsistence.[6] Eventually, the pleasure quarters lost geishas and teahouses and gained in unlicensed or free-agent prostitutes. Japan, like Europe, saw the open market supersede ritual.

Ritual faded, but not beauty. For the age was occupied with ennobling "technical necessities by artistic aims."[7] The market was not a denial of art; sellers sought to use beauty for their own ends. The Japanese department store Mitsukoshi placed a life-sized picture of a pretty girl in Shimbashi Station to invite people to buy.

Paris, like Tokyo, was in the business of selling beauty. It, too, was famous for women who could be bought and entertainment that ranged from an innocent song to an erotic liaison. Paris, like Tokyo, was a big city, an important city, and a city filled with foreigners and foreign goods. Paris was so noted for selling the daring and the new that the twentieth-century critic Walter Benjamin called Paris the "Capital of the Nineteenth Century," not for its beauty, but for its salesmanship.[8] Paris, like other capital cities of Europe, was international partly by design and partly by default. Latin history weighed heavy on Paris, remnant of an age when all of Europe shared a Catholic culture, and students traveled far to attend the great schools in Paris which were established in that former age. Once there, students like Frédéric Moreau in Flaubert's *Sentimental Education* inhaled the heady and perfumed air. They tasted political action and felt the touch of women both beautiful and available. Paris had been the glorious seat of monarchy, the headquarters of the Revolution; by the end of the nineteenth century it was the magnificent city of lights. Its size and physical beauty drew foreigners to it. In 1910 France was earning 350 million francs from its tourists compared to 200 million earned by Switzerland and 318 million by Italy.[9]

Paris drew visitors with its international expositions. Major countries were all represented at these exhibits. The Centennial Exposition of 1899, the one for which the Eiffel Tower was built, was filled with foreigners and foreign goods. Increased contact among European nations made each national capital international as railroad and mail routes depended upon the capital. The French sent letters abroad and other nations returned equal numbers of them. Foreigners not only visited, but moved to settle. In 1891 over 1 million foreign residents lived in France and over 170,000 foreigners were naturalized.[10]

Visitors also came singly, important foreigners whose influence was felt in Paris. Oscar Wilde found a home in Paris, and later Amedeo Modigliani did, as did scores of other artists, writers, and musicians. Parisians also borrowed from abroad. Maurice Chevalier began vaudeville in the early 1900s by studying parts from English acts and songs. English words and phrases such as "smoking jacket" or "lavatory" were chic. France had long before begun its admiration for things English. By the end of the century, there were Frenchmen so convinced of England's merits that they argued that France should borrow elements of the English educational system.

Late-nineteenth-century Europe was wound in a knot and Paris was its center. A web of treaties and alliances kept the European balance of power, and Paris and Parisians were held in that web: receiving missions and ambassadors; sending ambassadors; exchanging secret memoranda, ball invitations, consul reports. All foreign embassies to France were in Paris. A flourishing trade and investments also united Europe. French investment was for the most part European, although there were also substantial interests in Africa and Egypt. France received supplies of iron ore. Trade made foreign goods quite common. "Between 1893 and 1913 French imports from Germany increased threefold and exports to Germany doubled. In the 1890's, a quarter of the beer consumed in France was produced in Germany; the bulk of textile dyes used in France came from Germany. . . ."[11] So in addition to treaties and trade, Europe had in common tastes. Goods moved from place to place and so did people. The European monarchs, if no longer absolute, were still arbiters of form and they shared family ties. They shared French as a language. They shared Paris as a shopping showcase.

Of all of Paris' international allure, however, Paris' strongest seduction was its tradition of intellectual enlightenment and political democracy. The French Revolution had sworn brotherhood and the armies of the Revolution brought that message to much of Europe. Napoleon's reorganization of the law, education, and government gave Paris a clean, open outlook. Education meant more than birth and law more than privilege. It was this Paris, the Paris of raging presses, free speech, education, and democracy, that attracted political refugees from all over the world. Polish noblemen and Russian aristocrats, Polish and Italian workers, and eastern European Jews sought the fresh air of Paris, giving

Paris in return Polish newspapers, Russian bookstores, and increasing variety.

The rage for things Japanese began as collectors returned from the newly-opened East with vases and porcelain as well as lacquered boxes dubbed "japanned." The Impressionist painters of the 1870s were not introducing novelty when they put a vase or fan in the background so much as they were simply chronicling an interest of their age. Sir Rutherford Alcock, the first British consul general in Japan, took it upon himself to collect the handicrafts and arts he saw around him. He sent to London a total of 614 pieces, including lacquerware, porcelain, ironware, woodcraft pieces, picture books, maps, and toys, all of which were displayed at the International Exhibition beginning in May 1862.[12] Not only did international exhibitions introduce thousands of Europeans to Japanese style. The exhibitions promoted the sale of Japanese style. After the 1862 fair in London the Japanese objects were sold by the firm of Farmer and Rogers. (A young clerk in their employ named Liberty later had significant influence on English design.) Japan entered Paris in 1867 at another international exhibition. This time, too, the collection was afterward sold. In 1868 there was a sale at 41 rue de la Victoire made up of the 1,308 pieces of art, furniture, and porcelain which Paris had seen the year before.[13]

It was essentially the Parisian marketplace that introduced the East, just as the Tokyo marketplace introduced the West. At first, boutiques like the Porte Chinoise served tea and sold curios, more like exotic tea shops or cafés than stores, really. Later, however, dealers in Japanese art opened distinguished galleries. Monsieur and Madame Desoye themselves voyaged to Japan to buy for their store. The French essayist and publisher Edmond de Goncourt wrote of their store that it was the school for the Japanese movement in France and, he said in 1875, Madame Desoye was virtually a historic figure for her influence.[14] Through the stores and artists, the influence entered middle-class homes. While Japan looked to the West for Civilization and Enlightenment, France looked to the simple, sinuous lines of the East as the symbol of modernity.

Both Paris and Tokyo seemed to invite variety or novelty in any case. Foreigners visited. Foreigners came and stayed. Foreigners were imitated. Yet there is little reason to believe that foreigners were liked and no reason to believe that foreignness itself was valued. It was always the absorbed version, the rewritten, reworked, local version which won admiration. In Paris it was Maurice Chevalier singing English songs who won audiences, not the English vaudevillians. In Tokyo the initial excitement of Western styles eventually died and the most chic styles were updated Japanese styles. A contemporary Japanese writer, explaining Japanese customs at the turn of the century for curious Westerners, proudly explained how Japanese clothes were better, even as he described Western influence.[15] Both France and Japan waged colonial wars against peoples they considered inferiors. Cosmopolitan culture rests on variety—in fact, active interest in variety. But Japan and France, defensive and busy forging national identities, cared little for differentness, even in their capitals. Japanese identity rested on a mythic unity; all Japanese were descendants of the powerful Yamato clan of ancient times. If French identity could more easily be learned or acquired, it was just as single in purpose: French identity rested upon French culture, which meant, to a large extent, French language. The seemingly cosmopolitan capitals Paris and Tokyo did not have cosmopolitan culture. Their people saw themselves in terms of the rural values which were being taught as a national identity.

France and Japan at the turn of the century were rural countries. Most countries at the time were. Only about 10 percent of the whole Japanese population were living in cities in 1890, most of those in small cities. By the end of the Meiji era in 1913, only 17.5 percent lived in cities, even after old restraints on settling in cities had been removed.[16] Similarly, France on the eve of the First World War was an aggregate of rural provinces. The predominant values in both societies—that is, their beliefs in what is good, true, and beautiful—were influenced by rural or provincial life, and this overpowered even their capital cities. The following is a discussion of values, the rural values of Paris and Tokyo.

THE GOOD. Imagine the good measured by investment, a rough measure of the things people believe have worth. They put their money where their hearts are. Both Paris and Tokyo had plenty of capital for construction. There were virtual booms in both places in this period. Yet when it came time for industry, growth was slow. Private investment in industry was so sluggish that it fell to the governments of the two countries to build almost all transportation and communications and much other heavy industry. One interpretation of Meiji Japan argues that where modernization was superficial, like a haircut, it was taken up immediately, but other phases which required money, a strong economy, and deeper effort were slow to take hold.[17] Why? Why, if modernization was on everyone's mind, was private investment in industry weak? Why did it lag behind construction?

The answer is clearest in France. Capital investment in industry traditionally has been slow in France because people did not see value in it. Investment went into land. After Parisians were no longer related to country seats where they could spend holidays, they started buying country land. Value was in rural life. Not only economic value was in rural life, either. The worth of a man was tied to his country roots. Jean-Jacques Rousseau believed that natural man, the man without court life or the trappings of the city, was the man of dignity. He was private man, using only what he needed, returning to the earth his due. The French Declaration of the Rights of Man was founded on the ideas of Rousseau and the other philosophes, who defended Natural Man—often understood as Man in Nature. The Revolution may have taken hold in Paris, but the battle was about the countryside. Rural life, even in the nineteenth century, was valued over city life.

As for the rewards of industrial investment, the French had small interest. Distribution was so slow as to be nonexistent. Paris traded and Paris had a world of goods. But the small manufacturer saw little point in shipping his wares to a tiny village where there was no one to sell them. The tiny village would not sell the new goods because of habit or ignorance or simply lack of a salesman. And if there were no markets, why expand production? Distribution remained provincial and so did investment.

Provincial habits of production also affected investment in Japan. Western goods did not penetrate into the countryside for perhaps fifty or sixty years after city use.[18] Western goods seemed to need Western showcases and department stores, but these certainly were nowhere to be seen in the countryside. Western methods were equally resisted.

Modernization was slow, because in an age of radical change the old ways, meaning the rural ways, were respected.

THE TRUE. Think of the true as the strong and permanent, "true" meaning "loyal, unwavering." Truth is knowledge that remains. The true is what we see as lasting. The word itself sounds almost feudal— true-blooded, a servant true, a true weapon, true love. What is true in a feudal system is the military strength of regional lords, the power of knights loyal to their land and their leader. It is power based in landholding and a rural military. These were still the true in Meiji Japan and Third Republic France.

This is not to say that the samurai stayed as powerful under a new constitution as they had been in the past. Rather, the new military organization exploited its traditional rural ties. The military message was strongest and most successful in the countryside. The military virtues were admired and became increasingly popular as officers created or utilized national organizations to link local interests, military pride, and the new, growing nationalism.[19] It is one thing to admire discipline, quite another to put that discipline in the service of a nation. The Japanese military succeeded in doing exactly this.

The rural military, with its "cells" and reserves and militia, was a powerful influence in the nation as a whole. As the military took upon itself the task of defining the nation, the nation became more militaristic. Militarism and nationalism went hand in hand. Physical strength and defense were seen as the most important part of a national identity. Or, at least, that was a popular view in the countryside.

Likewise, in France the military was associated with a narrow definition of national identity and rural dignity—and military strength represented a dependable, everlasting truth. The infamous Dreyfus Case still stands as evidence of the influence of the "old" French military. Captain Alfred Dreyfus, a Jew whose family was originally from Alsace, was graduated from St. Cyr, the elite military academy of France, and in every way met the formal requirements for advancement and promotion. He had skill and discipline, but little charm and few friends. He was accused of delivering weapons secrets to the Germans, tried in 1894, and sent to Devil's Island, the fortress prison.

1 A nude goddess, one of Babylon's seductresses, paid homage by a worshiper and another deity.

2 The god Marduk portrayed as a king. Kings were godlike in ther knowledge and power.

3 King Ashurbanipal himself makes a symbolic contribution to the construction of a temple, so important was construction to Babylon's greatness.

4 Babylon in Nebuchadnezzar's time was a complex of buildings, temples, bridges, and roads: view from the western bank of the Euphrates (a) and from the north end of the procession street (b).

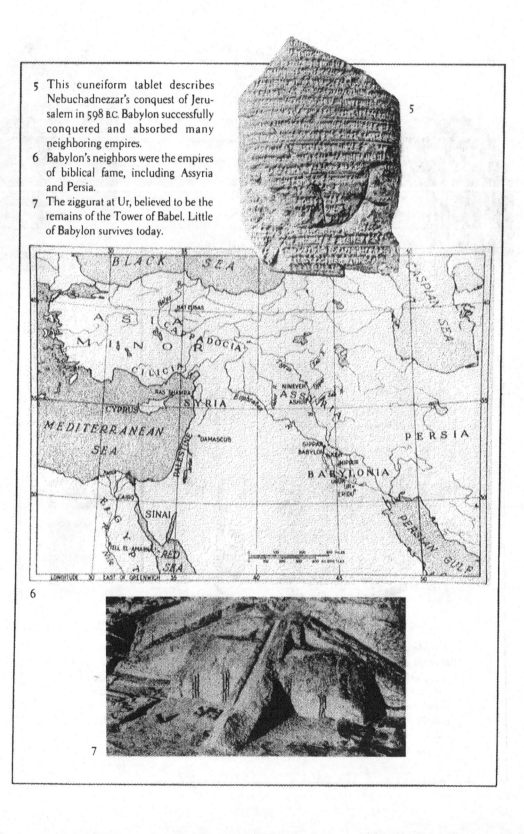

5 This cuneiform tablet describes Nebuchadnezzar's conquest of Jerusalem in 598 B.C. Babylon successfully conquered and absorbed many neighboring empires.

6 Babylon's neighbors were the empires of biblical fame, including Assyria and Persia.

7 The ziggurat at Ur, believed to be the remains of the Tower of Babel. Little of Babylon survives today.

8 Constantine and Justinian present their city to the Virgin, protector of Constantinople.

9 *Empress Theodora and Her Retinue* shows the elgance and majesty of the city's rulers.

10 The Byzantine Empire took pride in its urban settlements, as in this detail from *The City of Nazareth*.

11 Travelers and foreigners who flocked to Constantinople made it the most cosmopolitan city of its time.

12 Minority workers filled the textile mills, where they produced sophisticated silks such as the Pattern of Eagles.

13 The Empress Irene's fair complexion reveals her foreign birth in this mosaic, *The Virgin and Child Between the Emperor John II Comnenus and the Empress Irene.*

14 For centuries Jews have been involved in city life. This unidentified
fifteenth-century northern Italian
city included Jewish inhabitants.

15 The Jewish quarter in a German town
about 1428.

16 Jews were also involved in the
building of cities. Here, Jews work on
a building site in fifteenth-century
Germany.

17 Jews were sometimes an integral part of city life, as in Augsburg (a) or Amsterdam (b) but were often forced aside into ghettoes, as in Cracow (c). This 1938 photograph shows the entrance to the Jewish quarter.

18 Not until the eighteenth and nineteenth centuries were Jews granted rights as citizens (a), often at the instigation of the Napoleonic armies, as seen in Langendijk's etching, *Louis Bonaparte's Entry into Amsterdam, 1808* (b).

19a

19b   20

19 The emancipation brought Jews into the modern urban economy, as illustrated by
    clothing vendors at the market in Kazimierz nad Wista, circa 1920 **(a)** and Nalewski
    Street, in the Jewish quarter of Warsaw, 1938 **(b)**.

20 Jews were also significantly involved in modern politics. Labor Zionists march in this
    1932 May Day Parade in Chelm.

21

22

23b

23a

23c

21 The modern city became part of Jewish religious life. Moshe Raviv captures worshipers leaving the Altshtot (Old City) Synagogue on Wolborska Street, Lodz, 1937.

22 Even a *sukkah*, a ritual tent erected to celebrate the harvest, was painted with city scenes.

23 Emancipated Jews participated in the arts, as subjects, in Rembrandt's *The Jewish Bride* **(a)**; as patrons—Jews like Fanny von Arnstein hosted salons where artists and intellectuals gathered **(b)**; and as an eager audience **(c)**.

24

25

26

24 *Maximilian I and Family*. The Habsburg family made Vienna their capital.
25 *Maria Theresa and Her Family*, by Martin van Meytens II. Maria Theresa is seated at right; Joseph, her son and successor, is standing immediately to her left.
26 Magnificent gardens and architecture add to the cosmopolitan city's public dignity, as in this view of the Imperial Palace of Schoenbrunn by Belloto.

27a

27b

28

29

30

27 But public life goes beyond monuments to include Vienna markets **(a)** and social occasions: *Ball in the Winter Riding School* by Johann Nepomuk Hochle **(b)**.

28 *Grand Galop*. Music provided an excuse for balls, but it also gave Vienna a unifying interest, including the passion for the waltz.

29 The waltz took Vienna by storm and made its popularizer, Johann Strauss II, a hero.

30 *Beethoven, 1815*. One of Vienna's most famous immigrants.

31 *Station at Oise,* by Keisai Eisen (a). The Japanese bather is seductive, yet self-centered. In Henri Toulouse-Lautrec's *Elles: Femme au Tub* (b), Japanese influence goes beyond subject and perspective.

32 *The Artist Kitao Masanobu Relaxing at a Party* by Kitigawa Utamaro (a). The wealthy classes of Tokyo and Paris took more pride in their own image and progress than in foreign adventure. In Edgar Degas's *At the Milliner's,* the bourgeoisie is interested only in its own reflection (b).

33a

33b

34

35

33 *Opening of the First Railroad Station in Tokyo,* 1872 **(a)**. Both the Japanese and the French viewed foreign influence and technology with ambivalence. *Gare St. Lazare* **(b)**. The expanding railroads were an interesting subject, but for Claude Monet, no more interesting than the patterns of light and dark in the station.

34 *The Steerage, 1907,* by Alfred Stieglitz. More foreigners came to New York City than any other American city.

35 Old World immigrants, and their children, were eager to abandon Old World ways and escape their pasts.

36 Many aspired to New York elegance and the luxury of being American.
37 Public life in New York was outside, on the streets **(a)**. Music was outdoors **(b)**; even libraries, soul of the city's intellectual life, could be out of doors **(c)**.

38a

38 Young Italian girls worked in factories **(a)** or at home, as illustrated in these Lewis Hine photographs, *Making Pillow Lace, New York City, December 22, 1911* **(b)** and *Family Making Artificial Flower Wreaths in Their Tenement House* **(c)**.

39 Italian men often sought construction jobs, as seen in this 1910 photograph.

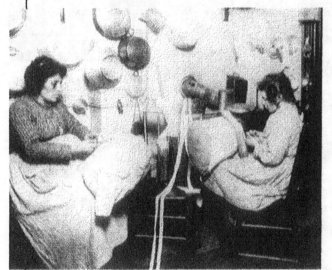

38b

38c

39

40

41

42a

42b

40 Langston Hughes, pictured here about 1927, was an important voice of the Harlem Renaissance.

41 The Silent Parade of 1917 protested the St. Louis Riots.

42 The new Harlem was a center of literature and drama. *Reading Room of the Schomburg Collection, 1920s* **(a)**. Charles S. Gilpin, Actor **(b)**.

43a

43b

44

43 Harlem's lively street life mirrored the public life of New York. Lenox Avenue at 134th Street **(a)** and *Negro News* **(b)**.

44 Connie's Inn, Harlem nightclub of the 1920. This empty room once held great performers such as Louis Armstrong and Fats Waller, but it was an irony of the new Harlem that they performed for all-white audiences.

Once again the battle was fought in Paris, but the issue was rural, feudal France. Courtrooms were full for years with evidence and counterevidence, attempts to obtain Dreyfus' release, to prove his innocence. Celebrities took sides, columnists speculated, Parisian children traded Dreyfus cards and played Dreyfus board games. Urban publicity surrounded the case. Yet the issue was the existence of the traditional, aristocratic army. Or, put another way, it was a last gasp of feudal France. Traditionally, the officers' corps consisted of aristocrats, landed gentlemen, men whose families always fought as officers. The military declared sovereignty over its choice of officers and their discipline. Dreyfus looked like a spy even if he was not one, in the the eyes of the French military—he was an outsider pretending to be an insider. He was not from an old, landed family and he was a Jew and he was from Alsace, no longer part of France.

Dreyfus was eventually freed, although he was so broken he died soon after his release. He had been framed by a military organization which hid and fabricated evidence, forged letters, and lied in order to prosecute him. When the officer who forged evidence committed suicide in his cell, though, it clouded France's interpretation of the case: was that officer simply proving his complicity, or was he a dignified soldier, a man of honor, martyr to the secrets of the military?

Military honor meant a lot. If history sees Dreyfus as a hero, not all of his contemporaries did. The country was deeply divided. It took the new technologies and greater threats of the First World War, not the Dreyfus Case, to modernize the military and take its command into urban, mechanized life. Until then it was the true-blooded, valiant knights, leaders of the land, who defined defense and what it was they believed they were defending.

THE BEAUTIFUL. Tokyo and Paris were beautiful in the context of their nations' aesthetics. True, both were cities of light, early to make use of gas lamps, then electricity. Their beauty, though, was judged by rural standards and rustic metaphors. The streets of flower and willow, the markets, the waterways—interest was not in the air or in the skylines, but close to the ground. Boulevards were grand when tree-lined, homes when graced with flowers, and holidays were best close to scenery in garden settings. The underlying myth of Paris or Tokyo was not the story of a meeting ground, gateway, or sanctified ground. They were the best their nations could offer, no more, no less.

Even at the turn of the century, at a time of urbanization, each nation's aesthetic traditions focused on the garden as the center of beauty and meaning. Both France and Japan had traditions of imposing meaning on nature. The garden meant, above all, power and privacy. So their garden cultures were quite opposed to everything the cosmopolitan city stood for: order as opposed to diversity, privacy as opposed to the public world, and, of course, agricultural, not urban, life.

The French garden tradition began in the Catholic Middle Ages, when private gardens reproduced the dimensions and symbolism of cloisters. Gardens were square and walled, for not only did they allude to the biblical gardens of Eden and Gethsemane, but the walled garden was also the symbol of the virgin bride, either in the Song of Songs or the Virgin Mary.[20] So the French garden represented private power even in these humble beginnings—the Eden of God's power, or the capture and shielding of love, virginity, and fertility. *The Romance of the Rose,* an early literary work, possibly the first European novel, takes place in a garden after the hero enters its walls. The capture of the rose is the conquest of the mistress.

Louis XIV's magnificent gardens at Versailles were a direct and successful display of power. As one expert on gardens explained:

> Indeed, the gardens rather than the chateau are what visitors were expected to admire, and from journals, travel accounts, memoirs and biographies one could cull a young bookfull of anecdotes concerning the visits which people made to the gardens, guided personally by the king, or in his suite, or going round with his representatives; making the whole tour, a partial tour, or inspecting a single feature in the gardens.[21]

If Catholicism and absolutism kept the French garden a powerful symbol, the Enlightenment and liberalism added to the garden's importance. The natural world took on significance for its beauty, for its purity. Voltaire's advice for Candide, to "cultivate your garden," became the

French watchword for privacy, peace, and liberty. And if it was the tiny, spiteful liberty of someone in a stalemated, centralized state, the only liberty left him, what of it? It was a beauty one could not live without. French utopians of the nineteenth century, like Fourier or Proudhon, never left out the garden plots, whether shared or divided. An urban world was not beautiful enough.

The end of the nineteenth century was a time of industrial growth and building in France. Yet the painting we think of as most characteristic of the age, Impressionism, is largely an ode to nature and gardens. The day trips which brought Parisian painters to the countryside depended upon the new trains and stations. And trains and stations often appear in their paintings. Most often, though, we see water lilies, gladioli, and irises, garden settings where the morning light plays on the path. Beauty was found in the highly ordered, structured gardens away from the throng, where petty tyrants ruled over petaled kingdoms.

The Japanese tradition, perhaps even more than the French, associated beauty with flowers and flower viewing. As in France, gardens were so well-loved and so meaningful that they were a national preoccupation. Everyone, no matter if he lived in city or country, counted his days in garden seasons. Tokyo never let go of its rural understanding of beauty and so, like Paris, the city could never claim undisputed primacy. The Japanese garden ordered people's lives. The garden represented an elaborate code, a plan to capture the essence of nature, and a refinement of the spirit. The garden was bound not by walls, but by codes and conventions. By the ninth century the ladies of the court had already devised a code of dress which enabled the colors of their kimonos to match the flowers they would be viewing.[22]

Just as much of Japanese culture had been Chinese in origin, so the Japanese garden had Chinese beginnings. The Chinese garden was intentionally symbolic in its smallest detail, always trying to capture man's position in relation to nature: subordinate, contemplative, observant, small. So in the Chinese garden the viewer could see only one scene at a time, never the whole.

The Chinese garden was home to the scholar-poet who searched nature for understanding. Its descendant, the Japanese garden, was home to the courtier-aristocrat who refined his nature by surrounding his house and grounds with landscape scenes. *The Tale of Genji,* a Japanese novel written about the time of *The Romance of the Rose,* is filled with gardens built by the hero to honor his lovers. Each garden is dedicated to a different season and is meant to convey the temperament and nature of each of the ladies, the most private of private gardens.

The landscape garden, with its rules and requirements—a guardian stone, a near mountain, a sandy beach, a cascade, etc.—was simplified and given added significance by Zen Buddhism. According to the Zen, not only did the garden as a whole convey reality, but each stone, each step conveyed Buddha or the whole physical world. The garden was still the focus of meaning and beauty, but by the fifteenth or sixteenth century it was sometimes so minimal as to be austere. It was the center of ceremony, pleasure, religion, beauty, subtlety, and, of course, nature.

Kyoto, the religious and imperial center, was the city of garden parks and glittering pavilions, yet old Edo also had its charms. When the capital was moved to newly renamed Tokyo, many residents of the city regretted the loss of its natural beauty, its canals and flowering trees. After the earthquake of 1923 destroyed much of the city, even more of the old garden city was built over. The reaction was more often regret than pride in progress. It was, after all, the death of refinement, all that the nation had believed beautiful.

So France and Japan respected the rural virtues. Those values influenced their capital cities. How, though, could those values so overwhelm the seductions of foreign influence that the capital cities were made less than cosmopolitan? Only under the influence of nationalism. Nationalist movements exalted the rural virtues, gained power through rural support and seated members in the national parliaments of both Meiji Japan and Third Republic France. Both governments, making fresh attempts at democracy, had constitutions which gave a lot of power to provincial representatives, representatives who were sometimes militant national- ists. The myth of nation, unlike the myth of empire or refuge or God's city or gateway or any other possible claim to legitimacy, is exclusive. If this is the city's claim to perfection, that it is the most unique in a unique nation, how can it love foreignness and favor the esoteric? So at the very moment when Tokyo and Paris might have been building a cosmopolitan character, they were swallowed in the age of nationalism. It is possible that no nation at the end of the nineteenth century could have overcome the growing militarism in Europe and Asia to value diversity and nurture a cosmopolitan city. The defeats that urged both France and Japan into the modern world, though, gave special vehemence to these countries' desires to mobilize their people with a single, strong identity. France and Japan were busy looking inward, convincing their people to believe in a nation, to produce for it, fight for it, feel something called patriotism. Looking inward, they were ambivalent at best, paranoid at worst, toward the outside. And a paranoid nation makes an awkward host to a cosmopolitan city.

The hinterland, up until this chapter, has appeared only as a blessing to cosmopolitan culture. It is a source of labor, resources, even genius. Now, with the age of nations, we see the other side. The hinterland can wield political power, can represent the force of tradition. Its people can be resentful as well as awe-struck. The hinterland can shape values. The hinterland can be used as a powerful symbol. It is the America that never was, with its even and clean picket fences and smiling farmers who never worry about drought. The hinterland is a powerful symbol. It is the America that never was, with its breezy wheat fields and lawns and gardens and sunrises where people who are up at sunrise have the leisure to watch sunrises. The hinterland makes for symbols so powerful they can be used against the outsider. The hinterland is the painterly countryside where sunlight plays on complacent lilies and weary irises. The lilies and irises seem so inviting—and yet—so self-absorbed.

VI

New York: The Hope of Opportunity

New York was a city of gold before it was a city of trade or industry or arts. If the myth of a gold-paved city gained currency, it was a myth well-founded. Not long after Peter Stuyvesant, governor of Dutch New Amsterdam, ordered a wall built across the colony's northern boundary, Wall Street became a center of wealth and power. It was the center of the federal government following the Revolution and home to Alexander Hamilton's bank, the Bank of New York and Trust Company, organized in 1784. Wall Street held the New York Stock Exchange after 1790, when Congress entrusted its bonds to New York banks. The same New York market later financed the War of 1812 and the Civil War. Boston may have had the ships, the schools, and the abolitionists; Philadelphia may have had political tradition; but New York had the gold.

So New York and its golden dreams exemplify another element of a cosmopolitan culture, an economic element: the hope of opportunity. New York has a sense of purpose, diversity, and a public life, like other great cities, like Babylon, Constantinople, and Vienna. New York also holds for its people, as these other cities did, the promise of gain. Daniel and scores of other adopted children in Babylon found their lives bettered. The scholar Michael Psellus and other newcomers to Constantinople improved their lot. Sigmund Freud rose to prominence in Vienna's public world. But New York will best explain why and how opportunity is part of a cosmopolitan culture because New York and success so often sound synonymous.

New York, the city of banking, helped to create New York, the city of trade. The city's strategic location on waterways and as a coastal harbor was a boon to trade. By the early 1800s the city was rich with cotton and fabric, sugar, and eventually clothes. Fifty years later, just before the Civil War, New York Harbor controlled 70 percent of American imports and 33 percent of exports.[1] Improvements in trade and transportation stimulated New York's manufacturers. And always, investment, money; it was ground into the history of the city, spun like a metallic thread through all of its suits, minted into a glittering reputation. In 1938, the very heart of the Depression, $650,252,600 in gold and silver entered the port of New York.

The glamour of New York was in its Midases. Jay Gould and J. P. Morgan, Jim Fisk and E. H. Harriman, these were men of legend and of enormous real power. Gould and Fisk's attempt in the 1860s to corner the gold market created a national panic and economic depression. That was in the days of the gold standard: all worth was measured in gold and New York held all the chips. Farms might fail, industries fall, or wars end bloodily; the banks grew and prospered.

That was the New York of Delmonico's, of glamorous send-offs for cross-Atlantic voyages, of Fifth Avenue mansions. And it is there still, in the society pages and business pages and home furnishings and fashion. New York's mission as the city of wealth and luxury gave New York a special myth and sense of purpose. The city was a place of wealth and glamour, where everything could be had for money.

But what about the other New York? Isn't New York also the city of refuge, where the tired and poor can huddle freely? If you guess that liberty in the form of aristocratic privilege came first and Emma Lazarus' poem, apologetically bestowing freedom on everyone else, later, you are mistaken. Emma Lazarus' poem "The New Colossus" and the Statue of Liberty were born together. In New York, freedom and compassion are twins. In 1883, when Bartholdi's famous statue was delivered to New York Harbor, the Congress voted money to help erect it, but no money for a pedestal. A committee of concerned New Yorkers attempting to raise enough for the pedestal arranged an auction. Committee members asked famous authors to write something appropriate and allow their works to be put up at auction.

They approached Emma Lazarus, a well-known, widely read poet of the day, along with many other authors. Lazarus was cool to the idea, not because she was hardhearted or uncharitable, but because she didn't take kindly to having her subjects dictated by committee. But a shrewd committee member saw the slow shift in her interests from classical odes to Jewish themes. The Lazarus family, he knew, was descended from Portuguese Jews who had arrived in New York in the 1600s. His argument convinced her: weren't the recent Jewish refugees from Russia the people who truly deserved the light from the statue's torch?

In fact, the news of the pogroms and terrors of 1881 had affected Emma Lazarus deeply. In 1882 she had published a response to an article by a Russian social scientist which defended the pogroms, claiming that Russian peasants killed only those Jews who interfered with their destruction of Jewish property. Emma Lazarus' published answer was cold with irony and satire. Her poetic answer, though, had all the heated emotion necessary for the foundation of an urban creed.

> Not like the brazen giant of Greek fame
> With conquering limbs astride from land to land;
> Here at our sea-washed, sunset gates shall stand
> A mighty woman with a torch, whose flame
> Is the imprisoned lightning, and her name
> Mother of Exiles. From her beacon-hand
> Glows world-wide welcome; her mild eyes command
> The air-bridged harbor that twin cities frame,
> "Keep, ancient lands, your storied pomp!" cries she
> With silent lips. "Give me your tired, your poor,
> Your huddled masses yearning to breathe free,
> The wretched refuse of your teeming shore,
> Send these, the homeless, tempest-tost to me,
> I lift my lamp beside the golden door!"[2]

"The New Colossus" was read at the auction, then again at the statue's dedication on October 28, 1886. It was not only successful—it became the unofficial New York anthem. It did not accompany the statue; it became the statue. The poet and critic James Russell Lowell wrote to Emma Lazarus two weeks after the sonnet was first recited:

> I must write again to say how much I like your sonnet about the statue—much better than I like the statue itself. But your sonnet gives its subject a *raison d'être* which it wanted before quite as

much as it wants a pedestal. You have set it on a noble one, saying admirably just the right word to be said. . . .[3]

Liberty may have been the theme of France's gift to the United States, but the theme became exile and refuge at the very moment the statue rose in New York Harbor. This powerful symbol and impassioned statement established New York City as a sanctuary. That was the meaning of New York.

The meaning was money. The meaning was refuge. It seems odd that one city could have two such different missions, founding myths of such different spirits. One legend says this is a city for the rich, another that this is a city of the poor. One says power, the other weakness. Wouldn't the rich feel degraded told that their golden city was a refuse heap? Wouldn't the poor feel cheated, told they'd arrived not at equality and safety but exploitation? New York's rise as a cosmopolitan city between 1900 and 1950 depended on belief in both of these creeds, both money and hope. In New York there was a mythic element which united money and hope: opportunity. The founding myth of cosmopolitan New York became the belief that dross could be spun into gold. The very wretched of the world became the privileged who dined at Delmonico's. Believe it, and the differences between rich and poor were fleeting and benign. Believe it, and the city was as open as a sunlit meadow. Believe it, and the streets were paved with gold.

The man who gave New Yorkers their lessons in the creed of opportunity was himself an exile in New York: Horatio Alger. His background was radically different from Emma Lazarus', except that he, too, was authorized to speak for his country. The Alger family, like the Lazarus family, had been in this country for centuries, but the Algers were Unitarian ministers from New England, trained at Harvard. Horatio Alger, Jr., had always been interested in writing, but was actually a Unitarian minister until he was dismissed in 1866, charged with engaging in sexual acts with young boys in his congregation. In shame and disgrace he left to live in New York—where he would not be known, where he could earn a living as a writer, where a stranger had a chance. Like Emma Lazarus, he never married and never had a family. Instead, he spent a life surrounded by boys—rich, poor, charges, orphans, adopted sons, beneficiaries—all of whom were models for characters in his novels. His novels were tales for young boys, they all took place in New York, at first, and virtually all of them shared a single plot: a newsboy/orphan/ragamuffin/bootblack resolves to live a clean life; he works hard, studies, meets a beneficent, wealthy adult, and is rewarded with a happy, secure, comfortable life.

Alger's books were fairly successful, but by the time of his death in 1898, they were out of fashion. Reformers believed their fantastic improbability had a bad effect on impressionable youths and many libraries actually barred Horatio Alger stories. The new century, though, was kinder to Alger. As the actual stories declined in popularity, the Alger legend grew. In the 1920s he was hailed as significant; in the 1930s the American historians Samuel Eliot Morison and Henry Steele Commager said that Alger had probably had a greater influence on the national character than any other writer except Mark Twain;[4] in the 1940s the American Schools and Colleges Association sponsored the Horatio Alger Awards, to honor people who had pulled themselves up by their bootstraps in the American tradition.[5] Horatio Alger thought of himself as an apologist for economic competition no more than Emma Lazarus thought of herself as a caption writer for a statue. Still, their works went far beyond them, providing people with a way of giving meaning to New York. New York was founded as a city of power and money where liberty allowed all to enter and try their hand at achieving success. This myth about the city was an invitation to diversity. Believe it, and you were any New Yorker's equal. Believe it, and you owed the city your heart.

GOLDEN DOOR

If immigration is a necessary ingredient for a cosmopolitan city, New York needs no explanation. Between 1880 and 1919 over 23 million Europeans entered the United States, and, of those, 17 million landed in New York.[6] In 1902 alone 286,000 Italians and 259,000 Russians entered New York. Many of the immigrants stayed in New York. In New York City in 1920 over half the males over twenty-one were of foreign birth. By 1940, when New York City's total population was about 7.5 million, 5 million of those reported being "of foreign stock" in that year's census. Two million of New York's residents at the time were Jews. The reasons the immigrants came have been carefully analyzed and romantically recorded. For many the upheavals of Europe in the throes of modernization left them no choice. Displaced from their land, ruined by famine, Irish and German immigrants asked only the chance to survive. Others left behind hatreds, wars, and hardship. Specific political events caused dislocations and threats. The wave of European revolutions in 1848, the Franco-Prussian War of 1870, the Risorgimento in 1870, the death of Alexander II and the coronation of the new czar in 1881, the failed 1905 Revolution in Russia, the 1911 Revolution in China, the 1922 coup d'état in Italy—all of these left in their wake refugees and political outcasts. Proponent or opponent, fighter or pacifist, anyone could find himself without family, without hopes, without livelihood. It is neither surprising that people had to leave their homes nor surprising that the United States was a strong choice, for some the only choice. The emigrés chose New York for its promise. But why did the United States welcome the emigrés?

The United States did not welcome them unreservedly. Nativist groups resisted loudly, appealing to the fear of people already in the country, sometimes successfully, as in the case of Asian exclusion. One nativist, A. L. Wayland, wrote:

> We allow every nation to pour its pestilential sewage into our reservoir; at last we so far arouse ourselves to strain out the Mongolian gnat at the Golden Gate while we open wide our mouth at the narrows to swallow the Italian camel, the Polish Dromedary, the Hungarian Elephant, and any pachyderms that present themselves.[7]

Nativism, fear of foreign attachments and foreigners, runs deep in American history. Even Thomas Jefferson feared that the new immigrants of the 1790s would "warp and bias" the direction of the new nation. Until the first quotas were set in 1921, the theory behind American policy was that any aliens had the right to enter unless there was a specific prohibition barring them. But even then Americans consistently fought for greater controls and more and more specific prohibitions. As much as the history of American immigrations was shaped by foreign events, economic and political, it was shaped by domestic prejudices and domestic disagreements.

The western states were the first to attempt to restrict immigration in order to keep out the Chinese. Mine owners and railroad builders had begun bringing in Chinese laborers in about 1850, and in 1852 California was already taxing Chinese miners, businesses, and individual immigrants. As fast as the Supreme Court defeated discriminatory practices, Californians demanded new ones. Throughout the 1860s, 1870s, and 1880s, Congress attempted to control and regulate Chinese immigration, but bills were vetoed by Presidents Hayes and Arthur. Finally, in 1887 Congress passed a bill which excluded new immigrants for ten years, ordered some immigrants deported, and refused citizenship to all remaining Chinese. The Exclusion Act, or Immigration Act, was renewed periodically until 1948.

Other early restrictions were not aimed at specific groups, but instead were used as tools to selectively bar various groups—admission was refused to idiots, the insane, paupers or persons likely to be a public charge, persons with contagious diseases, polygamists, persons of "moral turpitude." The Immigration Act of 1891 left room for interpretation in some matters, while clarifying others—unlimited immigration of friends and relatives of people already in the United States was stopped, and the federal government took charge of inspection and deportation. But immigration was increasing, even while acts in 1903 and 1907 tried to tighten the restrictions and keep immigrants out. Finally, the Immigration Act of 1917 tried to slow the new immigration—the waves of southern and eastern Europeans—by barring anarchists, revolutionaries, contract laborers, persons sponsored by a society or responding to ads for work. The First World War had created millions of refugees and potential immigrants; as the commissioner of the Hebrew Sheltering and Aid Society of America said, "If there were in existence a ship that could hold 3,000,000 human beings, the 3,000,000 Jews of Poland would board it to escape to America."[8] In 1921 American policy makers devised a quota system which would reverse the trend of immigration. The quota system was an answer to the growing numbers of immigrants and a sneer at their countries of origin. Only immigrants whose numbers totaled 3 percent of the foreign-born persons of a given nationality who were in the U.S. in 1910 could enter in a given year. Thus northern and western Europeans had an annual quota of about 200,000, southern and eastern Europeans about 155,000. By 1924 only 2 percent of the 1890 population was allowed per year.

The argument all along was that the "newer" immigrants—and Asians—were not "assimilable." They stayed in enclaves in the cities speaking foreign tongues, dressing in foreign dress, looking so . . . foreign. The argument came from the hinterland, and from Calvin Coolidge, who proclaimed, "America must be kept American."[9]

What, then, was golden about the golden door? If America was issuing an invitation, it was certainly a half-hearted one. Or perhaps the door itself was golden, but it opened onto emptiness. In New York, as in so many cosmopolitan cultures, tolerance was not widespread and invitations were not freely given. Tolerance is a result of diversity, not a cause. America's tolerance did not bring immigrants to American shores. But then, what did? Why did the United States in general and New York in particular accept any immigration at all? Why weren't ships turned back all of the time, instead of only some of the time? Why didn't pogroms and riots greet all immigrants who entered here, advised to abandon all hope?

Gold. Someone benefited; you can read it in the immigration laws themselves. The new immigrants helped other people make money. American steamship companies sold millions of passages. Railroads and mines used forced labor. Growing American industry benefited from cheap labor. Although assimilation was the strong nativist argument, the very first restrictions on European immigrations were designed to select a high-quality work force, not a cultural elite—sickness, moral laxity, and people who would be public charges were excluded. In other words, all able-bodied workers were admitted. The same was true of the early Chinese restrictions, which generally denied citizenship to the Chinese but allowed them to enter the country to work. Perhaps the strongest evidence that economic and not humanitarian motives were behind the golden door is found in American immigration policy in the 1930s. Despite growing fascisms which threatened millions of people in Europe and Asia, American immigration policy did not change. Quotas and exclusions were held intact. People outside America may have been suffering, but so was American business. Businesses in a slump could not afford to sponsor new workers or create new jobs. The golden door was a literal entrance made possible through love of money.

Except in New York, where diversity was growing and a cosmopolitan culture was building tolerance—there the invitation was more sincere. It came from relatives longing to see their families, friends convinced that the promise of the city was in good faith, foreign-born politicians gaining in power, lobbying for less restrictive laws. Thousands of workers sent money back to their families, begging them to come join them. Five of every six Russian Jews and over three-quarters of Italians stayed in big cities, especially New York, where their welcome was most sincere. The streets of the city welcomed the stranger, who recognized his fellow villagers, heard his language, and found work and a neighborhood that looked like home.

GOLDEN RULE

In 1660 William Dieft, the Dutch governor of New Netherland, remarked to the French Jesuit Isaac Jogues that there were eighteen languages spoken at or near Fort Amsterdam at the tip of Manhattan Island. There still are: not necessarily the same languages, but at least as many; nor has the number ever declined in the intervening three centuries. This is an essential fact of New York: a merchant metropolis with an extraordinarily heterogeneous population. The first shipload of settlers sent out by the Dutch was made up largely of French-speaking Protestants. British, Germans, Finns, Jews, Swedes, Africans, Italians, Irish followed, beginning a stream that has never yet stopped.[10]

This paragraph opens the first chapter of Nathan Glazer and Daniel P. Moynihan's sociological classic, *Beyond the Melting Pot.* New York, they say, is huge, heterogeneous, a complex arrangement of classes, cultures coming in contact with other cultures. Unique about New York, they say, is that not only does a small elite learn of other peoples through scattered representatives, but whole masses of people come in contact with other groups—everyone is visible. And yet there is no melting pot. The city is made of different groups—they write about "the Negroes, Puerto Ricans, Jews, Italians and Irish of New York City"—and the members of these groups do not give up their separate identities. They share the same city, but not the same habits or opportunities or work. The melting pot, an idea "as old as the Republic," never existed in New York.[11] New York was really about diversity.

So Glazer and Moynihan recognize something different about this mass heterogeneity, but they stop short of giving it a name. These many peoples shared the experience of living in a city of many peoples. They developed identities that the first immigrants did not have, could not have. As Glazer and Moynihan point out, in New York, "when one says Jews, one also means small shopkeepers, professionals, better-paid skilled workers in the garment industries. When one says Italians, one also means homeowners in Staten Island, the North Bronx, Brooklyn and Queens."[12] Ethnic groups became interest groups, political allies or adversaries. In order to arrive at this modus vivendi, they had to share the experience of living with one another. But what does that mean? How did New Yorkers between 1900 and 1950 "live together" in order to create a relatively peaceful, economically powerful city? What kind of public life drew such diverse groups into a common endeavor?

Actually, the immigrant groups did not literally live together. Recently, Nathan Glazer has commented that the mingling and mixing believed necessary for success in America has been overstated; there really was not all that much mingling or mixing.[13] New York was a city of neighborhoods and these neighborhoods were tight and homogeneous. In Little Italy in 1938, 98 percent of the heads of households in this area were of Italian birth or parentage, mainly from Sicily.[14] Similarly, Jewish neighborhoods in the Bronx during the 1930s were 97 or 98 percent Jewish, Spanish Harlem was about 85 percent Puerto Rican, and of the remaining 15 percent of Spanish Harlem, most were Spanish speakers from Latin America. Although some of this concentration was due to available housing and affordable rents, some was by choice. One group fled from the other it most feared; usually, groups that had been in the city longer, such as Irish, Germans, or blacks, moved uptown and away to escape incoming immigrants.

Similarly, although the New York system of public education was extensive and advanced, each group experienced it differently. The ideal image of black, white, yellow, and red children sharing the same school bench and all becoming some "other" thing—American—hardly describes the reality of the public school system during the first half of this century. First, different groups had varying degrees of attendance. Italian families in New York often came with rural skills and easily found work that was familiar enough and rewarding enough. Italian children, then, were often kept home to work. Jewish immigrants, by contrast, sent their children to school in prodigious numbers (although it must be remembered that more whole Jewish families immigrated and there were more Jewish children to attend school). Already urban, Jews also tended to put more value on education, although some resisted it as a threat to religious tradition. Finally, since many schools were neighborhood schools, diversity was diminished by residential segregation.

And yet public education had some interesting, unintended consequences. The schools might not have been teaching assimilation to a single standard, but they did teach cosmopolitan culture. Immigrant groups eyed one another with wary admiration; success was not American, but whatever seemed different and better. Thousands of young Jewish women aspired to the dignified and glamorous career of teaching public school after seeing their own teachers, the Irish whose ancestors had come to the United States not eighty years before and who now controlled much of public life and the civil service.[15] Success sometimes seemed Irish. Then again, the progress of Jewish students sometimes prompted other groups to see the American dream as Jewish. Public education was an indirect introduction to other peoples.

New York was filled with great public institutions, libraries, and museums open to everyone. Many of these were so important to the lives of New Yorkers that they could be called the city's centers of aspiration. In 1939 the American Museum of Natural History's activities—teaching and research exhibits—touched 43 million people. On an average day the main building of the New York Public Library hosted eleven thousand readers and visitors. In the museums and libraries almost everyone could find something intriguing or something familiar. In the 1930s the New York Writers' Project commented on the New York Public Library's vast collection of current newspapers from all parts of the world and the cosmopolitan readership they attracted.[16] Nobel laureates and other prominent scientists credit the Museum of Natural History as much as any school they attended for their early love of science. The great libraries and museums inspired children of any social class or ethnic group simply by being public and telling them that American science—and art and literature—included them. Even if not all groups visited and not all children were touched, the buildings were massive civic monuments known to everyone as expressions of faith in public life.

In the lives of most newcomers and ordinary workers, New York's shared life was simpler. It was the streets and subways, the endless motion of New York and its endless crowds. While neighborhoods were often homogeneous, broad avenues or boulevards usually intersected or joined them, avenues where contact with people from other neighborhoods was possible. The contact was not always welcome. In Washington Heights and in the South Bronx during the 1930s, street gangs fought for neighborhood control. Everyone knew, though, that control was short-lived and very local. Not only did neighborhoods change, but the broad avenues moved on and left you behind—on this block it was yours; on the next you were in foreign territory. Most public of all public institutions were the streets; you could use them, but they traveled on and beyond you. The streets were a show for those who could not afford tickets, an airy mead for tenement dwellers, an office for the business-minded and also a marketplace. Those who could afford a subway ride rode fast and direct through worlds unfamiliar, where riders even more unfamiliar entered the car. The subway system ran long and complete. Transportation in New York was a lesson in public life. As the classic *WPA Guide to New York City* says:

Drama resides in the endless flow of activity that crowds the cars and platforms. Beggars, singers, banjo-players, and candy-butchers vie for a few pennies, howl bargains, or stumble silently past the apathetic passengers. Occasionally, a particularly bright singing troupe or an unusually pathetic cripple will meet with warm response. At large stations, pitchmen attract crowds with infinite ease, and disappear before the greenhorn realizes he has been duped.[17]

The city was huge and unmanageable to the newcomer, the greenhorn. The streets and subways were only one way in which he was drawn into the whirl of unfamiliar life outside his neighborhood. Another was politics. Political activity in New York forced every potential voter into civic-mindedness. Party machines courted votes. Labor organizers recruited union members. Much of this was done in an immediate, personal way, strangers glad-handing strangers, speakers exhorting crowds of unfamiliar faces. Unexpected partnerships emerged from participatory democracy in New York. The Irish actively converted new voters to vote Democratic. During the first decades of the century, when many Jews were active socialists, the Irish maintained control of Democratic New York. Yet as the New Deal drew more Jews away from socialism, an Italian-Jewish alliance elected Fiorella LaGuardia mayor, even though many Jews still preferred the American Labor Party to the local Democratic machine. LaGuardia changed the composition of the civil service, making it less Irish, more Italian and Jewish. Since he made more positions competitive, civil service began to favor college graduates.

Meanwhile, Jewish labor organizers fought for Italian support. Jews and Italians, the largest immigrant groups in New York during the first half of the century, sometimes found themselves in the same industries. Attempts to increase union strength had to include both groups. The popular Italian politican Vito Marcantonio represented Italian and Puerto Rican constituents. Communist organizers from the Lower East Side sent liaisons to black Harlem, especially in the wake of the Scottsboro trial in the 1930s, where the treatment of several young black boys charged with rape in Scottsboro, Alabama, raised doubts about the possibility of justice in America. So one way or another, when a group wanted power, it turned to other groups. The task of governing the city, a public task if ever there was one, was a task which required tolerance.

Even the most insulated newcomers, women, perhaps, who spoke only the mother tongue (at a time when men were more educated, the mother tongue was literally the language of mothers), who never went out, never voted, never even became citizens, still had the marketplace.

Eventually, someone else's food reaches your market. A Jewish peddler wanders into your neighborhood to sell zippers, or an Italian iceman. Eventually, the market for housing introduces a strange landlord. If you work, the market for jobs introduces a foreign boss. If you own a shop, you negotiate with someone for something American—you sell sugar, you buy candy. New York was a city of trade. Eventually, you would want to expand your trade. You rented to someone else. You ate in an unfamiliar restaurant. The marketplace in New York drew in everyone who had hopes of a better life or curiosity or need. Eventually, the marketplace drew in everyone.

GOLDEN OPPORTUNITY

Because cosmopolitan culture is a culture of inclusion, because everyone who enters has access to the beliefs, the life of the city, everyone has a chance at success. Opportunity is necessary—not sufficient, but necessary—to a tolerant culture. For here is the secret of loyalty and love: inclusion. If you want patriotism and loyalty, you must make all citizens feel that they are members. Ages ago when men and governments experimented with rational thought and ideas of progress, they believed that they could create a more perfect union. They believed that a constitution could be framed that would be so good, so true, so beautiful, that citizens would love their country for its very beauty. Men (for it was an age of men) would sign up in support of their government because it was the best of all possible governments. Then the ties of membership would bind all men into a national brotherhood.

But has that ever been the case? When men and women feel excluded, they seldom support abstract ideals no matter how true or beautiful. They must believe, they must feel, they must know that their contributions are wanted, that their chances are equal. Then, when all are welcomed and included, there is love and gratitude. Newcomers to New York faced despair and many obstacles, some expected, some unimagined. Yet there is love and gratitude in the voices of the few old men and women who remain to tell of their first years here. New York gave them life because New York gave them opportunity. The chance to be better, to live better, was a reality in New York.

Not only was New York a wealthy, booming city, but the organization of its economic life was peculiarly open, even to strangers who spoke foreign tongues or who had few skills. Its geography, above all, determined the city's economic life. New York's superb harbor, along with its developed system of waterways and railroads, made the city a natural center of trade. Immigrants with no skills could find immediate work on the docks. Even the most down-and-out, destined for failure in any landlocked town, could make do, at least temporarily, in New York. Daniel Moynihan, commenting on the debilitating effects of alcohol among the worst off of the Irish immigrants, indirectly paid homage to the New York harbor. Drink might prevent a man from practicing law, or running a gambling ring, or directing a business, he said, but a stevedore could drink and still do his work.[18]

Immigrant communities replaced one another, hugging close to the port where they entered until they could gain a foothold. The harbor held opportunities other than handling cargo. Proximity to the docks meant proximity to incoming goods, to fruit, vegetables, fish, any perishables which could be bought cheap and in small quantities. A peddler with ambition and very little capital could buy one day's work, as long as he could get close to the dock. If he was successful, he could buy the next day. The harbor brought the tides of supply and demand—supplies of goods to sell, and always more newcomers who needed to eat.

New York's harbor character, however, had other consequences for the city's economic life. Heavy industry was impractical on an island; the cost of transporting equipment and heavy industrial products would have been prohibitive. Moreover, Manhattan Island could scarcely contain its growing population. Real estate on the island was in short supply and expensive. As the city expanded, the same became true of the boroughs. The cost of the space required to construct foundries or mills or any of the heavy industries common in other regions would be prohibitive. So New York was limited to light industry, business that could take place in small spaces. It was this that gave New York its peculiarly acorporate character. At the turn of the century, when the rest of the United States was coalescing into giant companies with corporate hierarchies, only two regions were untouched, the rural southeast and New York City.

New York was home to small business and light industry, particularly the garment industry. The idiosyncrasies of the garment industry tended to further reduce the size and stability of businesses. A description from the 1930s explained:

> The process of centralization and monopoly that shaped other large industries has not operated to any great extent in the garment trade, largely because the style factor makes it an extremely speculative business. Instead of the assembly-belt system that obtains, for example, in the automobile industry, garment production is relatively dependent on the skill of the operator, who in most cases sews the entire garment. The so-called manufacturer, or jobber, may do only a portion of the actual manufacturing. . . .[19]

The vagaries of fashion aside, the garment industry was minutely subdivided and most of the actual sewing (as opposed to designing or cutting) was contracted out; "out" at the time often meant home, in crowded tenements. Numerous middlemen controlled small groups or crews. The garment trade depended on small, independently controlled teams.

An immigrant around 1907 would have faced a New York that was in some ways hospitable. There was work. It was close to home. He might find work with a local contractor or padrone who knew his language. With only the smallest bit of capital he could begin as a peddler, then possibly move up to shopkeeper. He could become a citizen. There were schools for advancement. He could even become comfortable.

Yes, it was a refuge. But equality? Where were the Yankees? Was it possible to achieve the same wealth and dream the same dreams as those invisible few who owned the steamship lines, owned the railroads, ran the banks, and asked for quotas so that the "racial composition" of the country would remain in their favor?

New York between 1900 and 1950 was a city of opportunity, but, true to its cosmopolitan character, it was limited opportunity.

What is a land of opportunity? In a land of opportunity you are free to ply your trade. You are also free to do better than your parents. You are not free to leave behind your past, to become something new. The cosmopolitan city offers opportunity, but it offers limited opportunity. Those limits are the subject of the following discussion.

The Cinderella story is a rags-to-riches dream. Cinderella—there was a woman with opportunity. She had a trade. She cleaned the cinders, and like so many, many others (Miller, Schneider, Wright), her trade became her name. She was skilled in cleaning, resource management (hence the ease with which she found pumpkins, mice, etc., at the fairy godmother's command), and the general direction of a houschold, as well as in conflict and personnel management, which she practiced in dealings with her miserable stepsisters. Through a combination of luck and skill and charm she rose into a position where life was easier, more beautiful, and more enjoyable; she became the wife of a prince. What were her tasks in that position? The general management of a large household. As a princess, Cinderella was supposed to serve her prince just as earlier in her wretched life she did the bidding of her stepsisters and step-mother. In other words, her life was immensely improved, but she was still in the same trade. Does a miserable charwoman become a court astronomer? A Roman Catholic pope? An explorer? A sheepdog? Cinderella could move up, up to the highest domestic position in the world, but not over. Vertical, but not horizontal, mobility.

There is another kind of land of opportunity, one where everything is gold and fortune and happiness. A wealthy land where food is plenty and economic expansion gives a chance to those who have no trade. Each of the cities here has been such a land of plenty. Maybe Cinderella's good fortune was caused not by her own individual life, but by her surroundings. Maybe things were getting wealthier all the way around. But if this alone were opportunity, if this alone could explain Cinderella's happy marriage, our story would be very different. "Times are good for charwomen," we might say. We might even cluck our tongues and remark, "These days every charwoman marries a prince," meaning that a profusion of rich men has made life easy for many women, even the lowest. Each of the cities here has been built on fertile plains, navigable rivers, or hospitable harbors. Many of the strangers who flocked to them, increasing these cities' wealth, expected lands of gold or, at least, plenty. Each of the cities also had its own form of opportunity.

New York between 1900 and 1950 was a city of expansion. But if we stop our explanation there, we will not get to the heart of cosmopolitan culture. Even though opportunity could mean a land of plenty, it more often means the hope of mobility, the Cinderella story . . .

But let's begin at the beginning. What is so important about social mobility, and what does it have to do with opportunity?

The social world is a hierarchical world. Better and worse, more and less, higher and lower, people look at each other in this way. This is not to say that the world should be like that; it simply is. What is more, most people agree on the rankings even if they do not all approve of them. Class (income or economic position), status, and power are apparent to most people. Titles like king or baron or doctor tell you aloud what you privately guess. Even where there are no titles, there may be outward signs. There is no aristocracy in the United States and yet there is a distinctive hierarchy—so distinctive that in survey after survey people consistently agree on which are the "highest" and which the "lowest" jobs. A plumber is never as high on the list as a Supreme Court justice. Even a baseball player, who may earn more than a Supreme Court justice, is lower. Money and status do not always neatly coincide.

If you aggressively resist this idea of ranking, it may be on moral grounds, but you cannot deny that in the reality of American life a U.S. senator is treated differently from a worker at McDonald's. And if the hamburger cook is smarter? More patient? Taller, stronger, older? There are many different dimensions on which to rank people and many different settings. And yet the modern industrial world wants most to know your niche in the world of do and make—your occupation. If your occupation at the end of your working life is higher than your father's was at the end of his, your family has been upwardly mobile. So mobility is movement on the social scale and opportunity is the likelihood that you'll move up. Opportunity is the promise of social mobility.

There can be limits on opportunity. There is no reason to expect opportunity to be total or even just or in any way natural. Many of the world's people, remember, have scratched out a living wherever life left them, expecting nothing, hoping for little. What is more, promotion for merit is an ideal, seldom followed in its perfect form. For with all the bureaucracies of Babylon or Constantinople, for all the bureaucratic reforms of Napoleon or Emperor Joseph I, never has a bureaucracy matched its ideal form, ignoring personalities and personal attributes in favor of cool expertise.

Enter the United States, land of opportunity. Americans hold a mass of contradictory beliefs about their country and their own lives. One popular view of the United States is as a land of no class distinctions, a middle-class country of middle-class people who share middle-class ideals. This is a venerable view, promoted by the Founding Fathers, who eschewed aristocratic titles. Didn't George Washington himself reject the offer of a kingship? When the French social observer Alexis de Tocqueville toured the United States in the early nineteenth century, he believed he saw a cooperative, conformist country of middle-class communities. His association of democracy with equality has pride of place in the American dream; everyone must own a home because everyone must have the same stake in the community, or at least, some people still believe. Even though the American economy can barely sustain the illusion, even today most Americans in most surveys like to call themselves middle-class.

Can everyone be middle-class? What about the idea that each son does better than his father? In America, Americans believe, each generation does better than the last—or should. The American belief that life is supposed to improve, no matter how sincere, obviously conflicts with the idea that all Americans have about the same. (After all, one's parents, this idea implies, always have less than oneself.) Besides, advancement itself was never really a fact. A son's chance of rising socially may have been good in the United States in the 1940s, but it was roughly as good in France, Italy, Denmark, or England.[20] A son's chance of dropping socially was also comparable in Europe and the United States. There is downward mobility, too, remember.

Mobility studies study careers, and Americans are mad about careers. While for the scholars careers are just paths from one occupation to the next and the next, for the layman career has come to mean a direct move straight and upward with some underlying plan or goal. But this has not always been true; in fact the historic circumstances which allowed Americans to formulate this picture are very recent. Opportunity and career are only sometimes, and coincidentally, joined. Improvement in one's lot is not necessarily tied at all to an underlying plan or goal, or even to a straight path.

At the start of American history, people had crafts or trades or, for the pure of spirit, callings; for the less noble, simple employment. Benjamin Franklin, for instance, had a work life which could be called a career only in kind retrospect. He apprenticed to a printer, traveled, sought work, changed jobs now and again, published, tinkered. Like many of his age, he dabbled in science as an amateur. He was in public service as a dutiful citizen. But not only did he not have a career; he paid little attention to his occupation. His advice, the essential modern Protestant work ethic, was not to master one's task, but rather to appear decent and trustworthy. Exemplified in his own life, the fruits of such good appearances were not only increased trade, but perhaps a serendipitous chance at another job altogether . . . such as ambassador to France.

It is only a short step from Ben Franklin's words on good impressions to Horatio Alger's words on cleanliness and study. The bootblack who lives decently will be rewarded with decency, according to Alger. Yet that bootblack no more has a career than did Alger himself. At the end of the nineteenth century opportunity still meant chance. The world was still divided into those, like clergy, with a calling, those with crafts and trades, and those with work—simple laborers or factory hands. The modern idea of a direct route to some other position barely existed. Alger's calling as a minister failed him. He ended more important than his father. But he might not have. He viewed his success as a writer the same way he would view the rise of a bootblack or the marriage of a factory hand and the boss' daughter. Chance and hard work—some win, some lose.

Here is an American view of mobility which contradicts yet again the already contradictory hopes of jovial equality and generational change. Work and good luck. If some work harder or have better luck, how can all Americans be happily middle-class? If some lose or fall down on their luck, how can all sons do better than their fathers? American views of opportunity and success are hopelessly muddled. The good son (seldom daughter) pulls hard on his bootstraps in order to remain equal to and better than his father, equal to and better than his peers, all the while mastering no task except cleanliness and thrift and trusting his fate essentially to luck and the good regard of others—who are at once better, worse, and equal to him.

The twentieth century strengthened professions and professionalism, but the language was still the language of the Puritan calling. Crafts declined and automation reduced more craftsmen to factory hands. These workers, without trade or profession, still saw opportunity as chance and chance as random. There has been only one generation for whom opportunity seemed to come from a steady upward climb on a single path. These are the parents of the young people entering the work force today.

Those men and women who were children during the Depression were an exception rather than the rule of American mobility. First, because so many of them felt direct improvement in their own lifetimes, they believed that opportunity blossomed. Although the likelihood of a man rising up above his peers may not have changed, the whole standard of living had improved. In other words, they did feel they had a chance for a better life, but that is not necessarily social mobility.

Second, and more importantly, in a powerful, growing postwar economy, promotion-from-within was a reality. Not only did the labor movement successfully fight for seniority rules in many industries, but at the same time expanding corporations, government offices, even small businesses under the protection of New Deal legislation could accommodate more and better employees. A greater proportion of the men whose work lives stretched from roughly 1950 to 1980, more than any other group of workers in this century, stayed with one employer, promotion after promotion, throughout their careers. The causes of this direct climb range from the organization of corporate management in the 1950s to the growth of the American economy, the psychological effects of the Depression, even the housing market. More interesting here, though, is the effect: another contradictory addition to the American view of mobility.

This most recent view is that opportunity takes the form of a single, planned choice. Make the right choice, and your talents, and the economy, will buoy you up to a better life. Choose your skill, your employer, your goal. Children of the exceptional generation are busy choosing and planning for the steady climb. But what is mobility, really? Is it choice, chance, success, or staying put? It is all of these, obviously, as long as people are confused about opportunity. As long as opportunity means everything and nothing, it is an empty promise. Everyone in the United States knows that it is not equally possible for any child to grow up to be president. There are and have always been limits to opportunity in the United States.

The particular limit to opportunity which interests us here is the cultural division of labor. Different religious and ethnic groups tend to end up in different occupations in this country. Although it is an academic commonplace,[21] the subject is embarrassing and difficult in common conversation. People make jokes and wander into stereotypes when they try to describe their observations that many restaurants are owned by Greeks and many laundries are owned by Chinese. The subject is embarrassing and difficult because it is not supposed to exist. The idea of a cultural division of labor flies in the face of the idea of equal opportunity. And that is right. Opportunity in this country has been circumscribed by ethnicity.

Just as unemployment allows the economic system of free enterprise to work, the cultural division of labor allows the social system of cosmopolitanism to work. Unemployment, too, is disturbing and disquieting. Few people say out loud that it serves a grim purpose, and those few are seen as callous. Quietly, though, we have grown to accept "acceptable" levels of unemployment as the price of a "vigorous" economy—in other words, profits for corporate industry. If everyone were employed, competition for jobs would not be keen enough and the threat of losing a job would lose its bite. Unemployment makes plain society's lower limits.

The cultural division of labor makes plain society's upper limits. If any member of any group could reach any position, competition for positions would be too keen and the hope of success would lose its promise. Quietly, people grew to accept a cultural division of labor as the price of a certain social harmony. And that is why limited opportunity—that is, limited by a strong cultural division of labor—is in fact essential to cosmopolitan culture.

How exactly does the cultural division of labor limit opportunity? The cultural division of labor has a peculiar effect on success. Due to his habits and history, a member of a certain group will be more likely to enter a certain trade. Within that trade, he or she may advance to Olympic heights, achieving wealth, even power. The barrier occurs only if that member or his son or daughter tries to move horizontally rather than vertically, when he tries to enter a *different* trade or field. It's like the Cinderella story. You can go up, but not over. It certainly looks like success. It even looks like social mobility. It means that entering immigrants create wealth and contribute to the economy while competing only with one another.

The rest of this chapter is a discussion of how the cultural division of labor in New York between 1900 and 1950 contributed to its cosmopolitan character—how the cultural division of labor was set into place, which mechanisms kept it in place, and, finally, the fate of one group, Italian-Americans, in this city of cosmopolitan-style success.

As for Cinderella, who was she really? In 1870 she was an Irish girl whose brother took her to a party at the Democratic headquarters, where the ward leader took a fancy to her. In 1910 she was a Polish Jew who attended citizenship classes, where she sat next to the son of a furrier. In 1937 she was black, sent by the WPA to clean the house of an old woman in Harlem whose son was a doctor. She and her husband eventually bought a house in Queens and had two daughters and later six grandchildren. The daughters lived on Long Island. Three of the grandchildren became lawyers, one a teacher, one went into business, and one is still deciding. Two of the grandchildren vote Republican, three vote Democratic, one is registered Independent. Do fairy tales come true? You be the judge.

SOCIAL MOBILITY IN NEW YORK

Social mobility for immigrants to New York and their children was a fact, not a fairy tale. In Omaha, Atlanta, or Boston, no more than 22 percent of the population, both native and immigrant, advanced from blue-collar to white-collar jobs between 1880 and 1890. Immigrants who were on New York's lowest rung in 1880, however, had a 37 percent chance of reaching white-collar status within that decade.[22] And after

1900 New York's mobility statistics remained head and shoulders above all other cities. Most people could move out of manual labor in less than one generation.

Nathan Glazer has chronicled this change from working class to professional class among New York's Jews. Children of immigrants who arrived in New York in the early twentieth century tended not to replace their parents in unskilled or semiskilled work, Glazer discovered. Although in 1952 there was a sizable Jewish working class in New York, larger than in most cities, most of those factory workers or service workers were old—of the immigrant generation. By 1952 two-thirds of all Jewish men were out of manual labor—among their parents, the Jewish immigrants arriving between 1899 and 1910, almost two-thirds had been laborers, skilled or unskilled.[23]

The story of opportunity for other groups is roughly similar to the story of opportunity for the Jews. New York between 1900 and 1950 was not only expanding and raising people's standard of living, the city was actually taking sons and sometimes daughters up and away from the world of their parents. If not in one generation, then by the next, the groups of the great wave that peaked in 1907 and again in 1919 experienced firsthand part of the American dream. Stories of sacrifice and superhuman effort fill the annals of these years. Stories of generational conflict, more bitter and heartrending than anything since, accompanied this massive mobility. And funny stories, misunderstandings, frustrations, and language difficulties. All the while doing a little better with each step.

Doing better most often meant higher incomes. Manual labor like construction or unskilled factory work was poorly paid. While unions fought for living wages, manufacturers preyed on the needs of the poor—even during a strike, there were always some people who felt they needed money so badly that they would sacrifice solidarity and accept a pittance for any work at all. Eventually, unions did succeed in raising wages, but by that time increased education and language ability were already pulling the next generation into higher-paying managerial jobs.

The path to higher status and higher income, however, was remarkably straight and narrow: mobility was always vertical. The peddler bought a shop; his son expanded the business. The machine operator's son became a cutter or designer, boss or contractor; he opened his own factory. The junk dealer's son became an antiques dealer. The ditch digger became a landscaper; his son a landscape architect. The stellar rise of the managerial class can be explained in large part by continued expansion of small businesses and by the promotion of workers to owners within the same industry. According to the 1950 census, the sons of Italian immigrants were much more likely to be involved in clerical or sales work than their fathers. Where did this change come from, and why clerical and sales? Many sons, it can be inferred, found white-collar work in their fathers' businesses.

Even where the children entered the professions, they worked in traditional small, independent businesses or civil service. The second generation was not absorbed into corporate America. Just as some occupations, such as labor leader, remained Jewish, even after Jewish labor membership declined, other occupations, such as insurance executive, were seldom Jewish, long after immigrants' children—and grandchildren—were qualified. A 1960 study found that non-Jewish graduates of the Harvard Business School proportionately outnumbered Jewish graduates in executive positions in the leading American corporations by "better than 30 to 1."[24] In 1963 Glazer drew a similar conclusion: "In the great banks, insurance companies, public utilities, railroads and corporation head offices that are located in New York," he wrote, "few Jews are to be found."[25] What was true of Jews was even more true of Italians and other southern and eastern Europeans. The second generation was not absorbed into corporate America.

Upward mobility brought income, status, and prestige. What it did not bring was an even or homogeneous distribution of jobs. Opportunity had certainly touched the immigrants. Yet that opportunity was distinctly shaped by ethnicity. The cultural division of labor, which was set into place as different groups settled in New York, determined occupations for generations to come.

First, the fate of immigrants and their families was determined by the skills and experiences they brought with them. Of the Jewish immigrants entering the United States between 1899 and 1910, over 145,000 were tailors, 23,000 were shoemakers, and 17,000 were clerks and accountants. According to one historian, New York's already giant clothing industry "was their salvation, because it provided an outlet for their narrow abilities, allowing them to enter the economy at a higher level than other immigrants" of the same time.[26] In other words, when there was a natural fit between skills already held and areas of opportunity, the path of least resistance afforded an avenue to success. No matter that the immigrant was looking for a new life; a new life was not always open to him. So he took up his old work. Almost one in three newly arrived Jewish workers in 1907 lived thanks to the clothing trade. Immigrants, remember, were coming from an impoverished traditional world where trades open to them had been decreed by law and enforced by armies. Those who came often represented those occupations under the hardest conditions. Skilled Jewish craftsmen specifically were being denied work in the Russian Pale. Professionals less often found their way to American shores. In a twelve-year period fewer than 350 rabbis came to the United States from Russia, in contrast to the thousands and thousands of tailors.[27] The American clothing industry welcomed them when they accepted wages lower than any earlier immigrant groups were getting. Years down the road that business, filled with *landsmen,* gave them a place to invest.[28]

One would guess it was also experience which created peddlers, but that was not necessarily true. Although there had been Jewish peddlers and merchants in Europe, they were not the people who came. Only 5 percent of those entering the United States were merchants or dealers.[29] Rather, it was a New World opportunity which matched an Old World goal—at home the successful had been independent businessmen. The pushcart was the vehicle for the impoverished entrepreneur. "Tailors or mechanics who are out of work hire a pushcart until they find a position. Recently landed immigrants are advised by their friends to take a pushcart until they can establish themselves in some business," a *New York Times* reporter wrote.[30] The same was true of Italian immigrants. Few southern Italians or Sicilians had experience in trade: they were for the most part peasants escaping an impoverished rural life. The road from street trading to storefront sometimes even passed through systematic, organized peddling: for these immigrants an investor would buy several licenses, and hire peddlers by the day—these peddlers needed no experience, no capital, and not even the language ability to negotiate a license.

Some Italian immigrants competed for factory jobs and worked in low-paid service jobs, but over 42 percent of all Italian household heads around 1905 fed their families thanks to unskilled labor, that is, largely construction work. It was another example of old experience matching new opportunity. They had not come to a new world to do old jobs. But the jobs were there. The peasants who came had been farm laborers in the old country. They were physically able to do heavy work. They entered a city booming with construction—streets, bridges, subways— and the path of least resistance once again afforded a chance to save, invest, and succeed. One historian of New York called unskilled construction work "the great Italian beachhead into the American economy."[31] Over five thousand Italian workers were employed at the Bronx aqueduct project in 1904; more at Grand Central Terminal; even more on the railroads. Any work which demanded physical strength, such as moving or carrying ice, gave preference to people who had been peasants. The goal, though, was always clear: such work was a way to save money in order to get ahead, to open a business, to buy a tenement, to go back to Italy. True, old skills were useful, but the goal was advancement, not the re-creation of an old order.

Most Italian immigrants vehemently resisted farming. They had come from farms, but they intended never to go back to farms. Any construction work was preferable to agriculture. The few who did go into farming were extremely successful. Many of the vineyards in both upstate New York and California were expanded or begun by families with vineyard experience in Italy. Truck farms in New Jersey or Staten Island which supplied New York with produce were extremely profitable. It could even be argued that had more Italians capitalized on Old World farm experience, Italian social mobility overall would have been faster, profiting from another path of least resistance. The associations with farm life were so bad, however, the brutality and degradation so recent in memory, that few immigrants wanted it. Polish and Czech workers also resisted resorting to their traditional skills, mining and foundry work. Yet often out of desperation and necessity they ended up in the great foundry cities of the Midwest. In short, there was often no choice. There was work, but not the work one had hoped for, and the past weighed heavy on the immigrants.

Now all of this is not to explain success. This is not to say that there was more available work "back then," or that immigrants were better prepared "back then." Rather, we call on the Old World roots to show how it was that millions of people from one group made the same choice, how whole industries became full of one ethnicity or another. Here we see the cultural division of labor being set into place: certain workers choose to emigrate; those workers have a particular background; that background matches a particular New York endeavor. Even this would not be enough, though, without other influences.

New York's cultural division of labor was also constructed out of the hopes, fears, values, habits, and traditions of the immigrant generation, as well as their skills. Obvious constraints barred them from certain jobs—many eastern and southern Europeans faced a language barrier. Devout eastern European Jews needed time to pray and could not work on religious holidays. More subtle choices, too, based on past experience, determined their goals. Sicilian peasants had suffered not only deprivation in their native land, but grueling physical hardships. One of these hardships was walking to the fields in order to work, a walk that could be hours long. Sicilians in America consistently and vehemently chose to work close to home as soon as they established some sort of household. Near Elizabeth Street, on New York's Lower East Side, one factory drew almost four-fifths of its workers from the surrounding block.[32] Italians would travel for seasonal or temporary work, however. Jews would live a little farther from work, but, other than for sales or deliveries, would seldom follow work that traveled. The draw of business was that it could be conducted near the family.[33]

In this way values and attitudes helped determine the jobs that immigrants held—and the jobs their children held. Above all, it is impossible to overestimate the power of the family. Rare, very rare was the immigrant who saw his fate in terms of his own likes and dislikes. He was inextricably bound to other people, people he had to bring over, support, obey, or actively leave behind. Fathers and uncles and cousins, especially those who brought fellow workers to America at great personal expense, would not take kindly to being abandoned and insulted by their sons. Surely, over the course of time, the tradition of a family trade has lessened. And yet the advantages are so clear—connections, familiarity, union membership, when that is important—that they are still in force today. The sons of doctors become doctors. The sons of professors become professors. The sons of writers become writers. The sons of steelworkers work in steel plants, when that is possible. The sons of politicians become politicans. Even today.

Other traditional views and habits also influenced the immigrants and their children. Different groups had differing goals and saw different work as honorable. The Jewish value on education and the professions is often cited as a key to Jewish mobility. Even though a large number of Jewish immigrants were themselves illiterate, they had been trained to see scholars as admirable and scholarship as divinely blessed. The glory of America was not that any immigrant's son could become president— who knew?—but that any immigrant's son could become a rabbi. If not a rabbi, he could be his secular equivalent, a professional with high status. In addition, the newcomers faced before them the example of New York's German Jews, who had arrived at least a half-century before them. They were, above all, educated. Some jobs, like that of policeman, were distasteful because immigrants remembered law enforcement officers as tyrants in the old country. Italian immigrants, too, brought with them standards of success and failure which they gave to their children. Anyone in America, they believed, could be a respected, successful worker—an artisan, never a peasant. Eventually, this image of the Italian became widely held: he was a good, hard worker, never less, little more.[34] It is easy for the ousider to turn deeply held values into a stereotype. The outsider does not know the anguish which produced those values.

For anguish, pain, and fear also filled immigrant lives. Fear of change, fear of loss, fear of outsiders. The quickest route to success was always believed to be the one which depended least on others. Immigrant families succeeded best in independent businesses. Almost everyone was trying to escape the arbitrary demands of outside bosses. Risk takers, like those willing to emigrate, were independent decision makers. Almost none of the immigrants around 1907 became servants, even though some of the work they did take, like garbage collection, was dirty or distasteful.

However independent they tried to be, immigrants and their families were often simply coerced into certain trades or livelihoods. Women were forced into prostitution, when they were not forced into the needle trades by cruel, distant relatives or greedy jobbers. Representatives always met the boats at Ellis Island and recruited, or sometimes threatened, disembarking Italian laborers into signing up with a *padrone,* or construction contractor. Uncaring relatives deserted their wards, leaving them without friend and without promised employment. Letters to the *Jewish Daily Forward* during the early years of this century recount stories of such hardship and coercion.[35] The worst coercion of all, hunger, was eventually replaced by family pressures for the most part, but it had its characteristic effect: immigrants and their children took the low-paying work.

It would be impossible to ignore another emotional influence—prejudice. However capable an immigrant might be, in the eyes of the Yankee even the third and fourth generation might not "look quite right." There was prejudice and everyone knew it.[36] There was active discrimination. There was volatile diatribe in many publications. Moreover, the immigrants came from countries where the simplest activities of their American lives, like voting or arguing, were fraught with danger. How could they not fear arrest or worse for simply pushing too far? When Jews read anti-Semitic threats in the press, how could they not remember their recent experiences in Russia? Many of them held memories of extreme violence and bloodcurdling fear.[37] Many peoples carried memories of intense persecution. Immigrants rejoiced in new freedoms, but were not deaf to the American voices declaring them persona non grata. The American press in the early part of this century railed against the Italians as filthy, dangerous, and drains on the economy.[38] The press feared a nation overrun by Jews. The Yankee Henry Adams warned:

> The Russian Jews and the other Jews will completely control the finances and the Government of this country in ten years or they will all be dead . . . the hatred with which they are regarded . . . ought to be a warning to them. The people of this country . . . won't be starved and driven to the wall by Jews who are guilty of all crimes, tricks and wiles.[39]

Enough Americans believed this to fight to cut off immigration, to limit
the employment of Jews, and to make necessary an article in *Fortune*
magazine in 1936 devoted to Jewish wealth and financial influence.
Completely contrary to the popular fears, the study found, Jewish wealth
was concentrated not in finance, but in clothing manufacture, department stores, and entertainment (natural extensions of the cultural division of labor set in place earlier in the century).[40]

American opinion equated Jews and Italians, many of whom were
active socialists, with subversion, and the Sacco and Vanzetti Case of
1921 was ample proof to many Italians that American freedoms were not
open to immigrants and the children of immigrants. Nicola Sacco and
Bartolomeo Vanzetti were convicted of murder, but many people believed "the decision was based on their foreign birth and political beliefs." The judge in the case, Webster Thayer, boasted, "Did you see
what I did with those anarchistic bastards the other day?"[41]

Discrimination was present in the minds of parents and children when
they thought about the future. The cultural division of labor was set into
place with legacies of the past and thoughts about the future. The future
should be respectable, secure, and safe. Respectable by traditional standards, secure by the standards of the American economy, and safe from
persecution or torment. In other words, the cultural division of labor
depends in part on limited aspirations. They do this job, we do that. Jobs
like corporate management were inaccessible due to discrimination and
undesirable since discrimination caused anguish and insecurity. The
more education the children received, the more their aspirations
changed. Employment was less tied to family honor, and respectability
was held closer to American than Old World standards. The more you
fit in, the more you want to fit in, and ultimately assimilation was another
element of hope in the choice of occupation.

These were the constraints and qualifications surrounding economic
achievement in New York between 1900 and 1950. The result, remember, in the best of cases, was high income, some status, possibly security.
The immigrants and their children were not going to break into bastions
of Yankee respectability, including corporate America, at least for the
most part. The Yankees believed that and so did the immigrant parents.

Italian parents, Jewish parents, Ukrainian parents may have stressed different goals, but they all had in common the emphasis on security. When children grew frustrated, it was with the low, simple aspirations of their immigrant parents more often than with their insistence on achievement. For you see, even being a doctor is settling when you want to be a Great American Painter. The immigrant parents, though, did not believe that their children—an Italian, a Greek, a Jew—could really be or should really be in those Yankee positions. Such a leap seemed impossible. Mario Puzo's life in America was beyond his mother's wildest aspirations for him, as he recalls:

> My mother wanted me to be a railroad clerk. And that was her highest ambition; she would have settled for less. At the age of sixteen . . . when I let everybody know that I was going to be a great writer . . . she quite simply assumed that I had gone off my nut. She was illiterate and her peasant life in Italy made her believe that only a son of the nobility could possibly be a writer. . . .[42]

There was a tacit agreement that any immigrant's son could become president of the United States—but probably would not.

All of this sheds a new light on the old argument about crime. Crime, according to sociologists, is found among new immigrant groups because it is an open avenue to success in American values—money, power, some status—when other avenues are closed. It is a way of achieving the ends of American life when the acceptable means are not accessible.[43] What this crime argument has ignored is that the acceptable means were almost never accessible to immigrants. Even under the very best circumstances, there were so many constraints surrounding immigrant achievement that legitimate success could never go further than illegitimate success—money, some status, possibly security. Legitimate success had only one advantage, a big one for many immigrants: it was possible, eventually, to rub shoulders with other groups and to escape the watchful eye of tradition. While success might not guarantee assimilation, assimilation was unlikely without some degree of success. Crime, on the other hand, requires the most extreme secrecy and trust. Crime is always a family business. Ironically, strong family ties may prevent criminal activity not through moral teaching, but through the threat of suffocation. The only way to get out is legitimately—through the front door. There is no back way. Only closed-in yards and exits that are family controlled.

Ironically, then, crime was not only a means of upward mobility, it was also a mechanism for the perpetuation of the cultural division of labor. It was insider's work; it relied on trust and familiarity. It was one of three unusual historical circumstances which reinforced New York's strong cultural division of labor, three circumstances which kept ethnic groups localized into specific occupations, partly by drawing off workers who otherwise would have pushed, or would have been pushed, into Yankee mobility. The first circumstance was Prohibition and the growth of organized crime; the second was the Depression and the growth of the Works Progress Administration; the third was a conglomeration of other avenues of endeavor, including the Catholic Church. These alternative economic paths maintained groups' specific skills rather than extended them and so postponed still further the day of direct competition.

KEEPING OLD SKILLS

Just as one wave of immigrants followed another onto American shores, one wave followed the next into American crime.[44] Irish hoodlums organized into gangs, followed by Jewish hoodlums, followed by Italian. Crime as an avenue of success was the monopoly of no group. As each group achieved more legitimate money and power, though, it left off the more high-risk, low-status criminal work; at a certain point crime became such a threat to the whole group that they dropped it altogether or pushed out the criminals among them. Then there are the Italians. Sometimes crime was the only avenue open; sometimes Sicilians were denied jobs because people believed they were involved in criminal activities.[45] In either case, for one reason or another, New Yorkers got the idea that Italians had a monopoly on crime.[46] Everyone seemed to politely believe in the cultural division of labor. But how did Italian crime really fit into the cultural division of labor?

At the beginning of the century Italian crime in America looked very much like any petty crime anywhere. Most of the victims were also Italian, it was very local, and crimes were largely committed by street thugs who were bitter, frustrated, and saw a chance for quick gain. Some say Italian immigrants brought with them the suspicions of villagers and peasants who hated and feared outsiders and law officers. Of course, other groups brought with them similar feelings. Italians did bring with them memories of a violent country where protection was often necessary. In the old country protection often meant extortion, but that was a *modus operandi*, not a special group.

In other words, the methods were imported and so were a few criminals, but otherwise it looked like the crime of other immigrant groups. More Italians were not proven guilty of crime—but more Italians were arrested.[47] The bulk of Italian immigration consisted of young, single men, more than the numbers in other groups. Behind the arrest statistics Italians were no more nor less criminal than any other group.

In fact, after the First World War, Italian crime steadily declined. Enough people were earning enough money to move away from crowded ghettos. Through the teens and twenties Italian-Americans fanned out into Queens and Nassau County on Long Island, buying suburban property. Tightening immigration laws also reduced the ghetto populations, so that by around 1920 there were fewer Italian petty criminals and fewer potential victims. If history were even and uneventful, an odd thought, we could imagine a steady, slow increase in wealth and eventual assimilation. That did not happen. Instead, New York's uniquely strong cultural division of labor was perpetuated. One mechanism for its perpetuation was Prohibition and organized crime.

Just at the historical moment when Italian gangsters were ready to pass on the torch, so to speak, to the next criminal group, the Volstead Act of October 28, 1919, made liquor illegal, rendering illegality very close to America's heart. Before that, Italian crime was petty crime. After the law was enacted, young gang members set about filling America's demand for liquor, which was enormous.[48]

Once they became involved with crime on the large scale made possible by Prohibition, these new criminals could reach extraordinary heights of wealth and power. Instead of leading them deeper into American life, though, the Mafia, or Cosa Nostra, kept them strapped to their ethnic roots. First, the larger the organization, the greater the necessity for loyalty and secrecy. So while Italian-Americans not involved in these organizations were slowly assimilating, those on the inside were perpetuating village suspicions of one hundred years before. Mafia leaders who entered the United States from Italy during the 1920s naturally ran Italian-speaking organizations.

This picture describes some of the ambivalence which analysts find so baffling. Italians did not admire crime or criminals. What they wistfully admired was the ability to succeed—that is, be wealthy but still be Italian: talk the old way, live the old way. It is true that crime was an avenue of upward mobility, but it led only straight ahead—one never left the Organization to join something else. The appeal of Mario Puzo's *The Godfather* is not in its pretense of power or the saga of exploitation, but in the sentimental portrait of the old ways coexisting with American wealth and power. This would have been impossible in corporate America.

As for the outside world, organized crime provided a convenience seldom matched. First, it drew off some Italians who otherwise would have looked in other directions. Second, it succeeded in stigmatizing so many other Italians that the direct competition over wealth and power was again cut in half. Almost any public leader could be traced to a childhood friend who took a different route—creating scandal at any moment. Most importantly, it was an imaginary escape hatch in the minds of Italians and others—if an Italian really wanted to get rich, he need only become involved in crime. So while crime might buy third-generation law degrees, as some have suggested, it was not a quick route. It was a slow route. It was a thirty-year detour while New Yorkers grew used to one another.

Another slow road to success traveled via the New Deal. The Depression devastated the entire nation and New York was no exception. Almost 50 percent of all of New York's manufacturing and mechanical workers were on relief in 1934.[49] Even though the modernizing and mechanizing workplace had been loosening its reliance on manual labor, the manufacturing and mechanical workers still represented over one-third of all workers in the 1930s. So this group alone accounted for perhaps one million unemployed workers—in one city alone, not the whole country. Add to this the hefty percentages of unemployment in other occupations and that puts almost one-fifth of all New York workers, and their families, on relief. The danger of the Depression was in part economic; if a nation's work force is allowed to deteriorate through malnutrition, lack of education for the children, and lack of hope, that nation's economy may never recover. There was a very strong political danger, too, though, especially in New York. A country where children starve does not command the loyalty of its people. Socialism had its strongest adherents in this country just at that time when the government seemed to care so little for its people.

Franklin Roosevelt's New Deal was both an economic and a political solution. Employment programs stimulated the economy, but also kept the unemployed busy at public projects instead of political rallies or even riots. The goal of Roosevelt's New Deal was essentially conservative: to conserve skills and resources and to threaten economic and political institutions as little as possible—bread lines without bread riots, hope without anger. With this in mind the Works Progress Administration provided jobs for unemployed New Yorkers following one simple rule: give people jobs they were fitted to do. In other words, all skills would be kept and used.

The WPA helped many, many people and in the process created some of the greatest work New York had known. WPA doctors, nurses, caseworkers, and scientists created the largest preventive medicine program in the country, using local talent. The new Department of Public Health stood as a monument to public concern and public life. The public employment of the thirties and forties gave New York City and the whole nation some of its most dignified public buildings, public artwork, roads, bridges, dams—everything that now stands as the country's public core.

What the WPA did not do was retrain anyone or prepare any workers for the future. Everyone left just as he entered. At the very minimum this simply put a hold on social mobility; no one went anywhere.[50] In a more complex way it reinforced the cultural division of labor. Unskilled black women whose only experience was in cleaning houses were assigned houses to clean; unemployed Irish construction workers were put on construction jobs; and unemployed Jewish bookkeepers were given bookkeeping assignments, all with just even-handedness. The economic world was not as even-handed, however: even before the Depression, blue-collar and domestic work was declining as the white-collar world of clerks and managers grew in size, importance, and pay. By not retraining, by holding the world steady, the WPA was really letting some groups slide backward. Factory hands came out of the Second World War relatively lower on the social scale than when they had entered the Depression. The many southern blacks who had come north in the teens and the twenties remained as unskilled after the WPA as before it.

So far, it just sounds like a simple stranglehold. Bring in another generation, however, and it is industrial quicksand. Anyone whose parents were the first generation in this country and who turned, say, eighteen in 1930 faced a closed economy. There were no jobs. If his (or her) parents owned a store, the only job possible might be in the parents' store. If the family could do without his earnings, the Depression was a good time to nestle in professional school and prepare for better times. If the family did need the earnings, though, he might try to get a WPA job. What skills could he possibly claim? Only the skills he saw or tried alongside his family. So in order to get any job at all, he claimed to do what everyone he knew did. In this way, instead of training the next generation for the future, the WPA trained them for the past. Instead of preparing workers for a white-collar world, the WPA limited the ranks to already existing white-collar workers. That meant Jews, many more of whom entered the country with clerical or bookkeeping skills, benefited from more experience while Italians, who reached white-collar jobs only after one or two generations, were slowed down in their move to higher positions.

The Depression might have increased antagonism between immigrant groups because competition over jobs increased. And yet there were few massacres, no pogroms, and only some gang wars. That was partly thanks to the WPA, which acted to bring the next generation into the cultural division of labor and a world where different groups were believed to have different skills.

Different groups did have different skills where ritual and tradition were concerned. So the final mechanism that kept groups in different jobs between 1900 and 1950 was part of the internal mechanism of adjustment to life in America. All sorts of specialized ritual jobs serve different groups: priest, rabbi, cantor, mortician, herbal specialist, ritual bath cleaner, etc. All of these are needed at the beginning. As American life holds sway, some jobs fall away. The paradox of assimilation, though, is that more jobs are created, not fewer. Daniel Patrick Moynihan commented on this when he said that Catholics in America have consistently become more, not less, religious. The church, he said, diverted Irish-Americans from other more profitable mainstream paths.[51] The old matchmaker may be replaced by a hotel's social director, but the specialized job is not lost and the cultural division of labor remains intact. The ritual jobs divert the attention and energy of talented minority or ethnic members. The harder groups try to be American, the more they need specialized help: counselors to tell them where to attend school, nursing-home directors to take care of their parents, even plastic surgeons, if it comes to that. The cultural division of labor was perpetuated, with or without the second generation's approval, long after their parents brought skills and habits with them from the old country.

Of course, people did compete for jobs. Not all Italians were icemen and not all icemen were Italian. And yet the rough division of groups into different occupations had more than an economic effect. It had a strong psychological effect. The stranger was made recognizable. The stranger was understandable. The stranger was not a parasite, not an animal of prey, but someone who works. The stranger contributes just as you do. See? There he is in his laundry. There he is at his pushcart, in his store, struggling to feed his family.

As long as the stranger has a place, as long as he is recognizable and visible, he can be accepted. In New York there was a fluid kind of cultural adoption among immigrant groups by the 1940s. To paraphrase the New York comedian Lenny Bruce, if you were an iceman, you were Italian, no matter what you were born. A Puerto Rican with Jewish friends from college would be an honorary Jew. Millions of small daily exceptions were possible as long as people believed they understood one another—even if it was only their economic position which they really understood. Years later a New York rye bread advertised with a home-grown slogan: "You don't have to be Jewish to love Levy's." Needless to say, had they expected hostile disagreement, they would never have run the ad. Intermarriage was not always without problems—but it was frequent. And New York became a city not where an elite had access to new ideas and foreign customs, but where the day-to-day life of masses of people depended upon the kindness, or at least the cooperation, of strangers.

The second half of the century has had a different pattern. The Second World War reawakened Old World antagonisms in New York and started the slow, gradual growing consciousness of peoples—Jews after the Holocaust, former colonials after the decay of the old empires, American blacks after the civil rights movement. New groups—blacks and Puerto Ricans—predominated in New York and old groups faded. The suburbs claimed thousands of former GIs, who marched toward new houses, mortgage in hand. Housing shortages were so extreme that in 1963 New York City released its civil servants from the obligation to live within the city limits. Robert Moses, master builder, remade the face of New York and Long Island. The city went from metropolis to megalopolis.

The third generation, the baby-boom generation, has benefited from the enormous opportunity their grandparents and parents found. Yet as the cultural division of labor grows less powerful, competition is stiffer and more visible. Is it really harder now to become president of the United States? Yes. Once it was impossible. Near-impossible is always harder than impossible. Are class, status, and power more evenly divided now that education and style have made the immigrants' grandchildren resemble more closely those other immigrants who came before? Is opportunity the same—for schooling, for jobs, for honor? If you do not believe it, the glitter tarnishes. If you do not believe it, the streets lose their golden paving.

THE ITALIANS

It is possible to overstate the old country. It is possible to forget that traits for which Italian-Americans are best known have little to do with life in Italy before immigration. So many Italians emigrated to the United States that now the old country is more likely to mean Little Italy in New York or the North End in Boston. During the peak years of immigration in the early part of this century, more Italians entered the United States than members of any other group. The "urban villagers" who settled in America's cities, the old widows in black and the local big shots, seem to be the oldest representatives of an earlier age.[52] There was a time and a place before that, though. And all the most common common knowledge has little to do with that former life.

Americans associate Italian culture with food. Big, long happy meals cooked by ample, able mamas and grandmas—pizza, spaghetti, and sausage: this is Italian. Italians grow vegetables; everywhere they live there are gardens. Even Italian-Americans have come to believe these to be ancestral cultural traits. They have no roots on the other side, though. Most Italians in the late 1800s barely had enough to eat. For over two hundred years workers in the south of Italy and in Sicily lived on a diet roughly half of what an ordinary worker would require.[53] Meat was too expensive for a laborer who earned about $3.50 a week. Taxes were so high, crops so poor, natural conditions so hostile, that any food at all was a luxury. Even in the relatively well-off North, pellagra, a disease of vitamin deficiency, was a fact of life.

As for vegetable gardens, they were neither a hobby nor an income in the old country, nor did they represent a life of farming. Over 80 percent of Italians depended on agriculture, that is true, but they worked at infertile, tired grainfields or disease-ridden vineyards. A tomato or pepper coaxed from a vine was the only alternative to starvation during the difficult years between 1870 and 1900, when Italian agricultural production dropped and could not compete in the international market. It was neither pleasure nor industry that grew vegetables, it was hunger. Farming, meaning grain or grapes, was the Old World. Any Italians who took up agriculture in the New World grew only what had been more dependable—fruit or vegetables. When Italians turned to gardening in America, it was an urban adaptation. It was part of the new luxurious life which afforded them meat, a varied diet, free time, money for tools, a little fertile land—the realization of a dream, not the re-creation of any tradition.

And the cooks, the loving extended family, the warm communal life? "Extended family closeness and supportiveness, an ideal much admired and desired in the Italian South, was seldom attained because of the harsh economic and social conditions."[54] One-room hovels were home to whole families in Italy; there were no windows, no chimneys, and most of the room was taken up by one bed in which the whole family slept. Beneath the bed animals slept; above were babies hung in baskets, "so the room was divided into three layers: animals on the floor, people on the bed, and infants in the air."[55] There was no privacy; without privacy there can be little intimacy. There was competition over work, over land, in short, over the future. Even though a Sicilian proverb counseled, "The real relatives are those inside the house," inside the house there was often conflict. Beyond the house was suspicion, envy, and jealousy.

The warm, supportive urban village, like Little Italy in New York, which inspires nostalgia among later generations, had no village model in Italy. Group cooperation was not possible, since there was no group with which to cooperate. Italy had been divided for centuries into estates which were prizes of conquest, cities which were independent prince-doms, regions which were governed by foreign powers. The landlords, the princes, the foreign aristocrats took from the land whatever wealth they could and created few lasting bonds with land or people. If in their search for wealth they needed local agents or even thugs to strong-arm troublesome tenants, so be it. Local agents could seek favors with land-owners. Peasants with a scrap of land could seek favors with strong-arm men to protect them. Everyone could seek favors from the church. And where there is no money, no goods, no food, and a hostile, disorganized environment, there are always favors. Loving villagers? An American immigrant, visiting the Italian village of his birth, described it this way:

> It is dirty; you must always hide something or from someone; everyone lies about everything: wealth, eating, friendship, love, God. You are always under the eyes of someone who scrutinizes you, judges you, envies you, spies on you, throws curses against you, but smiles his ugly, toothless mouth out whenever he sees you.[56]

Catholicism, force that it was, inspired ambivalence in the Italy left by the immigrants. Priests were often privileged and seldom succeeded, if they even cared, in promoting the confidence of peasants. Landowner priests of the smallest holdings lorded over their inferiors. The church was one of very few avenues of mobility and even within the church a peasant's son had little opportunity. Suspicion and superstition were powerful rivals to religion. Immigrants became more religious, not less.

Even Italy itself as it lives in the imagination of modern Americans was a product of Italian-American rather than Italian experience. The land of sunny, ripe vineyards, urban factories, and minor military power did not exist before American immigrants sent money back to Italy, infusing it with much-needed capital. By the outbreak of World War I $750 million had been sent to Italy by workers in the United States.[57]

So what was the old Italy like? What did it have if everything Italian-American turns out to be more American than Italian? Which traditions survived? What could a peasant do in Italy to improve his lot in life and have hope of a life better than his father's? He could leave.

Migratory work was an established pattern in impoverished Italy. Men left for months at a time to follow agricultural and fishing seasons. As they did in dozens of countries where industry was supplanting agriculture, men went to the cities following the hope of work. Such a move was not unusual and was the least degrading of all leave-taking, which was itself an admission of failure. The cities of southern Italy, though, were almost as depressed as the countryside. The southern region, or the Mezzogiorno, lost as the North gained after the unification in 1870. Foreign domination had finally been overthrown and an all-Italian parliament convened, but it was led by the North and shaped by the middle class. Workers in southern cities fell further into poverty and frustration while new national tariffs favored northern industry. Nothing was put back into the South. A visitor to sulphur-mining operations in Sicily in 1904 saw only hand tools in use. Booker T. Washington, comparing recently freed slaves in American cities and the lowest class in southern Italian cities, believed the southern Italians to be more steeped in "dirt, degradation and ignorance."[58] The farther the migration, the more likely any chance of success.

Many Italians had migrated to South America, mostly Brazil and Argentina. As Brazil's and Argentina's economic positions declined, though, the fate of Italian workers was imperiled. Opportunities for work turned into work without pay and without escape. The Italian government tried to discourage emigration to Brazil, "a land of slaves and not of free and civilized men."[59] Disease and hardship were growing in South America. The Italian government put a temporary ban on migration to Brazil after an epidemic killed nine thousand immigrants. After 1895 the United States attracted most Italian emigrants. Between 1900 and 1914 over 3 million Italians traveled to the United States.

The move was economic from start to finish. Opportunity attracted the majority of emigrants, who were young workingmen. Many of these "birds of passage" expected to save up some money and return home; about half did return home. It was not democracy which drew them, no more than it drew them to Brazil or Argentina. And yet it was democracy which convinced them to stay. One immigrant recalled:

> I came to this country to make a fortune and return to settle in the old country. But I changed my mind when I saw that the great thing about this country is that it is good for the working man. . . . Here I can go out to eat in a restaurant and sit next to anyone I want. . . .[60]

After all, there is no difference between political and economic refugees. Poverty is not only physical violence, it is also psychological degradation.

Governments were active in the flow of workers to America. The development of steamships made the journey from Italy to the United States possible in one week. Governments eager to develop naval advances were equally eager to support the growth of steamship companies. But steamships need something to ship. Steamship agents and padroni, or leaders of work groups, went through the Italian countryside recruiting workers. The Italian government eagerly made treaties to ease the way for Italian workers to send money home. The postal agreement which allowed direct-mail money orders between the United States and Italy was de facto recognition that Italy stood to gain.

Tales about America as well as American money convinced Italians of possible success. Soon no recruiters were necessary. Men returned with full pockets. The Endicott Johnson shoe company was willing to send recruiters even when it broke American law, the Foran Anti–Contract Labor Law at the beginning of the century, a law designed to stop the entry of cheap labor. Then the company changed to an equally, if not more, effective system of labor recruitment—they told their immigrant workers that more work was available. Men with knowledge of America became common in Italy. Men with experience of America were admired; men with plans for America had prospects. Desirable single girls were eager to marry the men who returned for brides. An upper-class woman could even marry beneath her, lured by the promise of America. The stories were true. There were jobs in America.

Where they went in America was determined almost wholly by hopes for opportunity. Not only did they not settle in grain-growing regions, the Italian immigrants did not seek out Catholic regions, in particular, nor regions with the warm, sunny climate familiar to many of them. Instead, there was a direct relationship between the place where the money orders originated and the American destination of the villagers. If one village received most money from emigrants in Cleveland, others in that village packed for Cleveland. About 80 percent of all Italian immigrants settled in cities; that is where the jobs and money were. In 1900 New York had an Italian population of 145,433. By 1919 New York City was next to Naples the largest Italian city in the world.[61]

Life in the New York tenements was difficult. So was life on the work gangs led by padroni in and around New York. Both were squalid, crowded, and dangerous. Tuberculosis claimed the lives of thousands of Italian immigrants. Mortality was high for other reasons as well: dangerous physical labor, apartment buildings without safety features, and inadequate health care. People accustomed to bright sun never saw the light of day.

Yet New York represented an improvement even for the very first generation that arrived. There was food. There was work. Life was already better than it had been for their fathers. Moreover, there was social status and respect. The tenements not only had water on the premises and other amenities unknown in rural Italy; they represented a social world more inviting and challenging than the immigrants had ever seen. One could choose to live near people one liked. One could move away. One could become popular among a local group or gain in prestige by doing well, all without hurting another family member. Leisure time was possible. Within one generation families moved from pick-and-shovel work to factory work. People quickly moved away from the overcrowded, poorer neighborhoods on the Lower East Side to the Bronx, Brooklyn, and beyond. In 1905 statistician Eliot Lord wrote, "The thrift of the [New York] Italian is so exceptional that even boot-blacks and common laborers sometimes save enough to figure as tene-ment landlords."[62] The real-estate holdings of Italians in New York in 1905 were valued at $20 million. So there was opportunity.

MEN

Italian men came to the United States first and they came for work. Most were unskilled. In fact, the Italian men arriving in the United States were relatively more unskilled than other immigrant groups. In 1907 immigration from Italy accounted for one-quarter of all immigra-tion, yet Italian plumbers counted for only 1 in 150 arriving plumbers, 1 in 74 locksmiths, 1 in 26 plasterers.[63] Rather, skilled workers were stonecutters, masons, and shoemakers. Most, however, were unskilled. What opportunity greeted the unskilled men an observer noted:

> . . . the bootblacks, humblest of all, have not . . . plied their trade in Italy. But they found it open to them here (or occupied mainly by negroes) and they brought to it a pride in neat work which is in some sense a national attribute. In goodly numbers they entered the trade very early, at the time in fact when the street musicians, with their . . . monkeys, and ragpickers, were still the conspicuous types . . . in those quarters of New York where the foreign popula-tion dwelt. 473 out of the 474 foreign bootblacks . . . were Italians.[64]

By 1900 more arriving immigrants went into construction labor and more Italians already here were moving up to factory jobs from their street perches as bootblacks or ragpickers. Blue-collar work, even service work like barbering, increased, and yet in 1905 about half of all Italian household heads were doing unskilled, heavy labor, mainly construction work.

It was true that most workers coming were unskilled. Yet Italian men were also being systematically told that only unskilled, heavy labor was available. The padrone was a powerful figure. He had jobs to distribute when immigrants all sought jobs. Yet he was not the only one telling immigrants that the pick and shovel were the tools for success. The American press, voicing the concerns of American officials, warned that professionals or intellectuals should not come to America. Marion Gurney, a member of a prestigious New York commission, warned educated Italians that their skills were not wanted. She said that

> an accountant was cleaning hats in a shop on Houston Street; an actor and professor were compelled to wash dishes in a restaurant; an interior decorator was "wearing out his strength handling beer barrels," in a saloon; and his unfortunate brother, a former teacher, was a bartender. . . .[65]

A New York housing inspector also commented that there was no place for the educated Italian—he ended up a common laborer or simply on relief. Magazine articles warned that Italian doctors, teachers, and lawyers should not come.[66]

The effect of these stories, both the true and imagined, had to be to reinforce the original immigrant's idea that a professional goal was not particularly desirable.

> Peasant life in the Mezzogiorno had trained Italians to trim their aspirations to the prevailing winds. They did not think in terms of careers or professional life. Work was something one did in order to earn money. Life was not so much fulfilled by work as it was filled with its drudgery. The attitude was often passed on to children, even in New York's freer atmosphere.[67]

"New York's freer atmosphere" was not very free for Italian professionals. The professional, after all, did not succeed particularly well in America. Either the newspapers were exaggerating and it was just a discriminatory bent that made them tell Italian intellectuals they were unwanted—or it was true, Italian professionals did not do well in America. In either case, this had two results. The Italian community on the whole lost, since professionals did not bring their capital and skills. In the mind of the individual worker, however, America was all the better for it. What made America seem so free and full of opportunity was precisely this turnaround—he who was first at home was, the same as everyone else, last in America.

So a limit to opportunity—in this case a limit on the kinds of work open to Italians—actually created a feeling of justice, freedom, and belonging. This is the irony, the contradiction, if you will, that later forces a wedge into the cosmopolitan culture. How can a city be both fair and unfair, fair in its unfairness? How long can it last?

It can last as long as the belief that all workers have a chance and that America is a workingman's country can last, in the case of Italian men. And that can last as long as the cultural division of labor can keep Italians in the role of the wealthy workingman.

In New York, Italians successfully moved up from unskilled to skilled labor, but moved much more slowly to professional positions. Certainly, this is in part due to a wary ambivalence toward education and worry over subsistence. Yet it is also related to the egalitarian ethos which the immigrants associated with America—in the old country only the aristocracy was educated; in America, the land where the worker is rewarded, aristocracy is unnecessary. Why ape the aristocracy in a land where everyone can contribute? Italian-Americans became part of New York's cosmopolitan culture in this way—they believed that everyone could contribute. Since their focus was narrow—down to people from the same village or even family—this meant that everyone in the family had a future.

Once the cultural division of labor was set into place, sons followed fathers. Sons followed fathers into the family business, or established their own shops. Sons followed fathers into "male" crafts, like stonecutting or masonry. Then the mechanisms of mid-century appeared and the Depression took over. But skills and family attachments were preserved, not changed. Italians were especially touched by unemployment, since they were heavily concentrated in blue-collar jobs. Small businesses remained small, especially since profits were often used to buy buildings which could provide rental income. Better-educated sons sometimes left behind the small businesses in order to enter the professional paths open to them—independent practice or government work.

By the 1940s Italian-Americans had achieved national prominence as sports stars, singers, labor leaders, and business magnates, but the traditional cultural division of labor still held sway. Perhaps, as Nathan Glazer suggests, the power of the family made individual achievement difficult.[68] Yet in some fields it was difficult, in others impossible. Italian-Americans were not integrated into corporate management; they were barely represented on Wall Street; there were few in academia and few in politics. Individual reasons can be suggested for each endeavor: authority difficulties hinder hierarchical climbing; lack of intellectual tradition rules out academics; lack of wealth makes political power unlikely, etc., etc. Yet the simplest reason is the strongest: the second, even the third, generation did not have opportunities except those passed down from the immigrant generations—plus or minus a handful of exceptions. Italians in New York did accumulate wealth. But the move from wealthy contractor to investment analyst was not made between 1900 and 1950. Those were the years of the workingman.

WOMEN

And the working woman. Although Italian women were not among the first Italian immigrants, by the 1930s they represented the majority of new Italian immigrants. More Italian women worked than did women of any other group, since more continued to work after they were married. Fewer Italian women were engaged in prostitution than were women of any other group. They were uniquely tied to New York's light industry, especially the needle trades, especially the artificial flower business. One girl explained, "Everybody else I know worked in it. It is the Italian's trade, and then I thought that when I get married I can still keep up at home."[69] The Italian immigrant woman's life centered on home, no matter what the work. Her whereabouts were closely watched. Her father, brothers, or a potential husband might have brought her over with the express purpose of keeping house while they saved enough money to return. So while New York afforded women opportunities for both income and self-expression which they never had back home, those opportunities were carefully limited within the family and broadly limited outside it.

Marriage was not only traditional and necessary, if one were to be accepted, it was also the avenue of opportunity open to women—the only one in southern Italy and Sicily, the most important one in immigrant America. Many, many unhappy marriages were the result of the traditional economic ties that bound husband and wife—no prisoner could ever be grateful enough for her upkeep and no warder could ever work hard enough to fulfill the promise he made to support her. Moreover, husbands and wives did not know each other well, some were courted from abroad, and family opinion weighed heavily in any decision. Some traditional marriages were happy. Many, though, could at best be called stable or successful. In America, Italian women were not encouraged to learn English or go to school and so represented "the other side" to their husbands; they were the stable domestic life, the old language, the old ways.

They also represented increased economic opportunity. Their take-home work increased the family fortunes. Often the increased fortunes were used to educate sons. Self-realization, self-expression, any self at all was ruled out for the first- and second-generation Italian-American. At home she was discouraged from schooling and her aspirations were kept low. The few Italian women who aspired to teach said their subject would be sewing—traditional women's work. It was not the family alone, however, which reinforced this division of labor. Philanthropists who wanted to raise the skills of Italian workers opened the School of Italian Industries on MacDougal Street in Greenwich Village. They did not teach typing, nor any skill of the industrial future. Italians, they believed, belonged to the past and Italian women to the distant past.

The philanthropists themselves were wealthy American women who got the idea for the school while touring Italy in 1904. They "lamented" that the ability to make lace "should be lost upon box factories and sweatshops."[70] In other words, they assumed talents or skills were culturally inherited. Never mind that the only reason Italian women were in the needle trades was that it was an industry that involved light work at low wages. Never mind that Sicilian peasants did not own sewing machines. It was the goal of these American reformers to take Italians back to "Italian" work. They took on an embroidery teacher from Rome and opened the school in New York. Magazine articles praised the school for its phenomenal success, especially in "recognizing the Italians' ability to produce fine handicrafts."[71] Interestingly, the magazine writers spoke consciously of reviving the past and of the "antique" quality of the lace. One writer said that they "took advantage of the traditional deftness of the Italian women in the art of the needle in order to reproduce in America the Italian interpretation of that ancient feminine handicraft."[72]

The effect of this and other efforts to educate Italians in "their own" work was to create highly skilled women workers able to earn more money than their parents—even than their brothers—but unable to leave a very specific industry. The second, even third generation moved up, but not over. Skilled work was more lucrative, but it was still the needle trades.

As for the reformers, they had that qualified tolerance which makes cosmopolitan culture tenuous. They were not arguing that Italians should not immigrate, far from it. They were saying, If only those workers could provide for us this beautiful piece of Italy, then their presence here would be worth it. And after? When the lace is made one hundred times over and two generations of children graduate from college? The reformers did not want citizens; they wanted lacemakers.

Two positions of respect and power for Italian women blossomed in the United States—those were piety and widowhood. Both were paths of default when men left the field. Both are also intensely absorbing, whole worlds of endeavor which can distract women from trying something different. In their own way, they, too, kept alive a cultural division of labor in which Italian women had a simple, recognized place.

The ideals of the Catholic Church speak to the meek and powerless. For centuries women were Europe's meek and powerless and the church's strongest adherents, by force and by choice. In a world of bitter hardship and competiton, even the church was suspect. Yet in America, where there was more latitude and so much was uncertain, the church became a woman's ally in the struggle for status. Priests had enormous power and respect and their words could support a wife against her husband's opinion. The church and church functions were a justified reason to go out socially. But it was America, especially, which made piety possible. The missing aristocracy could not set standards for church dress and behavior—every woman who went to church in America was respectable. Husbands objected less and less as they saw that in America affiliation with an organization carried status. Their own affiliations may have been weak, finding work in independent shops or independent professional practices, but their wives' church activities could give them respectability. Thus American Catholics have become more, not less, religious, following that paradox of assimilation: the more you want to resemble the others, the more you must dig into your own past. Since Americans are organization people, you must find an organization. Americans are religious, so you must be as well. Your drive to be similar makes you more different.

Church and widowhood go hand in hand. The widow finds herself free and devotes time to the church. Many widows found this was the first time in their lives they were not under the constant direction of fathers, brothers, or husbands. If Italian widows are slow to give up the black clothes of perpetual mourning, it is because widowhood has its rewards in respect and newfound freedom. Many women found widowhood a sociable time of fulfilling friendships.[73] That which other women experienced in their youth, teen-age friendships with other women, was not possible for the immigrant generation and seldom for their daughters, who were kept close to the family and who married young. Unlike in Sicily, where it was best not to get too close to distant relatives, in America grandmothers and old aunts could form a cabal of opinions and judgments. America kept alive old ways by keeping alive old people. Since many immigrant men married women much younger than themselves, and since early marriages speeded up the time between generations, in 1950 a family's youngest member could be immediately influenced by his great-grandmother's opinion. She, in turn, could be simply elaborating upon her late husband's ideas—which he formed in Italy before the time of Garibaldi. Of course, a child might not listen.

CHILDREN

If Italian men and women lived out Emma Lazarus' ode to refuge, many fewer of their children lived out Horatio Alger's lyric to opportunity. Italian-American children were considered the scourge of the public schools, undisciplined, dangerous, and untalented. The schools, for their part, sought to make them American through simple indoctrination. As late as the 1940s and 1950s Vincent Panella, the son and grandson of immigrants, recalls, he was failing the public school "breakfast test": each student had to report what he ate for breakfast to ensure that it conformed to American standards—cereal, juice, toast, and an egg.[74] Forced Americanization went as far as attempts to convert immigrants to Protestantism.[75] Not as extreme were the private philanthropic attempts to teach English and prepare immigrants for naturalization carried out by the YMCA, the Italian-American Civic League of New York, and others.

There were some voices of opposition. Jane Robbins, a writer for *The Outlook* in 1906, warned against rushing Italian children into the "streetiness" and "cheap Americanism" which "so overwhelmed Italian youngsters in the cities."[76] Leonard Covello, the Italian educator who was principal of Benjamin Franklin High School in East Harlem between 1934 and 1957, introduced Italian in the New York schools. He feared the Italian heritage was being lost. He wrote, from his own experience in the New York public schools, "We were becoming Americans by learning how to be ashamed of our parents."[77] Yet the opposition voices were a dissonance in their age. It was an age when people believed they could successfully become American.

The 1930s and 1940s in New York were as amazing and confusing as they were everywhere else. The mass media made their full-scale appearance in movie houses. Clark Gable and Leslie Howard played out a rivalry both romantic and absurd to their immigrant audiences. These children barely left the borders of the city, let alone saw the Old South. Yet it was all there on the screen, American history, American wealth, world news. By the 1940s the old Italian theater, the puppet theater, even local interest in opera had given way to the big movie houses. All of the heroes and all of the excitement was in English. English was a thrill as well as a necessity for jobs and business. Even the old people tried an Italian-English pidgin, seeing the need. The old language, the old accents were an embarrassment to young people who wanted to be American. The old politics was also an embarrassment. There, right on the screen, where everyone could see, in every newsreel, was Mussolini, the fascist. At the same time, opinion in the home was divided and there was strong support for Mussolini. The second generation held tight to American nationalism; many grew politically conservative in order to be "more American than the Americans, more nationalist than the Mayflower descendants."[78]

Another old-fashioned embarrassment was their parents' suspicion and prejudice. By the 1930s and 1940s separate village-communities, reproduced from the southern Italian countryside, were no longer isolated. They shared churches and communicated in a rough Italian that the speaker of any dialect could understand. The children, though, wanted to be American, not just understood by another Italian. While the Old South was the America of the screen, the America close to home resembled Emma Lazarus' image, not Margaret Mitchell's. The more their parents expressed fear or suspicion over other groups, the more the second generation would embrace them, or at least try to, or at least say they did. Americans were not suspicious villagers, right? Of course, any old customs were laughable, because the movies laughed at them. But if everyone tried, then it was all right. I'll be Barbara Stanwyck and you'll be Fred MacMurray. Believe it and it's a deal; it won't matter what my parents are like and it won't matter what your parents are like. We're all from somewhere, right? We'll meet in a drugstore and go to a movie (neutral ground) and it will be all right.

Other groups were understandable because they had their jobs. They were interesting because they were different. Italians, who experienced the most unemployment during the Depression, showed the least conflict with other groups.[79] Since they were more concentrated in unskilled and skilled blue-collar work, they did not feel the direct competition of an increasingly white-collar world. Even the second generation was concentrated in blue-collar work. Even the third and fourth generations feel the effects. Father Andrew M. Greeley uncovered an odd result in his surveys stretching from 1963 to 1974: America's treatment of the Italians has been ambivalent. "Their educational and financial mobility is the highest in the country, but occupationally their mobility is less than average."[80] In other words, our Italian Horatio Alger hero begins as a helper on a moving van. He works hard, studies, and achieves that neat, American appearance so important to success by modeling himself after Cary Grant. Uncle Sam rewards him with a strong economy and finally bequeaths him a moving business. He is wealthy and wise, but still caught in an old cultural division of labor. How else explain high education, high income, and low-status work? His son goes to Fordham Law School or Georgetown or even Harvard, or to medical school. His earning power is high, but he is trapped by old predispositions, prejudices. He can achieve wealth, but not power. And then, in direct competition with the sons and daughters of the Yankee establishment as well as the sons and daughters of other immigrants, the world looks very different. The world tolerated differentness because everyone believed it would bring them ice or make them lace, because they believed every group had its own work. Eventually, the cosmopolitan outlook fades when opportunity bears its fruit.

VII

The Harlem
Renaissance:
A Dream Deferred

*T*he more I thought of it, the better I liked the idea myself. I had an overwhelming desire to see Harlem. More than Paris, or the Shakespeare country, or Berlin, or the Alps, I wanted to see Harlem, the greatest Negro city in the world. "Shuffle Along" had just burst into being, and I wanted to hear Florence Mills sing. So I told my father I'd rather go to Columbia [University] than to Switzerland.

—Langston Hughes[1]

In the teens of this century, when the poet Langston Hughes dreamed of Harlem, that was not the beginning of black New York. There had been blacks in New York since the Dutch settled there in the 1600s. And Langston Hughes was not a grandson of slaves, was not from the Delta or the Carolinas. He traveled everywhere, grew up in Cleveland, and came to New York from Mexico, where he had been living with his father, a man who had left America for its lack of opportunity. And yet Harlem was new in the teens, there was something new about it, and Hughes came to Harlem in the middle of a massive migration, especially from the rural South. Harlem, called Mecca, called Metropolis, called magnet, was another setting for the cosmopolitan dream.

COSMOPOLITAN HARLEM

Wallace Thurman, a journalist and critic and one of the most piercing observers of the Harlem scene, explained its attractions:

There is no Negro settlement anywhere comparable to Harlem, just as there is no other metropolis comparable to New York. As the great South Side black belt of Chicago spreads and smells with the same industrial clumsiness and stockyardish vigor of Chicago, so does the black belt of New York teem and rhyme with the cosmopolitan cross currents of the world's greatest city.[2]

There were other magnets and other cities swelled with newcomers, black and white, at the beginning of this century. Depressions at the end of the last century forced small farmers into bankruptcy. At the same time, improved technology made old farming practices obsolete. These developments affected all farmers, but repressive Jim Crow laws in the South made the lives of black southerners even more miserable. All the while industry in the North and Midwest promised a better life. When World War I and its war industries made the demand for labor boom, northern companies sent notices to the South; some even sent trains. The Mississipi Delta generally sent its sons and daughters to Chicago, and the South Atlantic states generally sent theirs to New York. Many stopped in cities along the way, but few went further.

Some cities in the Midwest mirrored the social conditions of the Delta: one or a few industries employed most of the blacks, who lived, for the most part, apart from the whites. In addition, an elite originally from Louisiana, half-whites or part-Indians, existed, who were proud and educated, but not worldly. So even Chicago, great black cultural center, was not called Black Metropolis.

Philadelphia and Washington had long traditions of a black presence. Yet they were not cosmopolitan. One controversial interpretation asserts that the longer the tradition, the more closed and snobbish the community. The "black bourgeoisie," this argument claims, those with long histories and light skins, sought to recreate the slave-world hierarchy, including the plantation owners' interest in scholarship and disdain for industry.[3] Black communities tended to have strong hierarchies and status distinctions. Washington and Philadelphia were refined and distinguished, but scorned outsiders. When Langston Hughes, a man who by chance already had been in several countries and spoke several languages, visited Washington, he said the black community there constituted as snobbish a group as he had ever met.[4]

Harlem in New York not only drew in more migrants, but it also promised what other cities did not: public life and a hope of mobility.

By 1930 New York City was home to more blacks than Birmingham, Memphis, and St. Louis combined. The black population of New York increased by 66 percent between 1910 and 1920; and in the next decade it expanded 115 percent. This was virtually all due to migration. In 1930 less than one-quarter of New York City's blacks had been born in New York State. Most newcomers were from Virginia and the Carolinas, but the Deep South was also represented. Over thirty-three hundred people came to New York through Washington, D.C., in 1930. And New York meant Harlem. In 1930 almost three-quarters of Manhattan's blacks lived in Harlem. Negroes everywhere saw Harlem as the Promised Land, the home of liberty.[5]

Everywhere included many foreign lands; in 1930 almost fifty-five thousand foreign-born blacks lived in New York. Ten times as many foreign-born blacks lived in New York as in any other American city. Haitians, Jamaicans, Trinidadians, families from Barbados, the Bahamas, the Virgin Islands; almost one-quarter of Harlem's blacks were foreign-born. Widely varying customs sometimes caused conflict, but different attitudes and experiences, particularly in business, expanded Harlem's horizons. Many foreigners came from countries where racial discrimination was not as familiar as class discrimination, and they refused to accept American racial slurs and degradation. They gave to Harlem an increased political awareness.

Diversity and the importance of newcomers created in New York's black population an excitement and awareness not present in other cities. Yet as in other cosmopolitan cities, diversity came before tolerance. New York had had its share of antiblack riots and massacres, including repression following a bitter slave revolt and draft riots during the Civil War. What is more, blacks for years had been barred from living in most Manhattan neighborhoods and had faced serious crowding due to this housing discrimination.

Black New York moved north along Manhattan Island, starting from the southern tip, where most blacks were living when slavery was abolished in New York in 1827. As New York City expanded, the black population moved or was pushed northward. By the 1890s most blacks lived on the West Side between the Twenties and the Sixties. "Almost all the blacks in Manhattan were herded together in squalid tenements on the West Side."[6] Whites would not rent or sell to blacks, and that included Harlem. But as new white immigrant populations moved into the lowest-rent tenements, blacks looked for better housing. On the West Side blacks were systematically charged higher rents for the worst buildings. *Harper's Weekly* ran a story on this abuse in 1900.

> Property is not rented to negroes in New York until white people will no longer have it. Then rents are put up from thirty to fifty per cent, and negroes are permitted to take a street or sometimes a neighborhood. There are really not many negro sections, and all that exist are fearfully crowded.[7]

But the growing population of the city started moving uptown and they pushed the blacks farther uptown.

Harlem, or the Manhattan streets between 110th and 158th streets and between the East River and Morningside Drive, was a distant outpost at this time. The part around Lenox Avenue had been only partly built up and it was inaccessible. The announcement in 1900, however, of a subway tunnel to be built up Lenox Avenue started wild speculation and a rage of construction. By 1904 almost everything was being improved. But the buildings were empty. The speculators had overbid. Their solution was to exploit racial prejudice: by renting high to blacks, they could recoup their losses and drive out whatever white tenants there were in order to reap higher black rents. Black renters valued the chance to live in a nicer and, more importantly, less crowded environment.

Probably the men most influential in creating black Harlem were black realtors, who convinced white landlords to allow blacks to rent their property. Although white landlords stood to gain, even by their own reckoning, they were loath to begin renting to blacks. Black realtors, chief among them Philip A. Payton, Jr., vouched for the reliability of their clients. Philip Payton was a college graduate from Massachusetts when he came to New York in 1899. The only jobs he could get were as a barber, a slot-machine attendant, and a porter. It was his inspiration that blacks needed a black broker in New York. A company he shared, the Afro-American Realty Company, and later his own business, brought more and more blacks into Harlem. In 1914 the St. James Presbyterian Church, a black congregation on West Fifty-first Street, moved to West 137th Street to answer the demands of a slowly growing black population there.

But Harlem was soon as overcrowded as the West Side had been, since few neighborhoods allowed black tenants and virtually all new migrants ended up in Harlem. The crush created high rents, which were accompanied by low wages. Even the most elegant parts once again became "everything neighborhoods," where hoodlums and numbers runners lived amid movie stars and ministers. While in Washington, D.C., the "respectable community" was able to isolate itself, and in other cities social class divided black neighborhoods, all New York's blacks were huddled in the same buildings.[8]

This was undoubtedly difficult for the many working people struggling against their criminal neighbors. And yet the class diversity in Harlem added to New York's unique position as Black Metropolis. College graduates and intellectual innocents wandered directly into the meanest, strangest side of life. Malcolm X, who entered the world of drugs and crime in New York's Harlem, and the fictional main character of Ralph Ellison's *Invisible Man* share this in common—they enter educated, are touched by violence and unhappiness, and become politicized. Harlem gave its intellectuals a whole world. Langston Hughes saw that Harlem was only partly a choice for blacks:

> Harlem was like a great magnet for the Negro intellectual, pulling him from everywhere. Or perhaps the magnet was New York— but once in New York, he had to live in Harlem.[9]

Harlem drew in students, writers, and artists, who came so they could be close to the publishing world or the schools or libraries.

Born in Missouri, schooled in Cleveland and Mexico, Langston Hughes had his heart set specifically on Harlem. Columbia University was the closest school, so he went there. But he spent more time in the lectures, shows, streets, cabarets, and homes of Harlem than he did at Columbia. After a year he quit the school for the city.

The novelist Zora Neale Hurston was born in Eatonville, Florida, studied at Howard University in Washington, D.C., and went to New York in 1925. She won a scholarship to Barnard to study under the famous anthropologist Franz Boas, and while at Barnard she worked for a novelist, Fannie Hurst, and submitted stories to magazines. Her choice of New York seems hardly accidental.

The poet Countee Cullen was a New York product; he began his career as a poet while a student at De Witt Clinton High School. He, too, was dependent on the city's resources—its schools, its publishers and, along with the newcomers, its critics and publicists.

And there were thousands of others whose names are less known or unknown altogether. New York University, City College, and Columbia had black students. Harlem was a world of amateurs, where waiters and porters were poets and artists.

> Since the well advertised "literary renaissance," it is almost a Negro Greenwich Village. . . . Every other person one meets is writing a novel, a poem or a drama. And there is seemingly no end to artists who do oils, pianists who pound out Rachmaninoff's Prelude in C Sharp Minor, and singers, with long faces and rolling eyes, who sing spirituals,[10]

wrote Wallace Thurman, who was born in Salt Lake City—and found his way to Harlem.

Renaissance. New Negro. A change was coming over black America in the early part of this century. It happened fastest and most brilliantly in Harlem, but it was a change destined for everyone. Ralph Ellison's *Invisible Man* describes the plight of modern man generally, but most painfully that of the black man in America. Black men and women were invisible. While changing beds and emptying ashtrays, bussing tables and sweeping floors, black people were ignored. Whites talked and laughed, shouted secrets in front of maids, changed plans in front of porters, as if they could not see or hear or feel. To the white audience blacks had no features, they were minstrels or mammy dolls. Whites projected onto black Americans their own beliefs, their own fears or feelings. And yet for all the pain of being invisible, it was so much better than being singled out and hurt. Invisibility was a defense America created for itself. A lie.

During the early part of this century blacks became visible. With a dose of northern confidence, an addition of Jamaican pride, and a changing sense of history, black men and women started to recognize themselves. The experience of the First World War changed the way many blacks saw America and themselves. They were willing to fight for freedom; where was the freedom at home? A black combat unit was the only American unit to win the French Legion of Honor medal for bravery: blacks were any Americans' equals. It was realizations like this that made black men and women found some of the most enduring political organizations of this century, including the National Association for the Advancement of Colored People and the Urban League. Blacks started historical associations and marketed black dolls. They sought a visible identity.

In 1917 three events in New York City marked a new, visible black presence, and this began the era known as the Harlem Renaissance. First, a Silent Protest Parade took place, a massive rally, peaceful and highly visible, that marked the discouragement of veterans who returned home to find fewer rights than they had fought for in Europe. Secondly, the poetry of Claude McKay first appeared in print. McKay wrote not as an apologist or scribe for black southern dialect, but as a voice celebrating Harlem and singing of confidence. And thirdly, blacks appeared on the Broadway stage in a trilogy by the white playwright Ridgely Torrence. All at once, what blacks thought and said and felt was important. Blacks marched, not as a work force, but as a political force; they spoke, not as an oddity, but as an oracle; and they performed, not as minstrels, but unmasked, cloaked in only their own lives, what one historian has called "that sadly neglected storehouse of dramatic material, the life of the American Negro."[11]

New York became the center of black writing, music, drama, criticism. Young's Book Exchange on West 135th Street was a leading black bookstore in the leading black city. In 1921 the musical revue *Shuffle Along* hit Broadway—not only were all the performers black, but it was written, music and script, by blacks Eubie Blake and Noble Sissle. It was this show that brought the young Langston Hughes to New York. It represented, for him as for many Americans, the new, visible presence, the excitement, the rebirth, of Harlem.

The poetry and fiction, essays, plays, even the songs and dances and paintings of the artistic flowering known as the Harlem Renaissance had two unique themes: what it felt like to be black and, more particularly, what it felt like to be black in Harlem. There had been black art before, even beyond the folk art almost every American already knew in 1900—spirituals, Uncle Remus stories, and work songs. Jupiter Hammon, a slave in New York, had published poetry as early as 1760, and another slave, Phillis Wheatley, published in 1773 the second volume of poems published by a woman in America. Over thirty black poets wrote and published before Paul Laurence Dunbar, the acclaimed poet who died in 1906. Yet Hammon's poems were religious, Wheatley's were classical odes and elegies, and even Dunbar stayed close to white tradition, except his pastoral odes were set in the South and peopled by blacks. The new Harlem poets were not concerned with pathos or humor, particularly, nor any of the other clichés that situated blacks round the cabin door, singing, laughing, and playing banjo. The subject that interested them was the subjective experience of their people, what blacks were thinking, feeling, and what they wanted to hear.[12]

Claude McKay wrote about a lynching. The subject of Countee Cullen's poem "Heritage" was black history and its relevance to modern-day blacks:

> What is Africa to me:
> Copper sun or scarlet sea
> Jungle star or jungle track,
> Strong bronzed men, or regal black
> Women from whose loins I sprang
> When the birds of Eden sang?[13]

Wallace Thurman's novel *The Blacker the Berry*, about distinctions and despair within the black community, took its title from a black, not classical, aphorism: the blacker the berry, the sweeter the juice.

When the new artists did not speak for all blacks, they spoke for Harlem. Harlem itself was a symbol and a topic of undying interest, as can be seen simply in the titles of books from that time. McKay wrote a book of poems called *Harlem Shadows,* as well as the nonfictional *Harlem: Negro Metropolis.* James Weldon Johnson, another author and essayist, wrote about *Black Manhattan.* Wallace Thurman wrote on *Negro Life in New York's Harlem.* Even if the catchy tunes in black musical revues, like Eubie Blake's famous tune "I'm Just Wild About Harry," were not always pointed or poignant, they were often about life in Harlem. Fats Waller's song "This Joint is Jumpin' " advises the listener to check your hat and dance, but not before explaining that Harlem is the scene of the action.

Black life and black Harlem were celebrated with a burst of energy and emotion. Both were captivating. Interpreted in drama by Paul Robeson and Charles Gilpin, sung by Bessie Smith and Ethel Waters and Florence Mills, the emotions of black men and women became visible and audible. As for Harlem itself, it was beautiful with its wide boulevards and promenades, and stone buildings, monuments of belonging. The elite glittered through crowded streets, stars, and debutantes. But it was also horrible, just as America itself was both beautiful and horrible. Claude McKay, originally from Jamaica, wrote ambivalently of "America":

> Although she feeds me bread of bitterness,
> And sinks into my throat her tiger's tooth,
> Stealing my breath of life, I will confess
> I love this cultured hell that tests my youth.[14]

It was difficult to live in Harlem, but it was a thrill. And it was America, the American dream. Claude McKay, even through his ambivalence, recognized Harlem's importance:

> Harlem is more than the Negro capital of the nation. It is the Negro capital of the world. And as New York is the most glorious experiment on earth of different races and divers groups of humanity

struggling and scrambling to live together, so Harlem is the most interesting sample of black humanity marching along with white humanity.[15]

WHITE MONEY: MINGLING

Not only was Harlem more diverse itself than other great black communities; it was more connected to its surrounding white population. As James Weldon Johnson optimistically wrote in 1930:

> These two hundred thousand Negroes have made themselves an integral part of New York citizenry. They have achieved political independence and without fear vote for either Republicans, Democrats, Socialists or Communists. They are represented in the Board of Aldermen by two members.[16]

They were also represented in the State Assembly, the Civil Service Commission, public schools, the police force, hospital staffs of physicians and nurses, and the Hospital Board. True, the blacks went home to Harlem. But Harlem made its presence felt all over New York and it was drawn into the vortex of New York public life.

In fact, it was the white publishing world, white audiences, and a large dose of white interest that made Harlem not just an artists' colony, but a phenomenon. The white playwright Eugene O'Neill's *Emperor Jones* in 1920 and *All God's Chillun Got Wings* in 1924 were the first showcases for the black actors Gilpin and Robeson. Equally important to the Harlem Renaissance was the decisive influence of white editors and publishers. Charles S. Johnson, the black editor of the National Urban League magazine, *Opportunity,* sponsored a dinner in April of 1924 to introduce emerging writers to the most significant black men of letters and to white editors and critics.[17] The black intellectuals W. E. B. Du Bois, James Weldon Johnson, and Alain Locke attended. But so did the editors of the important white magazines of the day, who promptly imported downtown what they saw and heard. Paul U. Kellogg of the *Survey Graphic* was so impressed that he devoted the entire issue of March 1925 to what he called "Harlem—the Mecca of the New Negro." Not only did this provide an outlet for black writers; it increased white fascination with Harlem.

One white writer and literary critic, Carl Van Vechten, was personally responsible for promoting the work of black artists. He talked the editor of *Vanity Fair* into printing some of the first poems by Countee Cullen and Langston Hughes. He encouraged Alfred Knopf to bring out Hughes' first collection of poetry. He wrote prefaces, reviews, articles, and finally novels, all creating a white audience for Harlem. His novel *Nigger Heaven* sold a hundred thousand copies overnight.[18] The title was crude and controversial, but the book itself, about an educated Harlem couple, a librarian and a novelist, was a nuanced and sympathetic picture of middle-class Harlem, a picture which drew whites closer to fascination.

And why not? Van Vechten threw parties where black artists and writers were introduced to their white counterparts. These parties may have been daring, but they were parties, after all, in an age of parties. Playboys of the Roaring Twenties started traveling uptown to see chorus lines of blacks "in their element." Magazines like the *New Yorker* wrote guides to the Harlem clubs with advice like "Go late. Better not to dress." Wallace Thurman acknowledged this in his guide to Harlem:

> Much has been written and said about night life in Harlem. It has become the leitmotif of sophisticated conversation and shop girl intimacies. To call yourself a New Yorker you must have been to Harlem at least once. Every up-to-date person knows Harlem. . . .[19]

And so this search for adventure, this bittersweet cosmopolitanism, brought to Harlem jobs wrapped in ambivalence and payrolls heavy with irony. High-yaller chorus girls entertained white audiences in clubs where blacks were not admitted. The famed Cotton Club created jobs for scores of musicians, dancers, singers, waiters—blacks could do everything except watch. While white money circulated among waiters in Harlem, whites owned all of the dance palaces and restaurants.

Young black artists saw the contradictions and sensed their uneasy position. Zora Neale Hurston coined the ironic term "niggerati" for all the young writers and artists so quickly being wined and dined by white society. At the same time, they went to rent parties, where everyone informed by an invitation or word of mouth came to dance and chip in some small sum, supposedly to help pay the rent. Social scientists have verified that rents were in fact so exorbitant that rent parties as well as boarders were an economic necessity.[20] Yet Langston Hughes had another explanation. He said that blacks had been edged out of their own clubs and that rent parties were the place where blacks could feel at home.[21]

Langston Hughes sensed the ambivalence and sadness of cosmopolitan life. He was famous for the same reasons the Harlem Renaissance was publicized: the white world's budding interest in heterogeneity and its insensitive curiosity. Black poets were poets, that much was sure. But what had made them famous? Was it their talent or their white editors and readers or both? And what about the others, the poets who were still waiters, the elite who thought they were finally entering white society? The dream seemed askew.

What happens to a dream deferred?

Does it dry up
like a raisin in the sun?
Or fester like a sore—
And then run?

Does it stink like rotten meat?
Or crust and sugar over—
like a syrupy sweet?

Maybe it just sags
like a heavy load.
Or does it explode?[22]

BLACK MONEY: MOBILITY

Harlem was home to many wealthy, successful people, including members of the professions and some wise investors. Perhaps most famous of the Harlem fortunes was Madame C. J. Walker's. Typical of the empires of the underdog, she rose on a vertical ladder that turned to neither side. Sarah Breedlove McWilliams Walker began as a laundress, but turned her laundry techniques into techniques for straightening hair. Her special treatment made her a millionaire. Her daughter, A'Lelia Walker, not only was a prominent socialite, but turned a floor of her mansion into a retreat for artists and writers and financed substantial creativity. There was an elite of letters and distinction. Yet the opportunities for fame and fortune were for the most part limited to those that required only a keen wit or a shrewd eye. There were in Harlem, as there are everywhere, two kinds of businessmen: those who specialize in the future, and those dealers in down-home, who specialize in the past. Both are selling dreams.

The black philanthropist Caspar Holstein donated the award money for the most popular, prestigious, and widespread literary contests, the very contests which encouraged and promoted black artists in Harlem. He also informally supported many struggling artists, gave liberally to colleges and charities, was an exalted member of the Elks, a welcomed member of high society, and owner of the Turf Club, one of the most popular black clubs in Harlem. All of this had to do with growth and potential and so did the main source of his wealth: numbers. He was one of the six or so great numbers bankers of black New York.

At that time almost no one considered the game harmful; in fact, it is similar to the state-run lotteries today. Yet, even more than modern lotteries, it distinctly made a business out of people's dreams and hunches. Numbers was played by betting on a three-digit number. The winning three digits came from the Wall Street closing averages. In this way even the poorest New Yorker, betting one penny, felt the thrill of the stock market boom of the 1920s and felt himself one with the richest people in America. Far from feeling a thrill of illegality, it was the thrill of inclusion that players felt.

The illegality of numbers was also part of its success. Since the game was not controlled by the white majority, it was a place where blacks could be employed, and even make millions. It is already a cliché that crime is a path of minority mobility—not a way out of respectable society, but a way into it. Caspar Holstein succeeded at this, at least until white gangsters saw the game as profitable and pushed their way uptown.

The numbers bankers were not the only shrewd businessmen to capitalize on hopes and dreams. Have you heard the word of Father Divine? Or the preaching of the Reverend Doctor Becton? Or the promise of a black kingdom in Africa delivered by Marcus Garvey? These were city men who found their way to leadership and success by selling ideas. Not one was originally from New York. New York, though, transformed these men and their messages. New York drew them in and gave them fame.

The Reverend Becton settled in Harlem in the twenties. He was handsome. He was well-dressed. He was articulate. He hosted the World's Gospel Feast, a message which was sensual and appealing. One witness wrote, "Women, responsive to his agile movements and his well-modulated, persuasive voice, swayed like reeds."[23] Becton's justification was spiritual, but the source of his success was Harlem itself, where the arguments that "God ain't broke," or that "if Jesus were alive, he would dress like me," made sense. It was the age when all evangelists, black and white, saw God as successful and rich. Harlem, where there was a market for hopes and ideas and gossip, was the center of the black world—why not the center of God's kingdom? Becton's preaching was not only inspired and exciting, it was also lucrative. With each "consecrated dime" his mission—and pocketbook—expanded. He would take from the poor no coin larger than a dime, seven for a week. With the money he bought real estate for his church and for himself. His apartment was as exciting and mysterious as he was himself, and the source of as much gossip.

A golden gate led from an immense music and reception room into his private rooms, which he called the Holy Chambers. His white-and-gold bathroom resembled an oriental bazaar with fine cushions.[24]

George W. Becton was kidnapped and killed by two white men. Like many stories of daring skill and success in Harlem, this one was brought to an end by white intervention. The crowds disburse and the ideas return to the thin air whence they came.

Father Divine, or the man who was George Baker in Georgia or Florida or Virginia, wherever his home really was, moved to New York early in this century, where he led a cult of followers who believed him to be God. Claude McKay asked:

> Who is this God of Harlem? He is a near midget of a brown man whose will dictates the ritual of life in scores of New York houses, places named kingdoms, and in hundreds of extensions and connections in city and country throughout several states.[25]

Father Divine's promise of heaven on earth appealed to both blacks and whites. In fact, his first New York "kingdom," in Sayville, Long Island, was hounded, harassed, and eventually closed not on grounds of fraud or fakery, but for the mingling of black and white followers, which the neighbors thought obscene. After Father Divine's dramatic arrest and release (dramatic because the presiding judge was stricken by a heart attack, for which Father Divine, as God, claimed credit), Harlem welcomed him. The odd symbolism and cult behavior, the women called angels, the celibacy demanded of adherents, Divine's claims to be God, all of this has attracted the attention of those who study cults and religion, especially black religion. And the question "Why do men and women believe?" is always fresh on people's lips. Yet there is another side to Father Divine's story, not about black religion, but black economics, about chances for mobility and chances for success.

Father Divine had an economic scheme. Since his believers were meant to experience heaven on earth, it was perfectly consistent that he should offer free food and free shelter to thousands of people. He fed so many poor that he claimed that the New Deal owed him a tremendous debt for keeping thousands off the welfare rolls. Not only did his missions provide free meals for followers, but they cooked for any others willing to pay ten or fifteen cents for a hot meal. The houses, too, were open to nonfollowers willing to pay for board. Father Divine's heaven on earth was a second economy in Harlem, where the religion, if not fully self-supporting, was at least an active business concern. And then there were the contributions of followers, who often made large donations or signed over their estates, beefing up the coffers of the Righteous Government for the Divinites and, at the same time, Father's Divine's private purse. Since most followers had to work outside Divine's mission, the surest way to control their incomes was to declare money worthless and meaningless.[26] When followers turned over their funds, they did not record it, see it, feel it, or regret it. They were sworn to forswear money.

The cynic will ask, Why go to such lengths for wealth and power? Why not simply open restaurants and boarding houses, create a beneficent business empire? Maybe a nobody, especially a black nobody like Father Divine, would have had no chance in the majority business world. And he might not have been able to raise enough capital to get started. Father Divine started as a man of ideas, and nothing more, and traveled as far as New York would let him and made a success of those ideas.

Marcus Garvey's mission was not heaven in America, but redemption in Africa. Garvey lectured, argued, wrote, convinced, and spoke on behalf of black separatism and the migration of American blacks to Africa. Thousands upon thousands listened, agreed, read his newspaper, and contributed to his black shipping line. Garvey had arrived in New York from Jamaica in around 1915. He founded the Universal Negro Improvement Association with a nucleus of intellectuals interested in history, and in 1918 he founded the *Negro World* newspaper. In a few months the newspaper established itself as the leading national black weekly.[27] Garvey was first of all a man selling ideas and Harlem was where ideas could be sold. The fact that the Black Star Line, the all-black shipping line destined to take black America back to its origins, foundered, does not change the fact that he was a powerful leader. His influence—his international influence—was vast. It does not matter whether it was graft, cult of personality, or incompetence that killed the economic concern. Garvey's story is the same as Divine's—a black man could succeed selling ideas, but once he gained real economic power, he was vulnerable.

These idea sellers of Harlem remain controversial figures, subject even now to a variety of interpretations. To some they were frauds, con artists who made a buck by hoodwinking the ordinary citizen. Father Divine and Marcus Garvey both ran afoul of the American courts and some take this as proof enough. To others they were merely misguided, tempted, well-meaning but weak. The writer Claude McKay quotes the scholar James Weldon Johnson on the subject of Marcus Garvey:

> To this man came an opportunity such as comes to few men, and he clutched greedily at the glitter and let the substance slip from his fingers.[28]

But still others see these men as great leaders. Not only did they succeed in moving many people, they were also able to create resources starting with absolutely nothing. Within the avenues open to them, within the constraints of being black in America, they succeeded. Their names will live. Their names will live far longer than those of the professionals and real-estate investors whose dignity did not survive the Depression.

And then there is the past, the dealers in down-home. Some people in Harlem survived and thrived by making the past available in the present. All the women who took in boarders and provided home cooking were on a road to respectability using one resource that everyone had. They eased the move from rural to cosmopolitan. The protagonist in Ralph Ellison's *Invisible Man* benefits from a warm-hearted landlady, but encounters his first sweet memory of home when he buys yams from a street vendor. The yam vendor, selling a food so humble as to be undignified, was selling familiarity and welcome. Pig Foot Mary, as she was called, started a successful business by selling pigs' feet from a dilapidated cart and ended up a wealthy businesswoman.

Why couldn't more black businesses catch on and hold on? Why did success appear to crown drifters and luftmenschen, writers and ministers, leaving no place for so-called pillars of society? Or, to put it in the coldest way, the hardest way: once Harlem was a thriving cosmopolitan center, filled with money, art, and music—what happened? Why do people now think of pimps and not professionals when they think of the black world of New York? Harlem, the ghetto, was made, not born. Why were there so few paths to glory?

Looking at those people who sold the past, we can begin to understand why more black businesses did not thrive: there was a limit to the shared past they could sell. Each group brought to New York its tastes and demands, and more often than not the first roads to success were businesses that catered to that group. Specialized tastes in food demand specialized groceries. Foreign languages demand able-tongued store owners. And so one explanation for the slow growth of black business in Harlem is that black culture was American culture. Any English-speaking store owner could sell there. As soon as cosmopolitanism embarrassed rural tastes, any restaurant could thrive. The most stylish residents of Harlem met in the Bamboo Inn, a club with a Chinese kitchen.

But there are other explanations, which range from the dispassionate to the controversial. First, American blacks, even in as big a center as Harlem, had trouble raising enough money to begin a business. According to one economic historian, traditional loan societies had existed in Africa, but they were forgotten during the three hundred years of American slavery. If American slaves retained few of their economic traditions, Jamaican slaves, on the other hand, supported themselves and traded among themselves. So Jamaicans retained the traditions of cooperative investment which made small business possible. They went to Harlem and opened businesses.[29] New York City during the first half of this century was especially amenable to small businesses; it had the lowest percentage of corporate control in the United States, along with the South Atlantic states.[30] Yet without some way of pooling enough capital to begin—through informal loan arrangements or loan association or lotteries—it was difficult. This is one way of understanding Caspar Holstein and Becton and Divine, even Marcus Garvey. Lacking an established, informal tradition of creating big capital, they used whatever habits were at hand. Tradition or the past is a clue to the success of these men who specialized in the future.

More disturbing is E. Franklin Frazier's controversial *Black Bourgeoisie*, which argues that the myth of business was more appealing to blacks than the fact.[31] Successful, elite blacks, adapting the values of the plantation owners whom they had traditionally observed, emphasized beauty, scholarship, and a living intellectual tradition, but viewed business as dirty and ungentlemanly. Given the opportunity, blacks became lawyers and doctors, Frazier claimed, but seldom businessmen. When Frazier was writing, in the 1950s, blacks owned only 18.6 percent of the 10,319 businesses in Harlem. Claude McKay writing in the 1940s also commented on this fact. As he said, "There is no other American community in which the huge bulk of local business, from the smallest to the largest, is operated by outsiders."[32] Lack of capital? Many women in Harlem took in washing. They had all the tubs and laundry lines and the business required little else. Yet there was no commercial laundry in Harlem until an Asian-American opened one. Similarly, waiters and busboys and cooks did not open restaurants and carpenters did not open hardware stores.

Each of these explanations relies on the legacy of the past—first a tradition of borrowing is lost, then a false tradition of aristocratic values is learned. There is still another example of the weight of history—the power of racial discrimination. Blacks were barred from making many investments, just as the poorer among them were barred from many jobs. Also, while other groups could expand their clientele, black tradesmen could seldom compete with whites for white markets. But the weight of discrimination must be balanced against the weight of hope. Chicago or Philadelphia had more independent black business, but less cultural awareness and less optimism. It was in Harlem that the cosmopolitan dream took hold in the black community, the dream of tolerance along with beauty, excitement along with stability, and the dream of a public world of public cooperation. The Harlem Renaissance did not end for lack of confidence, but for overconfidence. If busboys did not open their own restaurants, it was in part because they believed that the white restaurants would always employ them.

The actress Jane White, daughter of the Harlem intellectual Walter White, describing her girlhood, painted a picture of warmth, elegance, grace, and hope. She believed there would be no limits to her success in the theater or anywhere. She believed mobility was unlimited, opportunity unlimited, as long as men and women cooperated, regardless of color. She was surprised to find discrimination and limits to opportunity.

> It came as a shock to me that there were barriers against my becoming one of the great stars of all time. Because I thought I'd done all the things right. But it's not that simple, is it? I'm harking back to a time before the truth became known—when there was a self-esteem, an enormous self-assuredness, an enormous optimism.[33]

Harlem was cosmopolitan not only in its diversity, but in its opportunities. On close examination, however, its opportunities were more dreams than realities, possibilities for a future that was not very dependable. Just like all cosmopolitan centers, Harlem in its renaissance was held together by a hope, an optimism about the future.

DEPRESSION

Its dream of cooperation and integration made Harlem peculiarly vulnerable to the effects of the Depression, but so did the barriers of color and the weight of history. Both Harlem's economy and a large part of its glamour were dependent to a significant extent on white involvement. When the Depression settled in, the white world shut its doors, twice: there was no more money to spend in clubs uptown, and downtown establishments fired black employees. Unemployment wreaks havoc everywhere. While other areas and other groups recovered, though, Harlem, the glamorous center of cosmopolitan blacks, was a casualty of the Depression.

What happened to other groups? Many members were unemployed and yet someone, somewhere, held enough capital to start up again in better times. Someone still owned the sewing machine. Someone still held onto the grocery store. He might have fired all the employees, cut back to a single countertop, but some member of the group had made a foothold. Even in the worst of times people still had to eat. And someone made money during the Depression, loan sharks and bankers at the very least.

Black Harlem, though, with relatively few independent employers, retained relatively little capital. What is more, the wealthiest black investors had made their fortunes in Harlem real estate, whose value dropped precipitously along with the fortunes of the Black Metropolis. There was nothing left to hold. By 1950 Harlem was no longer great, only crowded. The musicians, poets, and scholars who had helped make Harlem a brilliant black city had died, and with them they took away all the idealism, the sense of achievement, the positive self-image, and the hope, of their era.[34]

What was left was life's prosaic side, the ghetto conditions that follow whenever discrimination pushes a group into a small space. Harlem became just a small space in New York, pushed into direct competition with other neighborhoods. Direct economic competition broke New York as it broke other cosmopolitan cultures, foundered on their dreams. Direct economic competition replaced the cultural division of labor, for better or worse. Direct economic competition broke the myth that everything would be all right as long as black men danced and black women sang, Italians made shoes, and Jews mended suits. That Joe Louis, he was one hell of a fighter.

Langston Hughes had yet another statement of the dream of a cosmopolitan city. Newcomers dream and wonder, but their opportunities are limited. What happens to a dream deferred? he asks again. Look around you.

> Good morning, daddy:
> I was born here, he said,
> watched Harlem grow
> until colored folks spread
> from river to river
> across the middle of Manhattan
> out of Penn Station
> dark tenth of a nation,
> planes from Puerto Rico,
> and holds of boats, Chico,
> up from Cuba Haiti Jamaica,
> in buses marked New York

from Georgia Florida Louisiana
to Harlem Brooklyn the Bronx
but most of all to Harlem
dusky sash across Manhattan
I've seen them come dark

    wondering
    wide-eyed
    dreaming

out of Penn Station—
but the trains are late.
The gates open—
Yet there're bars
at each gate.

What happens to a dream deferred?

Daddy, ain't you heard?[35]

Conclusions

The Fate of the Stranger

*T*he story is ended and it sounds so sad. These cities do not last. If they really succeed—if their mission is compelling, immigration strong, public life pervasive, and opportunity present—then they fall under their own weight. The tensions and strains of cosmopolitan culture cannot survive when the dream is cashed in. But you knew that, didn't you?

Everyone has a favorite explanation for the decline of the great cosmopolitan centers. Each of the great cities in this book has its own traditional ending. And on close examination, they are all the same. According to standard scholarly works and rule-of-thumb interpretations, these cities decayed at their core. They died from an inner rot, the rot of too many peoples, with too many conflicting interests. All the cities but New York actually collapsed under the conquest of war, their golden ages ended in defeat. But behind each defeat, according to their chroniclers, was loss of will, and behind each loss of will, the confusion of cross-purposes. In each case minority peoples are seen as treacherous to a government's unity; that is the lesson history appears to teach.

Babylon fell as divine retribution. And what was the sin for which God was punishing the city? The story is summarized in the myth of the Tower of Babel: it is somehow unnatural for many peoples to work together. Whenever they attempt to cooperate, the result is chaos. Even though there is no linguistic evidence at all to show that the English word "babble" comes from the Sumerian and Hebrew "Babel," American intellectuals cling to the myth as if it were law. In America we follow the Puritan interpretation. Difference is chaos. Multilingualism is babble, nonsense. We have inherited the biblical interpretation of Jerome, through Erasmus, through the voices of the Protestant Reformation. For them Daniel was a prophet of revenge and not an adopted child who bridged the Hebrew and Chaldean cultures. For the national churches of our own age which grew up justifying both Jerome's Bible and the nation-state, Babylon was not a source of strength, but weakness, its Chaldean astronomy not curiosity, but heresy. And its exiles and minority peoples were no more than the cause of war and divine wrath. When Darius the Mede finally conquered Babylon and the city capitulated, torn by enemies from all directions, the city of monuments and meaning was no more. But were its people, intermarried, mingled in religious observance, were they glad to see their city gone? Could Daniel or a figure like Daniel have rejoiced in the destruction of his adopted home? That is, is Daniel automatically a traitor because he was born speaking another language? Our own history appears to say yes.

Constantinople, likewise, fell when it lost its Roman core, according to Byzantinists. Mercenaries and minorities within the army made plots inescapable and whole regions became untrustworthy. Internal rebellion is blamed by many experts; the final defeat by the Ottomans was inevitable due to weakness within the empire. The elite, with no will to fight, abandoned their post. Much of the blame is laid at the door of the Armenians, who "Easternized" the empire. They were present in large numbers in the army and many held religious beliefs outside the imperial orthodoxy. The policy of bargaining with the barbarians, exchanging gifts for diplomatic consideration, is also considered a sign of decay. The empire was not tolerant; diversity itself is blamed for Byzantium's loss of will and its retreat into artifice. When the Ottomans took the city, they captured not a unified government, scholars argue, but a golden tree of golden boughs of golden birds barely keeping awake a drowsy emperor with their pretty cacophony.

Babylon, the golden cup, and Constantinople, the golden bough, are joined in historical argument by Vienna, the Habsburgs' golden capital. Vienna, more than any other cosmopolitan city, was lost because of its internal conflicts, if you follow academic debate. A large part of Oscar Jászi's influential book *The Dissolution of the Habsburg Monarchy* is devoted to "centrifugal" forces—that is, the tendency of the nationalist movements to pull outward, pulling the empire apart. To the extent that Maria Theresa allowed national languages to flourish, she was fomenting discord; to the extent that she demanded German be spoken, she was antagonizing her subjects. Jászi's analysis of the decay of the Austro-

Hungarian Empire has long served as an analysis of the origins of the First World War. After all, it was a Serbian nationalist who fired the war's first shot and his target was Austrian unity. The fate of the Austro-Hungarian Empire has become an argument for the necessity of national self-determination. Joseph II's attempts at bureaucracy could never restrain the conflicting interests of his subject peoples, scholars argue. Just because Joseph wanted the best possible bureaucrats did not mean that a Czech and a Pole could work side by side or share the same view of government, historians point out. Viennese musical genius? Sheer accident. Public life? People today distrust large groups; they see in them the march of time or, worse, the march toward totalitarian regimes. Instead of the lilt of a waltz or the joy of a symphony, scholars hear in Vienna the discord of peoples at odds with their government.

New York, like the others, has its decline theorists. Bilingual education and the demands of so-called special interests figure in the explanations produced by both scholars and journalists. Discussions of New York's decline most often refer to the intense financial difficulties of the mid-1970s, when the city barely held together as a governing unit because the state and federal governments had to take over so many of its debts and accounts. More generally, though, there is a sense that the city's physical structure—its roads, bridges, harbors, warehouses—began a slow decay and its social structure followed suit. What was once a middle-class city of working people is splitting into haves and have-nots, critics note. A popular explanation has been the city's minorities—from the most racist explanation, that some groups do not know how to care for property, to the more subtle "unmeltable ethnics" argument, that some people just "stick out." Some observers suggest that the older immigrant groups, such as the Italians and the Russian Jews, were somehow better able to adapt to the city than were more recent immigrants, such as the Puerto Ricans. These observers ignore the cultural division of labor; they do not say that a cultural division of labor limited immigrants' opportunities, but rather that people were happier with less. Of course, some people think that all of New York's minorities are disruptive. Jesse Jackson's slur against New York during his 1984 presidential campaign, when he called New York "Hymietown," was just one expression of a national perception that what is wrong with New York is that its minorities are too recognizable—too diverse. The constant bickering of local politicians and local newscasters and neighborhood interest groups and unions and industries—hasn't it all robbed the golden city of its glow?

All of these arguments imply the same simple fact: history teaches us not to trust strangers. Didn't a rash increase in foreigners without shared values cause the decline of many great cities?

No.

As this book has tried to show in city after city, great centers are great precisely because they welcome strangers. When they fall, as they eventually do, it is not because these strangers are foreign to the city's shared values, but just the opposite. They fall because the strangers do take on the shared values. They buy into the cosmopolitan dream. But the dream is deferred. The more compelling the city's purpose, the more extensive its diversity, the stronger its public life, then the more its minorities feel a sense of belonging and cooperation. If a city fell due to centrifugal forces, that is, strains pulling it away from cooperation, the first casualty would be its public life; its schools would empty, parades go unwatched, political offices would go begging for want of candidates. Instead, in the cosmopolitan cities we examined, all of these public institutions became battlegrounds. People did believe the promises and did participate. As one generation replaced another, however, they despaired of their chance to realize their dreams. The dream of total participation was pushed off, year after year, generation after generation. A minority group's members were drawn closer and closer to the center, but never quite made it. They were trapped in the same cultural division of labor which at first seemed so harmonious. The light cloak of economic specialization, to paraphrase Max Weber on bureaucracy, became an iron cage.

The cosmopolitan city successfully absorbed newcomers. Immigrants believed the myth, became part of a heterogeneous whole, and took part in a vital public life. They contributed to the wealth of their city by becoming specialists. Once incorporated into the efforts of the city, the minority members wanted rewards as well. Once educated, they wanted better jobs, more recognition. They began to compete over real resources. But there are never enough resources. The cosmopolitan dream falters when faced with real heightened economic and political competition. Competition can mean competition to own as well as competition to work. It can mean conflict among individuals for high positions or fights between family firms for shares of a market. It can mean regional or neighborhood disputes over resources like water or electric power. But in any case it is heightened conflict due to heightened contact. It is the strain of the public world.

Economic competition unravels cosmopolitan culture. Hard times alone do not do it. If only one group suffers or if the cultural divisions stay intact, then the world stays in place. It is not happiness or equality or justice that we are measuring, but a way of looking at strangers. It is when the strangers are seen as a direct threat and nothing seems certain that the fabric of cosmopolitan life shreds. In other words, there is within the cosmopolitan culture itself the pattern that gives people opportunity and then threatens it. Outsiders become insiders and insiders compete. They competed in banking in ancient Babylon, in politics and the army in Constantinople, in publishing and government in Vienna, and in government and education in New York.

Even had Babylon not fallen in war, its golden age as a great city would have been threatened by its own system of inclusion. More and more, the city's practice of adoption was leaving its Sumerian religious origins and becoming an economic weapon, a way of subverting wills and subsuming debts. When the great banking families had more members, greater resources, and more power than the throne, what would have happened to the city's sense of purpose? Maybe if there had not been the growing expenses of war, the unhindered development of Chaldean mathematics and astronomy, in a blossoming educational system which invited more exiles and newcomers, would have challenged the old order—including assumptions about strangers.

Constantinople's minorities, too, did not want out of but into its institutions. Armenians and other Easterners systematically studied Byzantine learning, vied for Byzantine office, and rose to positions of prominence. Constantinople's weakness was its attempt to keep the Armenians powerless out of fear. Instead of rewarding Armenian officers, Byzantine officials suspiciously passed them over: a recipe for disaffection in the army. The tactical mistake of seeking military and economic aid from the Christian West was due to narrow-mindedness, not a confusion of interests or an excess of voices. Competition rendered Constantinople sclerotic and paranoid. Diversity made it great; fear made it weak.

Did minorities tear at Vienna's core? Far from retreating from Vienna's stress on music and education, the minorities passionately sought inclusion. Jewish families in Vienna became foremost in supporting concerts, in publishing music, even seeking to preserve public values by holding public office. The same was true of the Czechs, Serbs, Macedonians, and Moravians who came to Vienna. The Austro-Hungarian Empire was too slow, not too fast, in incorporating its minority peoples. As more educated minority members experienced the empire's preference for German culture and the effects of German nationalism, they saw their own dreams put aside.

New York, as well, gave its minorities limited opportunity—opportunity great enough to hold the promise of a better life, but restricted when the time came to enter New York's corporate community.

It is not unusual to see the life of a city as its economy or a city's dynamic as competition. Many theorists, including Adam Smith, father of the marketplace, have seen the city as the marketplace. Karl Marx, who praised the bourgeoisie for their enterprises so necessary to history, focused on the city. It was the city where workers could band together to defeat the very bourgeoisie who brought them there. Marxist thinkers have written on the competitive marketplace-city as the birthplace of capitalism. And recent works as well have either defended cities for their economic benefits or fretted for their shriveling economic base. If Adam Smith said it, it would be called the invisible hand. If Karl Marx said it, it would be economic determinism. In either case, it is the importance of economics in all realms and it would neatly explain cosmopolitan cities through resources and competition. First there was labor, then labor became expensive, then cities fell.

The cosmopolitan city, though, is a distinctly social creation. Part idea, part demographics, part social organization, and part economic pattern—it is all there. Economic explanation is important, but it is only one tension in a fragile and beautiful city. If workers were channeled into a cultural division of labor, for example, but the city had no founding myth, their work could not so easily be justified. Imagine Italian immigrants on construction jobs in New York without the hope of a better life. A public life without opportunity would not make minority groups feel a sense of belonging, only obligation. Imagine Viennese forced to attend concert after concert without the chance of music lessons, recruitment as musicians, or openings in the Imperial Boys' Choir. Migration without a public life does not contribute to a feeling of opportunity, but could simply create a laboring underclass. Imagine exile in Babylon, where the Hebrews were held as slaves, unable to share in the rituals of the Chaldeans. The tensions and contradictions within and among all these elements also contribute to the city. Literal equality is not possible where there is a cultural division of labor, yet a feeling of fairness may be just as powerful. At least for a while. In Vienna people believed in opportunity, so much so that the aspirations of Jewish schoolchildren, like Sigmund Freud, were unbounded. A generation later the successes of some and the frustrations of others set the stage for intolerance in Vienna.

Is pessimism, then, the only conclusion? Does tolerance lead only to intolerance or curiosity to narrow-mindedness? Why trouble over a project as expensive in effort as a cosmopolitan culture if it leads only to sadness? The story of great cities is so big and broad, so classically tragic. Or, as one critic said, it is so world-historical, so Decline-and-Fall. Haven't we escaped that obsession with tragedy on a grand scale? Who wants it, anyway?

We want it. The stranger in all of us dreams of a chance to belong. The gilt-edged dream of the tolerant city is neither what is nor what is not—it sometimes is, it could be; it is a wish to be fulfilled. "Dream" is the word to describe social life, the ordinary world of work, touched by culture, the realm of symbols and ideas. It is a hope. What happens to a dream deferred? When what could be cannot be, the power of anger, of sadness, frustration, swells people's hearts. Dreams are powerful. And we cannot live without hopes.

Today in America two dreams compete for the faith of the people. One is the cosmopolitan dream, in which all people are welcome, all people contribute, and city life is valued and desired. The other is the American dream, the dream of self-sufficiency and independence. At one time, perhaps, the two worked together. But you cannot have both imported goods and no imported goods. You cannot have both language instruction in the schools and no language instruction, only the three R's. You cannot both love your Central American neighbors and deny them sanctuary. Cosmopolitan culture, flawed as it is, is a culture kind to strangers. The people of cosmopolitan cities are inherently no more generous, loving, or thoughtful than any other. Their increased knowledge of things foreign simply results, temporarily, in tolerance. Couldn't we adapt some elements of cosmopolitan culture and make our world more tolerant?

The American dream might once have included tolerance—for religion, for privacy. Privacy, though, does not create great bustling centers of art and achievement. Which American cities can lay claim to a lasting greatness? There are not many. In recent decades Americans have been retreating into village life. Recently, the largest population growth has been in suburbs or exurbs, not cities, and the American move to the Southwest has been a move out of cities, not into them. Are we so afraid of strangers? The grandchildren of people who came to the United States one hundred or even fifty years ago are no longer interested in the advantages a port city gave them. Port cities have lost their power, anyway, what with air travel and large-scale trucking. Amid complaints that the world has become too big or too complex, people seek out smaller social groups and wider spaces. The New Deal has split in two over the fifty years since the Depression. What was once a Democratic attempt to conserve the country, both its resources and its people, has fragmented into two separate efforts, resources or people. Cities are believed to eat into the countryside. More importantly, city dwellers eat into the countryside. The language of "limits to growth" has colored American humanity, even among those who consider themselves enlightened or cosmopolitan.

A truly cosmopolitan culture, one that enjoys variety and permits a wide range of behaviors and opinions, could not afford to strangle its cities. That is the lesson of the cities in this book: migration and diversity add luster and genius to a city. Many of the same people who argue that our cities are overcrowded are too quick to argue that the whole nation is overcrowded. They elevate lack of adequate planning to an argument to restrict immigration. Leave aside political fashion and ask honestly, what would happen if American borders were open, if all who sought refuge were accepted? Oddly, people who know firsthand the vastness of the United States still say there isn't enough space. Enough space for what? Enough space for ghost towns and broken old houses no one bothers to clear? Enough space so that each man, woman, and child can lay claim to a quarter of an acre? Suddenly, space is more important than human life; it was not so when their ancestors needed refuge, or else they would not be here. The language of limits to growth is used to hide fear, resentment, and competition. That is fine. But alone on your quarter-acre you may forget that it is diversity which creates great culture, diversity which creates tolerance. Space was an argument against cosmopolitanism once before, when Germany sought *Lebensraum* and "cosmopolitan" was a code word for "enemy."

Why not welcome diversity and immigration? Immigration is usually discussed as a labor issue, usually negatively. For over one hundred years American officials have been claiming that immigrants degrade the lives of American laborers by stealing jobs, depressing wages, and, in the case of the sweatshop system, by worsening working conditions. The American economy has consistently denied these charges. Labor problems have beset American industry, to be sure, but these problems have not been caused by immigration itself. Substandard wages or excessively expensive union labor, ill treatment of workers or the flight of capital to foreign labor sources—these problems exist independent of migration statistics. Look around. The lives of American laborers have not been destroyed. The lives of all Americans were enormously improved by the railroads crossing the country, the availability of inexpensive, ready-to-wear clothing, and the bridges, tunnels, and roads—all created by foreign-born workers. The lives of workers themselves improved thanks to strong unions—supported and often started by immigrants. Immigration does not drain the economy. It expands the economy.

Nativists argue that jobs are taken from American workers. Yet on close examination the jobs most in jeopardy are those of skilled laborers, specifically not the jobs masses of immigrants seek. For better or worse, immigrants, often educationally disadvantaged and certainly unfamiliar with American customs, expect the low-skill jobs and accept the low-pay jobs hoping, as earlier immigrants did, to move up or move back. American workers eighty years ago did not want the back-breaking jobs digging ditches which Italian immigrants took, and few American workers today are competing with Mexicans to pick fruit or clean stables at race tracks. The jobs for which labor unions are fighting, such as the skilled and semiskilled work in auto plants or steel mills, are disappearing due to past management decisions and changes in the American economy, not immigration.

As for the service and white-collar economy, immigrants contribute to its growth. They eat at McDonald's, create work for everyone from insurance salesmen to movie ticket takers, send their children to school, even necessitate more police. All of these are American jobs. Immigrants open stores and their entrepreneurship expands the economy. Even though economists and sociologists have rehashed these arguments many times and conclude that immigrants help rather than hurt, immigration is again and again called a labor issue.

Sometimes immigration is called an issue in international affairs. Then nativists fear that our shores are flooded by the "wrong" side, that we should allow only friends to enter the country. The inverted logic of this argument suggests that refugees from Communist countries should be welcomed because they show how bad life is under communism, while refugees from democratic allies should be shunned; letting them enter would be an admission that democratic countries have difficulties. This is related to the idea that we should welcome only political refugees, not economic refugees. It is a remarkable coincidence how effectively this keeps out black, brown, and yellow people.

It is time for immigration to be discussed as an issue of civil liberties. Tolerance which welcomes strangers safeguards the native. Unfortunately, most historical evidence in the United States is embarrassingly negative. The case of Sacco and Vanzetti shows that when the hatred of foreigners is intense, the American justice system is thrown aside. The same American government of the 1940s which did not actively welcome European Jewish refugees imprisoned its own Japanese-American citizens. More recently, when Haitians and homosexuals were targeted as high-risk AIDS groups, many Haitians were already behind barbed wire, being kept in prison-camp conditions at detention centers in

Florida for trying to enter the country. Demands for quarantine for all possible AIDS risks followed quickly. In California, 1986 legislation proposed to quarantine potential AIDS populations, a short step to the imprisonment of American homosexuals. How much easier is it to erode the rights of Americans when foreigners are already treated with cruelty or disdain?

Tolerance must be read into American civil liberties and questions of immigration, especially as American support for immigration is declining. In a *New York Times* survey of July 1, 1986, the Northeast was the region least threatened by immigration. The Midwest and Northwest were eager to cut immigration. Among whites the single best predictor of opinion was how long their families had been in the United States. The longer they had been here, the less they accepted any newcomers. Blacks, however, supported immigration. Despite recent conflicts and bitterness between Asian immigrant store owners and inner-city blacks, blacks still supported immigration. They did not believe their jobs were threatened, even though blacks are often found among the unskilled. The experience of black Americans is still the experience of the stranger. Black support for immigration shows sympathy for the stranger. Such support expresses the hope that where the stranger is welcome, maybe all men will be treated fairly. A more diverse society is a more tolerant one.

Several years ago a representative of the Commission on Civil Rights was making a routine inquiry, telephoning local officials in every state in order to monitor civil rights violations. When he got through to a local sheriff in Montana, the sheriff reassured him, "Oh, we don't have any civil rights here." We could laugh at the simple man's expense, but how wrong was he? He associated "civil rights" with "those different ones." Without those others, some people don't see a need for all the fuss. They just assume that everyone is the same. Wants the same. Believes the same. The tighter the circle is drawn, the more the people inside are squeezed.

There was a time when Americans were believed to be open, generous, hospitable people. Not everyone rushed to welcome a stranger, but someone always did. The whole country never shared the love of things and people foreign that marks a cosmopolitan culture, but one or two cities had some or all of the elements. We still have the chance. Perhaps we will leave aside our preoccupation with sin long enough to learn from Babylon—not what makes a city die, but what makes it live. Perhaps cities will be rebuilt and Americans will say, Where the stranger is welcome, there I can breathe free. Perhaps not. Then it will be at another time, in another place, that the dream of the golden city will reappear.

Notes and Sources

INTRODUCTION

1. Lewis Mumford, *The City in History* (New York: Harcourt Brace Jovanovich, 1961). See especially the description of the origins of cities as cemeteries and shrines, page 7. Mumford's use of the term Necropolis, or city of the dead, summarizes both past and present criticisms of the city.

2. Carlo M. Cipolla, *Before the Industrial Revolution* (New York: Norton, 1976), page 156.

3. Giovanni Boccaccio, *The Decameron*, trans. Richard Aldington (Garden City, N.Y.: Doubleday, 1930; Laurel-Dell ed.), page 33.

4. Boccaccio, page 36.

5. John Gardner, *The Life and Times of Chaucer* (New York: Vintage, 1978), page 52.

6. I am thinking here of Jean-Jacques Rousseau's "A Discourse on the Origins of Inequality" (*The Social Contract and Discourses*, trans. G. D. H. Cole [London: J. M. Dent, 1973], especially pages 104 and 108), but other writings are consistent. For artifice and court life see Norbert Elias' *The History of Manners*, Vol. I of *The Civilizing Process*, trans. Edmund Jephcott (New York: Pantheon, 1978), and *The Court Society*, trans. Edmund Jephcott (New York: Pantheon, 1983). The idea of vice and the city is explored in Carl E. Schorske's essay "The Idea of the City in European Thought: Voltaire to Spengler," in *The Historian and the City*, ed. Oscar Handlin and John Buchard (Cambridge, Mass.: MIT Press, 1963), pages 95–114.

7. For an analysis of American attitudes toward city life, see Morton White's essay "Two Stages in the Critique of the American City," in Handlin and

Buchard's *The Historian and the City*, pages 84–93. Perry Miller's anthology, *The Transcendentalists* (Cambridge, Mass.: Harvard University Press, 1950), contains classic statements for nature and against artifice.

8. Elizabeth Palmer Peabody, "Plan of the West Roxbury Community," excerpted in Miller, *The Transcendentalists*, page 466.

9. Adrienne Koch, ed., *Jefferson* (Englewood Cliffs, N.J.: Prentice-Hall, 1971), see especially Jefferson's words on cities and manufacture, pages 28–29.

10. Edmund Burke, Thomas Carlyle, and John Ruskin are often cited as conservative critics of urban life. See Steven Marcus' *Engels, Manchester and the Working Class* (New York: Vintage, 1974) for a discussion.

11. Karl Marx and Friedrich Engels, *The Communist Manifesto*, trans. Samuel Moore (New York: Washington Square, 1964), page 61.

12. Cited in Raymond Oberlé, "Mulhouse, Alsatian Manchester of the 18th and 19th Centuries," *Elan* (Strasbourg), nos. 3–4 (March–April 1981), page 7. My own translation.

13. See the essays by Georg Simmel ("The Metropolis and Mental Life") and Louis Wirth ("Urbanism as a Way of Life") in Richard Sennett's collection, *Classic Essays on the Culture of Cities* (New York: Appleton-Century-Crofts, 1969).

14. The importance of apartment-house windows was especially questioned during the controversial Kitty Genovese murder in New York. Windows and watchful neighbors are also a key element of Jane Jacobs' argument in *The Death and Life of Great American Cities* (New York: Random House, 1961). See Chapter 2, "The Uses of Sidewalks: Safety," especially page 35.

15. Georg Simmel, "The Metropolis and Mental Life," in Sennett, *Classic Essays*, pages 47–60.

16. Richard Sennett's *The Fall of Public Man* (New York: Knopf, 1976) is seminal to this work, and many of the book's themes, including the significance of public life, will be supported here. Above all, however, Sennett's use of Georg

Simmel's ideas of impersonality and freedom give meaning to his book. On pages 337–340, Sennett summarizes the dangers of intimacy, and how intimacy can spell tyranny.

17. David Riesman, Nathan Glazer, and Reuel Denney, *The Lonely Crowd* (New Haven, Conn.: Yale University Press, 1950). The conclusion best captures the moral argument, especially page 373, where the authors say that the other-directed "no more assuage their loneliness in a crowd of peers than one can assuage one's thirst by drinking sea water."

18. Oswald Spengler, "The Soul of the City," in Sennett, *Classic Essays*, page 65.

19. Schorske, "The Idea of the City in European Thought," page 114.

20. Lewis Mumford, *The Culture of Cities* (New York: Harcourt Brace Jovanovich, 1970), pages 11–12, describes cities as the antidote to barbarism, fascism; pages 358 ff. distinguish between regional and cosmopolitan character.

21. Niccolò Machiavelli, *The Prince*, trans. George Bull (New York: Penguin, 1975), pages 130–133, explains how the wise prince opposes blind fortune by using reason and will.

22. Henri Pirenne, *Medieval Cities*, trans. Frank D. Halsey (Princeton, N.J.: Princeton University Press, 1952). For an overview of the significance of the middle class and trade to city-building see pages 213–218.

23. Pirenne, page 151.

24. Marcus, pages 4–5.

25. Lucien Febvre and Henri-Jean Martin, *The Coming of the Book*, trans. David Gerard (London: NLB, 1976). The discussion of printers and their travels from one city to the next, pages 167–180, is of particular interest.

26. Howard S. Becker and Irving Louis Horowitz, "The Culture of Civility: San Francisco," in *Cities in Change*, ed. John Walton and Donald E. Carns (Boston: Allyn and Bacon, 1973), pages 243–252.

27. In addition to Walton and Carns' volume, see Claude S. Fischer's article "Toward a Subcultural Theory of Urbanism" (*American Journal of Sociology* 80, no. 6 [May 1975], pages 1319–1341) for its comprehensive introduction and bibliography.

28. Alfred Schutz, "The Stranger," in *Readings in Sociology*, ed. Brigitte Berger (New York: Basic Books, 1974), pages 20–24.

29. See the work of Paul DiMaggio at Yale University on the Boston Symphony Orchestra, and his articles coauthored with Richard Petersen.

CHAPTER I: BABYLON

1. Adapted from Rivkah Harris, "Notes on the Slave Names of Old Babylonian Sippar," *Journal of Cuneiform Studies* 29, no. 1 (1977), pages 46–51.

2. Herodotus, *The Histories*, trans. Aubrey de Sélincourt (Harmondsworth: Penguin, 1954), pages 93 ff.

3. James Dougherty, *The Fivesquare City: The City in the Religious Imagination* (South Bend, Ind.: University of Notre Dame Press, 1980), passim.

4. Herodotus, page 93.

5. Erik Eckholm, "Mesopotamia: Cradle of Haute Cuisine?" *New York Times*, May 15, 1985, pages C1 ff.

6. Herodotus, page 93.

7. J. A. Brinkman, "Babylonia 1000–748 B.C.," in *The Cambridge Ancient History* (Cambridge: Cambridge University Press, 1982), vol. 3, page 283.

8. Kamil 'Alwan, "The Vaulted Structures or the So-called Hanging Gardens," *Sumer* 35 (1979), pages 134–136; Wolfgang Nagel, "Where Were the Hanging Gardens Located in Babylon?" *Sumer* 35 (1979), pages 241–242.

9. They are now held in retirement in the Archaeological Museum, Istanbul, Turkey, division of the Ancient Near East.

10. A. Leo Oppenheim, *Ancient Mesopotamia* (Chicago: University of Chicago Press, 1964), pages 87–88.

11. Oppenheim, page 88.

12. Herodotus, page 91.

13. "The Code of Hammurabi," trans. Theophile J. Meek, in James B. Pritchard, ed., *The Ancient Near East* (Princeton: Princeton University Press, 1958), vol. 1, page 161.

14. Karl Deutsch, lecturing at Harvard University, Cambridge, Massachusetts, Spring 1977.

15. Oppenheim, page 88.

16. Robert William Rogers, *The Religion of Babylonia and Assyria* (New York: Eaton and Mains, 1908), page 49.

17. Helen Trenkvalder, "Some Remarks on the Place Name Babil," *Sumer* 35 (1979), pages 239–240.

18. Cited in W. G. Lambert, "Celibacy in the World's Oldest Proverbs," *Bulletin of the American Schools of Oriental Research*, no. 169 (Feb. 1963), pages 63–64.

19. Archibald Henry Sayce, *Babylonians and Assyrians: Life and Customs* (New York: Charles Scribner's Sons, 1899), page 214.

20. Sayce, pages 2–5.

21. Cristiano Grotanelli, "Aesop in Babylon," *Berliner Beitrage zum Vorderen Orient* (Berlin: Dietrich Reimer Verlag, 1982), pages 555–572.

22. Samuel Noah Kramer, "Rivalry and Superiority: Two Dominant Features of the Sumerian Culture Pattern," in Anthony F. C. Wallace, ed., *Men and Cultures* (Philadelphia: University of Pennsylvania Press, 1960), pages 287–291.

23. Kramer, page 291.

24. "The Code of Hammurabi," pages 160–161.

25. Sayce, page 41.

26. Sayce, pages 44, 57.

27. "A Pessimistic Dialogue Between Master and Servant," trans. Robert H. Pfeiffer, in *The Ancient Near East*, vol. 1, pages 250–252.

28. "A Pessimistic Dialogue," pages 250–252.

29. "The Epic of Gilgamesh," trans. E. A. Speiser in *The Ancient Near East*, vol. 1, pages 40–75; quotation cited page 51.

30. Sayce, pages 188–189; 81.

31. Edwin M. Yamauchi, *Greece and Babylon: Early Contacts Between the Aegean and the Near East* (Grand Rapids, Mich.: Baker Book House, 1967), page 75.

32. Sayce, page 190.

33. John Campbell, "The Celt in Ancient Egypt and Babylonia," *Transactions of the Canadian Institute* (Toronto: Canadian Institute, 1898), vol. 5, pages 89–103.

34. Rivkah Harris, *Ancient Sippar: A Demographic Study of an Old-Babylonian City (1894–1595 B.C.)* (Istanbul: Nederlands Historisch-Archaeologische Institut, 1975), pages 333, 341.

35. M. A. Dandamayev, "Social Stratification in Babylonia (7–4th c. B.C.)," in *Wirtschaft und Gesellschaft im Alten Vorderasien* (Budapest: Akadémiai Kïadó, 1976), pages 433–444; M. A. Dandamayev, "About Life Expectancy in Babylonia in the First Millennium B.C.," in *Death in Mesopotamia* (Copenhagen: Akademisk Forlag, 1980), pages 183–186.

36. Brinkman, page 290.

37. Yamauchi, page 85.

38. "The Creation Epic," trans. E. A. Speiser in *The Ancient Near East*, vol. 1, pages 37–39; quotation cited page 37.

39. Brinkman, page 291.

40. The volume "Wisdom, Revelation and Doubt: Perspectives on the First Millennium, B.C." (*Daedalus* 104, no. 2 [Spring 1975]) is in part a lengthy dialogue on how and when the ideas of Max Weber, including disenchantment, apply. See especially Benjamin Schwart, "The Age of Transcendence" (pages 1–8); V. Nikiprowetzky, "Ethical Monotheism" (pages 69–89); Paul Garelli, "The Changing Facets of Conservative Mesopotamian Thought" (pages 47–56); and A. Leo Oppenheim, "The Position of the Intellectual in Mesopotamian Society" (pages 37–46).

41. Raymond Philip Dougherty, *Nabonidus and Belshazzar* (New York: AMS Press, 1929), page 7; Bahija K. Ismail, "Structures of the Babylonian King Nabopolassar," *Sumer* 35 (1979), pages 167–168.

42. Mohammed Nasir, "The So-called Summer Palace (Nebuchadnezzar's Life Palace)," *Sumer* 35 (1979), pages 158–159.

43. Steven M. Gettke, *Messages to a Nation in Crisis* (Washington, D.C.: University Press of America, 1982), passim.

44. John C. Trever, in "Prophecy and the Book of Daniel" (*Biblical Archaeologist* 48, no. 2 [June 1985], pages 91–92), says that a change in the meaning of prophecy took place around 400 B.C., when revelation seemed over and prophecy came to mean prediction.

45. E. W. Nicholson, *Preaching to the Exiles* (Oxford: Basil Blackwell, 1970), page 127.

46. Laurent Wisser, *Jérémie, Critique de la Vie Sociale* (Geneva: Editions Labor et Fides, 1982), pages 248–249.

47. Joyce G. Baldwin, *Daniel: An Introduction and Commentary* (Madison, Wis.: Intervarsity Press, 1978), passim.

48. Yamauchi, page 89.

49. Trever, page 92.

50. Baldwin, page 78.

51. Helmut Minkowski, "The Tower of Babel: Fact and Fantasy," *Geographical Magazine* 27, no. 8 (Dec. 1955), pages 390–400.

52. *Jerome's Commentary on Daniel,* trans. Gleason L. Archer, Jr. (Grand Rapids, Mich.: Baker Book House, 1958), page 20.

53. R. Dougherty, page 7.

54. Although Belshazzar has disappeared from later historical references, he sometimes appears as Baltasar, a form very close to Balthasar, one of the three kings who are supposed to have visited the infant Jesus. Some versions of the story say kings, some say wise men, some, vying for certain historical realism, say astronomers, drawn by the star of Bethlehem. Belshazzar is a good model for all three, a king interested in astronomy, a Chaldean who trusted magicians and stars and praised the gods of gold, silver, brass, iron, wood, stone— some possible gifts for the infant Messiah whom the Gods blessed with a special star. Never mind that Belshazzar lived hundreds of years earlier. He is a good model.

55. *Jerome's Commentary,* page 20.

56. Trever, page 92.

57. John Huizinga, *Erasmus and the Age of Reformation* (New York: Harper and Row, 1957), page 48.

58. Lucien Febvre and Henri-Jean Martin, *The Coming of the Book,* concludes with a discussion of the decline of Latin printing and the rise of the German vernacular, including the German writings of Luther, pages 320–332.

59. Huizinga, page 48.

60. See Michael Walzer, *The Revolution of the Saints* (New York: Atheneum, 1972), for a discussion of Puritan fervor used in the cause of nation-building. On pages 22–65, Chapter Two, he provides a perceptive and convincing analysis of Calvinism used as a political tool, one of social science's strongest statements linking cultural ideas and political action.

CHAPTER II: CONSTANTINOPLE

1. William Butler Yeats, "Sailing to Byzantium," from *The Tower*, reprinted in *Poems of William Butler Yeats*, ed. A. Norman Jeffares (London: Macmillan, 1963), pages 101–102.

2. Dean A. Miller, *Imperial Constantinople* (New York: Wiley, 1969), page 193.

3. Steven Runciman, *Byzantine Civilization* (New York: New American Library, 1956), pages 146–151.

4. R. J. H. Jenkins, "Social Life in the Byzantine Empire," in *The Cambridge Medieval History*, vol. 6, *The Byzantine Empire*, ed. J. M. Hussey (Cambridge: Cambridge University Press, 1967), Part II, "Government, Church and Civilization," page 80.

5. J. M. Hussey, *The Byzantine World* (New York: Harper and Row, 1961), pages 147, 151.

6. Hussey, *The Byzantine World*, page 150.

7. *The Alexiad of Anna Comnena*, trans. E. R. A. Sewter (Harmondsworth: Penguin, 1969), mentions soldiers of many nationalities, page 61, and is of special interest for its claim that Constantinople is first among cities, even more important than Rome, page 62.

8. Ernest Barker, *Social and Political Thought in Byzantium* (Oxford: Clarendon Press, 1957), page 18.

9. Speros Vryonis, Jr., "Travelers as a Source for the Societies of the Middle East: 900–1600," *Charanis Studies: Essays in Honor of Peter Charanis*, ed.

Angeliki E. Laiou-Thomadakis (New Brunswick, N.J.: Rutgers University Press, 1980), pages 287–288.

10. Hussey, *The Byzantine World*, page 152.

11. Runciman, page 188.

12. Runciman, pages 185–186.

13. Barker, page 103.

14. Barker, pages 52–53.

15. Samuel Hazzard Cross and Olgerd P. Sherbowitz-Wetzor, trans. and ed., *The Russian Primary Chronicle, Laurentian Text* (Cambridge, Mass.: Medieval Academy of America, 1953), page 83.

16. Cross and Sherbowitz-Wetzor, page 82.

17. Liuprand, "The Embassy to Constantinople," *The Works of Liuprand of Cremona*, ed. F. A. Wright (London: George Routledge and Sons, 1930), page 246.

18. Liuprand, page 246.

19. Cross and Sherbowitz-Wetzor, page 82.

20. Liuprand, page 247.

21. Liuprand, page 247.

22. Jenkins, page 101: Runciman, page 158.

23. Marc Bloch, *The Royal Touch*, trans. J. E. Anderson (London: Routledge and Kegan Paul, 1973), describes the figure of the king as sacred in the middle ages, pages 28, 30 ff., with specific reference to the Byzantine emperors, pages 271–274.

24. Ernst Hartwig Kantorowicz, in *The King's Two Bodies* (Princeton, N.J.: Princeton University Press, 1957), provides a scholarly and amusing explanation

of the "halo of perpetuity" which crowned many figures in Byzantine paintings, pages 78–86.

25. Harry J. Magoulias, *Byzantine Christianity: Emperor, Church and the West* (Chicago: Rand McNally, 1970), page 16.

26. J. M. Hussey and T. A. Hart, "Byzantine Theological Speculation and Spirituality," in *The Cambridge Medieval History*, vol. 6, *The Byzantine Empire*, ed. J. M. Hussey (Cambridge: Cambridge University Press, 1967), Part II, "Government, Church and Civilization," page 197.

27. Magoulias, page 53.

28. *The Alexiad of Anna Comnena*, page 463.

29. *The Alexiad of Anna Comnena*, page 465.

30. *The Alexiad of Anna Comnena*, page 466.

31. Clifford Geertz, *The Interpretation of Cultures* (New York: Basic Books, 1973). This entire work is of enormous import in any discussion of the power of ideas, but especially interesting here is the insight that the individual's understanding of history and time is crucial to his picture of the world, page 389.

32. Peter Charanis, "Cultural Diversity and the Breakdown of Byzantine Power in Asia Minor," *Dumbarton Oaks Papers* (Washington, D.C.: Dumbarton Oaks Center for Byzantine Studies, 1975), no. 29, pages 11–12.

33. Miller, page 193.

34. Speros Vryonis, Jr., *The Decline of Hellenism in Asia Minor* (Berkeley: University of California Press, 1971), page 53.

35. Joshua Starr, *The Jews in the Byzantine Empire* (Athens: Verlag der "Byzantinisch-Neugriechischen Jahrbucher," 1939), page 36.

36. Peter Charanis, "Observations on the Demography of the Byzantine Empire," *Proceedings of the XIIIth International Congress of Byzantine Studies*, eds. J. M. Hussey, D. Oblensky, and S. Runciman (London: Oxford University Press, 1967), page 449.

37. Peter Charanis, *The Armenians in the Byzantine Empire* (Lisbon: Livaria Bertrand, 1963), page 23.

38. Miller, page 20.

39. Miller, page 123.

40. Jenkins, page 88.

41. Charanis, "Observations," page 461.

42. Charanis, "Observations," page 463.

43. Starr, page 8.

44. Starr, page 8.

45. Starr, page 190.

46. Starr, see Appendix of Documents, pages 242–244.

47. Starr, appendix.

48. Starr, appendix.

49. Charanis, *Armenians*, page 13.

50. Charanis, *Armenians*, page 36.

51. Charanis, *Armenians*, page 27–28.

52. Vryonis, *Decline*, page 54.

53. Vryonis, *Decline*, page 53.

54. Charanis, *Armenians*, page 34.

55. David Jacoby, of the Hebrew University of Jerusalem, lectured on "Byzantium—History and Civilization," at Princeton University, Princeton, New Jersey, in the spring of 1976. His lecture of April 5, 1976, on the "State, Law, and

Administration" (unpublished) was noteworthy for its analysis of "barbarians" within the administrative hierarchy.

56. Marc Bloch, *Feudal Society,* trans. L. A. Manyon (Chicago: University of Chicago Press, 1961), page 39. Vol. I begins a discussion of the effects of the long era of invasions and the change to a peacetime economy.

57. Jacoby, lecture, May 7, 1976 (unpublished).

58. Michael Psellus, *Fourteen Byzantine Rulers,* trans. E. R. A. Sewter (Harmondsworth: Penguin, 1966), page 65.

59. Psellus, page 65.

CHAPTER III: THE JEW AND THE CITY

1. Yosef Levanon, *The Jewish Travellers in the Twelfth Century* (Lanham, Md.: University Press of America, 1980), page 18.

2. Bernard Lewis, *Race and Color in Islam* (New York: Harper and Row, 1971).

3. "Ghetto," *Encyclopedia of the Social Sciences,* ed. Edwin R. A. Seligman (New York: Macmillan, 1938), pages 646–650.

4. *The Memoirs of Gluckel of Hameln,* trans. Marvin Lowenthal (New York: Schocken, 1977). Gluckel begins her account, page 1, with a sincere and revealing statement of purpose, signaling how unusual and unique this work is for its time.

5. Walter Laqueur, *A History of Zionism* (New York: Schocken, 1972), page 25.

6. Laqueur, page 26.

7. Laqueur, page 25.

8. Laqueur, page 67.

9. Issac Babel, *Benya Krik, the Gangster, and Other Stories,* ed. Avraham Yarmolinsky (New York: Schocken, 1969), pages 41–42.

10. Robert Alter, *After the Tradition* (New York: Dutton, 1969). Alter's analysis of the "myth of the Jew," page 38, and the use of dreams in all fiction, not just Jewish fiction, page 23, does not dispute the fact that many writers, including Freud, did in fact interpret the Jewish experience through dream imagery. Jewish popular culture was also preoccupied with dream interpretation.

11. Isaac Bashevis Singer, *The Magician of Lublin,* trans. Elaine Gottlieb and Josef Singer (New York: Noonday Press, 1960), passim.

12. Alter, page 42.

13. "New York," *The Encyclopedia Judaica* (Jerusalem: Keter, 1972), page 1123.

14. Nathan Glazer in *Beyond the Melting Pot,* ed. Glazer and Daniel P. Moynihan (Cambridge, Mass.: MIT Press, 1970), pages 161–162.

CHAPTER IV: VIENNA

1. Sigmund Freud, from *Gesammelte Werke,* quoted in Ernest Jones, *The Life and Work of Sigmund Freud,* (New York: Basic Books, 1953), Vol. 1, page 5.

2. Edward Crankshaw, *Maria Theresa* (New York: Atheneum, 1986), page 175.

3. Carl Schorske, *Fin-de-Siècle Vienna* (New York: Vintage, 1981). This entire work is vital to any understanding of Vienna, but of special interest is Schorske's analysis of Freud, pages 181 ff.

4. Max Rosenbaum, et al., *Anna O.: Fourteen Contemporary Reinterpretations* (New York: Free Press, 1984). The life of the real Anna O. sheds light on life in Vienna, pages 1–4, and reveals an active, powerful woman of accomplishment, pages 19–20.

5. Alice M. Hanson, *Musical Life in Biedermeier Vienna* (Cambridge: Cambridge University Press, 1985), page 14.

6. John Murray Cuddihy, *The Ordeal of Civility* (New York: Delta, 1974).

7. Jones, page 5.

8. Daniel Bell has analyzed this at length and presented this view at Harvard University in a reading course on Max Weber and Intellectuals, spring 1978.

9. Oscar Jászi, *The Dissolution of the Hapsburg Empire* (Chicago: University of Chicago Press, 1929), page 34.

10. Walter Consuelo Langsam, *The Napoleonic Wars and German Nationalism in Austria* (New York: Columbia University Press, 1930), pages 140, 141, 142.

11. Crankshaw, page 336.

12. Crankshaw, page 8.

13. Jászi, page 82.

14. Langsam, page 193.

15. Jászi, page 34.

16. Jászi, page 273–274.

17. Hanson, page 9.

18. Marcel Brion, *Daily Life In the Vienna of Mozart and Schubert,* trans. Jean Stewart (London: George Weidenfeld and Nicolson, 1961), passim.

19. Ernst Roth, *A Tale of Three Cities* (London: Cassel, 1971), page 45.

20. Baroness de Staël-Holstein, *Germany* (London: John Murray, 1813; English trans.), Vol. 1, page 75.

21. de Staël, page 93.

22. de Staël, page 93.

23. Brion, page 4.

24. de Staël, pages 71–72.

25. Crankshaw, page 311.

26. A good example of this new Enlightenment perspective is Voltaire's essay "Micromegas," in *The Portable Voltaire*, ed. Ben Ray Redman and trans. H. I. Woolf (New York: Viking, 1977), pages 413–435.

27. Crankshaw, page 306.

28. Crankshaw, page 307.

29. Victor-Louis Tapie, *The Rise and Fall of the Hapsburg Monarchy*, trans. Stephen Hardman (New York: Praeger, 1971), page 201.

30. Crankshaw, page 307.

31. Crankshaw, page 20.

32. Tapie, page 197.

33. Robert Darnton has written on the significance of printers and printing, particularly in *The Great Cat Massacre* (New York: Basic Books, 1984), pages 75 ff., and in *The Literary Underground of the Old Regime* (Cambridge, Mass.: Harvard University Press, 1982), pages 148–166, in which he describes both the work and leisure of these men. Their role is so great that in the summary of their importance, page 166, Darnton calls printers the "forgotten collaborators" of Europe's literary awakening.

34. Tapie, pages 197, 198.

35. See works by Lee Rainwater, James Coleman, Otis Dudley Duncan.

36. Casanova, quoted in Saul K. Padover, *The Revolutionary Emperor: Joseph the Second, 1741–1790*, pages 101–102.

37. Padover, page 190.

38. Padover, page 183.

39. Padover, page 253.

40. Eugen Weber, *Peasants into Frenchmen* (Palo Alto, Calif.: Stanford University Press, 1976). By the end of the First World War, strangers had become part of French life; up until then migration was little and strangers few. See pages 290–291.

41. Padover, page 257.

42. Padover, page 217.

43. Padover, page 181.

44. Padover, page 186.

45. "Max Weber on Bureaucracy," in *From Max Weber,* ed. H. H. Gerth and C. Wright Mills (New York: Oxford University Press, 1946), pages 196–244.

46. Langsam, pages 186–187.

47. Tapie, page 259.

48. Stella Musulin, *Vienna in the Age of Metternich* (London: Faber and Faber, 1975), page 160.

49. Tapie, page 274.

50. Hanson, page 70.

51. Hanson, page 71.

52. Hanson, pages 82–83.

53. Crankshaw, page 183.

54. Hanson, page 106.

55. Brion, page 64.

56. Crankshaw, page 183.

57. Hanson, page 101.

58. Brion, page 66.

59. Hanson, page 84.

60. Brion, page 183.

61. Brion, page 188–189.

62. Brion, page 193.

63. Hanson, pages 20–22.

64. Hanson, pages 20–22.

65. Charles Osborne, *Schubert and His Vienna* (New York: Knopf, 1985), page 12.

CHAPTER V: PARIS AND TOKYO

1. Edward Seidensticker, *Low City, High City* (San Francisco: Donald S. Ellis, 1985), pages 69–70.

2. Seidensticker, page 73.

3. Seidensticker, page 94.

4. Seidensticker, page 109.

5. Seidensticker, page 169.

6. Seidensticker, page 171.

7. Walter Benjamin, "Paris, Capital of the Nineteenth Century," in *Reflections*, ed. Peter Demetz (New York: Harcourt Brace Jovanovich, 1978), pages 146–162.

8. Benjamin, page 159.

9. Theodore Zeldin, *France 1848–1945: Intellect and Pride* (Oxford: Oxford University Press, 1980), page 86.

10. Zeldin, pages 16, 100.

11. Zeldin, page 118.

12. Haga Toru, "The Diplomatic Background of Japonisme: The Case of Sir Rutherford Alcock," trans. Lynne E. Riggs, in *Japonisme in Art*, ed. Society for the Study of Japonisme (Tokyo: Committee for the Year 2001, 1980), page 39.

13. Genevieve Lacambre, "Les Milieux Japonisants à Paris 1860–1880," in *Japonisme in Art*, page 45.

14. Lacambre, page 46.

15. Jukichi Inouye, *Home Life in Tokyo* (Tokyo: Tokyo Printing Co., 1910). The discussion of women's hairstyles, pages 110, 111, 112, is a strong example of the extent of Western influence. The blackening of teeth, denoting constancy, since black is the only color that remains unchanged, was soon to go out of style under Western influence, page 120.

16. Shibusawa Keizo, ed., *Japanese Life and Culture in the Meiji Era*, trans. Charles S. Terry (Tokyo: Obunsha, 1958), page 333.

17. Edwin O. Reischauer, *Japan Past and Present*, 2nd ed. (New York: Knopf, 1953), page 13.

18. Keizo, page 337.

19. Richard J. Smethurst, *A Social Basis for Prewar Japanese Militarism* (Berkeley: University of California Press, 1974), page xiv.

20. Christopher Thacker, *The History of Gardens* (Berkeley: University of California Press, 1979), page 83.

21. Thacker, page 149.

22. Thacker, page 63.

CHAPTER VI: NEW YORK

1. Oscar Handlin, *The Newcomers* (Cambridge, Mass.: Harvard University Press, 1959), page 9.

2. Emma Lazarus, "The New Colossus," quoted in Don Vogel, *Emma Lazarus* (Boston: Twayne, 1980), page 158.

3. Vogel, page 159.

4. Gary Scharnhorst with Jack Bales, *The Lost Life of Horatio Alger, Jr.* (Bloomington: Indiana University Press, 1985), pages 152–153.

5. Scharnhorst and Bales, page 155.

6. Thomas Kessner, *The Golden Door* (New York: Oxford University Press, 1977), page 7.

7. Kessner, page 8.

8. Marion T. Bennett, *American Immigration Policies* (Washington, D.C.: Public Affairs Press, 1963), page 40.

9. Bennett, page 49.

10. Glazer and Moynihan, page 1.

11. Glazer and Moynihan, page 288.

12. Glazer and Moynihan, page 17.

13. Nathan Glazer quoted in Larry Rohter, "Scholar Finds Few Changes in Immigrants' Challenges," *New York Times*, July 28, 1986, II, 4:5.

14. *The WPA Guide to New York City* (New York: Pantheon, 1982; original copyright 1939 by the Guilds Committee for Federal Writers' Publications), page 118.

15. Moynihan in Glazer and Moynihan, page 217.

16. *WPA Guide,* page 328.

17. *WPA Guide,* page 328.

18. Moynihan in Glazer and Moynihan, page 257.

19. *WPA Guide,* page 162.

20. S. M. Lipset and Hans Zetterberg, "A Theory of Social Mobility," in *Sociological Theory,* 3rd ed., eds. Lewis A. Coser and Bernard Rosenberg (New York: Macmillan, 1969), page 435.

21. See Glazer and Moynihan, passim.

22. Kessner, page 165.

23. Glazer and Moynihan, pages 144 ff.; Kessner, pages 33–34.

24. Glazer in Glazer and Moynihan, page 148.

25. Glazer in Glazer and Moynihan, page 147.

26. Kessner, page 63.

27. Kessner, page 38.

28. Kessner, page 63.

29. Kessner, page 38.

30. Quoted in Kessner, page 61.

31. Kessner, page 58.

32. Donna R. Gobaccia, *From Sicily to Elizabeth Street* (Albany, N.Y.: State University of New York Press, 1984). Families lived close together, closer than in Sicily, pages 80–81. They had little desire to segregate by wealth, but did live in clusters by occupation, page 78.

33. Glazer in Glazer and Moynihan, page 147.

34. Robert J. Wechman, *The Economic Development of the Italian-American* (Champaign, Ill.: Stipes, 1983), passim.

35. Isaac Metzker, ed., *A Bintel Brief: Sixty Years of Letters* (Garden City, N.Y.: Doubleday, 1941). The early letters are the most poignant, especially stories of arrival in America, such as the letter on pages 40–42, or the letters about life as a peddler, pages 42–43. Romance or its lack, pages 69–70, and the vulnerability of young women, page 72, were also common themes.

36. See Glazer, pages 147 ff.; Wechman, page 32.

37. Metzker, passim.

38. Salvatore Mondello, *The Italian Immigrant in Urban America 1880–1920, As Reported in the Contemporary Periodical Press* (New York: Arno, 1980), passim.

39. Quoted in Kessner, page 39.

40. Glazer in Glazer and Moynihan, page 151.

41. Humbert S. Nelli, *From Immigrants to Ethnics* (Oxford: Oxford University Press, 1983), page 155.

42. Quoted in Kessner, page 40.

43. Daniel Bell, "Crime as an American Way of Life," in *The End of Ideology* (New York: Free Press, 1962), pages 127–150.

44. Bell, *The End of Ideology*, pages 127–150.

45. Bell, *The End of Ideology*, pages 127–150; Mondello, passim.

46. Glazer in Glazer and Moynihan, page 151.

47. Wechman, page 32.

48. Wechman, pages 32–33.

49. Ronald H. Bayer, *Neighbors in Conflict* (Baltimore: Johns Hopkins University Press, 1978), page 11.

50. Barbara Blumberg, *The New Deal and the Unemployed: The View from New York City* (Lewisburg, Pa.: Bucknell University Press, 1979), pages 284 ff.

51. Moynihan in Glazer and Moynihan, page 257.

52. Herbert Gans, *The Urban Villagers* (New York: Free Press, 1962), defines an urban village, page 4, and describes its key features, stability and familiarity, page 15.

53. Luciano J. Iorizzo and Salvatore Mondello, *The Italian-Americans* (Boston: Twayne, 1980), page 60.

54. Nelli, page 28.

55. Carlo Levi quoted by Nelli, page 21.

56. Nelli, page 21.

57. Iorizzo and Mondello, page 65.

58. Iorizzo and Mondello, page 62.

59. Iorizzo and Mondello, page 62.

60. Iorizzo and Mondello, page 64.

61. Wechman, page 59.

62. Nelli, page 63.

63. Wechman, page 76.

64. Wechman, page 77.

65. Mondello, *The Italian Immigrant*, page 65.

66. Mondello, *Immigrant,* page 66.

67. Kessner, page 80.

68. Glazer in Glazer and Moynihan, page 197.

69. Kessner, page 79.

70. Mondello, *Immigrant,* page 186.

71. Mondello, *Immigrant,* page 186.

72. Mondello, *Immigrant,* page 188.

73. Michelle DiPalo, unpublished research, Harvard University, 1979.

74. Vincent Panella, *The Other Side: Growing Up Italian in America* (Garden City, N.Y.: Doubleday, 1979). Panella talks openly about the effect of the gangster image, page 29, and about attending school with other groups, especially Jews, page 30. He also relates the experiences of his relatives who were newcomers to the country and their work in "pick and shovel" and peddling, pages 53–54.

75. Mondello, *Immigrant,* page 188.

76. Mondello, *Immigrant,* page 231.

77. Iorizzo and Mondello, page 118.

78. Glazer in Glazer and Moynihan, pages 214–215.

79. Bayer, page 11.

80. Iorizzo and Mondello, page 234.

CHAPTER VII: HARLEM

1. Langston Hughes, *The Big Sea* (New York: Hill and Wang, 1940), page 62.

2. Wallace Thurman, *Negro Life in New York's Harlem* (Girard, Kans.: Haldeman-Julius Publications), page 5.

3. E. Franklin Frazier, *Black Bourgeoisie* (New York: Collier, 1962), presents a controversial analysis of the roots of the American Negro elite on pages 31–38 and explains this group's desire to conform to American ideals. For a somewhat pessimistic, though trenchant, overview, see pages 192–195.

4. Hughes, *Big Sea*, pages 206–207.

5. Gilbert Osofsky, *Harlem: The Making of a Ghetto* (New York: Harper and Row, 1971), page 128.

6. Jervis Anderson, *This Was Harlem* (New York: Farrar, Straus and Giroux, 1981), page 7.

7. Anderson, page 11.

8. Anderson, page 8.

9. Hughes, *Big Sea*, page 240.

10. Thurman, page 62.

11. Anderson, page 113.

12. James Weldon Johnson, *Black Manhattan* (New York: Atheneum, 1972; originally published 1930), page 263.

13. Johnson, page 268.

14. Johnson, page 265.

15. Claude McKay, *Harlem: Negro Metropolis* (New York: Harvest, 1968; originally published 1940), page 16.

16. Johnson, pages 281–282.

17. Anderson, page 200.

18. Anderson, page 217.

19. Thurman, page 24.

20. See Osofsky, page 128. Also Seth M. Scheiner, *Negro Mecca* (New York: New York University Press, 1965), provides a historical treatment up to 1920 on pages 1–12. The argument concludes with a sense of decay; even by 1927 housing was deteriorating, Scheiner says, page 38.

21. Hughes, *Big Sea*, pages 248–249.

22. Langston Hughes, "Harlem," *The Panther and the Lash* (New York: Knopf, 1974), page 14.

23. McKay, page 84.

24. McKay, page 84.

25. McKay, page 32.

26. McKay, pages 53–54.

27. McKay, page 198.

28. McKay, page 180.

29. Ivan H. Light, *Ethnic Enterprise in America* (Berkeley: University of California Press, 1972), especially the discussion of credit associations, pages 19–44.

30. Moses Rischin, *The Promised City* (New York: Corinth, 1962), especially for the argument about New York's unique cosmopolitan nature, pages 17–18.

31. Frazier, see especially the Introduction.

32. McKay, page 89.

33. Anderson, page 346.

34. Anderson, page 347.

35. Langston Hughes, "Good Morning," *Selected Poems of Langston Hughes* (New York: Knopf, 1981), page 269.

PERMISSIONS AND PICTURE CREDITS *(continued from copyright page)*

edited by Richard J. Finneran. Copyright 1928 by Macmillan Publishing Company, renewed 1956 by Georgie Yeats. Reprinted in English throughout the world except the U.S.A. by permission of A.P. Watt Ltd. on behalf of Michael B. Yeats and Macmillan London Ltd.

Picture Credits: *frontispiece:* Alfred Stieglitz, "The City of Ambition, New York" (1910) (The Dorothy Norman Collection); *following page 184:* nude goddess (Egyptian Museum, Cairo); the god Marduk (F. H. Weissbach, *Babylonische Miscellan,* Leipzig, 1903, p. 16); King Ashurbanipal (The British Museum, London); restoration of Babylon, from a painting (Oriental Institute, Chicago); restoration of Babylon (E. Unger, *Babylon die heilige Stadt,* Berlin, 1931, frontispiece); cuneiform tablet (The British Museum, London); map of the ancient Near East (A. Heidel, *The Babylonian Genesis,* Chicago, 1951, frontispiece); the ziggurat at Ur (J. B. Pritchard, ed., *The Ancient Near East,* Princeton, 1958, fig. 58); Constantine and Justinian, mosaic over the doorway of the south vestibule, St. Sophia, Istanbul (Ayasofya Museum, Istanbul); *The Empress Theodora and Her Retinue,* mosaic in the choir, San Vitale, Ravenna (Museo Nazionale, Ravenna); *The City of Nazareth,* detail, the outer narthex, Kahrieh Djami, Istanbul (Kariye Mosque, Istanbul); map of Byzantine Constantinople (Topkapi Palace Museum, Istanbul); detail of the silk Shroud of St. Germain l'Auxerrois in the Church of St. Eusebius, Auxerre, France, tenth century (Giraudon Photos, Inc.); *The Virgin and Child between the Emperor John II Comnenus and the Empress Irene,* twelfth-century mosaic in the south gallery, St. Sophia, Istanbul (Ayasofya Museum, Istanbul); Northern Italy in the fifteenth century, illuminated Hebrew manuscript, c. 1470 (Bezalel National Art Museum, Jerusalem); houses of the Jewish quarter, Germany, c. 1428 (Museum für Hamburgische Geschichte, Staats- und Universitätsbibliothek, Hamburg); building site in Germany, illuminated Hebrew manuscript, c. 1460 (The British Library, London); Jewish streets in Augsburg (A. Rubens, *A Jewish Iconography,* London, 1982, cat. #1298); German synagogues in Amsterdam (A. Rubens, *A Jewish Iconography,* cat. #1604); Roman Vishniac, "Entrance to the Jewish Quarter in Cracow, 1938"; map of the emancipation of European Jewry (M. Gilbert, *Jewish History Atlas,* New York, n.d.); Langendijk, *Louis Bonaparte's Entry into Amsterdam, 1808* (Rijksmuseum, Amsterdam); Alter Kacyzne, "Sale of Clothing at the Market in Kazimierz nad Wista, c. 1920"; Roman Vishniac, "Business Courtyard on Nalewski Street, Jewish Quarter of Warsaw, 1938"; "Labor Zionists March in May Day Parade, Chelm, 1932" (L. Cobroszycki and B. Kirshenblatt-Gimblett, *Image Before My Eyes,* New York, 1977, p. 192); Moshe Raviv, "Worshipers Leaving the Altshtot (Old City) Synagogue on Wolborska Street, Lodz, 1937"; *Sukkah,* south Germany, early nineteenth century, painted with cityscape (Bezalel National Art Museum, Jerusalem); Rembrandt, *The Jewish Bride* (Rijksmuseum, Amsterdam); Fanny von Arnstein (A. Rubens, *A Jewish Iconography,* cat. #17); Jacob Epstein, "In these cafes they meet . . ." (Hutchins Hapgood, *The Spirit of the Ghetto,* rev. ed, New York, 1976); Bernhard Strigel, *Maximilian I and Family* (Academia de Bellas Artes de San Fernando, Madrid); Martin van Meytens II, *Maria Theresa and Her Family,* 1760 (Schoenbrunn Palace, Vienna); Belloto, *The Imperial Palace of Schoenbrunn from the Gardens,* 1759–1760 (Kunsthistorisches Museum, Vienna); Belloto, *The Corn Market, Vienna,* 1760 (Kunsthistorisches Museum, Vienna); Johann Nepomuk Hochle, *Ball in the Winter Riding School,* 1815 (Albertina, Vienna); A contemporary lithograph of Johann Strauss the Elder (Historisches Museum der Stadt Wien, Vienna); Theo Zasche, *Johann Strauss II* (Bildarchiv Osterreichische Nationalbibliothek, Vienna); W. J. Mahler, *Beethoven,* 1815 (Beethovenhaus, Bonn); Keisai Eisen, *Station at Oise* (Japonisme in Art, Tokyo, 1980); Henri de Toulouse-Lautrec, *Elles: Femme au Tub* (Fogg Art Museum, Harvard University); Kitigawa Utamaro, *The Artist Kitao Masanobu Relaxing at a Party* (The Metropolitan Museum of Art, New York, Frederick C. Hewitt Fund, 1912); Edgar Degas, *At the Milliners* (The Metropolitan Museum of Art, New York, Havemeyer Bequest, 1929); Hiroshige, *Opening of the First Railroad in Tokyo, 1872* (The British Museum, London); Claude Monet, *Gare St. Lazare* (Art Institute of Chicago); Alfred Stieglitz, "The Steerage, 1907" (The Dorothy Norman Collection); Jacob Epstein, "The Old Man" (Hutchins Hapgood, *The Spirit of the Ghetto,* rev. ed., New York, 1976); John Sloan, *Connoisseurs of Prints,* 1905 (*New York Etchings, 1905–1949,* M-127); Alexander Alland, "Main Drag" (*Portrait of New York,* New York, 1939); John Sloan, *Flute Player,* 1905 (*New York Etchings, 1905–1949,* M-125); Carlos Andersen, *Outdoor Library* (Bryant Park); Lewis W. Hine, "Artificial Flower Factory" (George Eastman House, Lewis W. Hine Collection); Lewis W. Hine, "Making Pillow Lace, New York City, December 22, 1911" (Collection of Walter and Naomi Rosenblum); Lewis W. Hine, "Family Making Artificial Flower Wreaths in Their Tenement House" (George Eastman House, Lewis W. Hine Collection); Lewis W. Hine, "Labor Agency, New York City, 1910" (Collection of Walter and Naomi Rosenblum); Langston Hughes, c. 1927 (Schomburg Center for Research in Black Culture, New York); silent parade (Schomburg Center for Research in Black Culture, New York); *Reading Room* (Schomburg Center for Research in Black Culture, New York); Charles S. Gilpin (Schomburg Center for Research in Black Culture, New York); Lenox Avenue at 134th Street, c. 1920 (Schomburg Center for Research in Black Culture, New York); Alexander Alland, *Negro News (Portrait of New York);* "Connie's Inn, Harlem Nightclub of the 1920s" (Schomburg Center for Research in Black Culture, New York)

Every reasonable effort has been made to trace holders of any existing copyrights. If an existing copyright has been inadvertently overlooked, the claimant is requested to contact the author.

Printed in the United States
By Bookmasters